S0-BKE-150

The Reader's Corner

The Reader's Corner

ESSAYS FOR DEVELOPING READERS

Second Edition

Carol Kanar

Valencia Community College

Houghton Mifflin Company   BOSTON   NEW YORK

Publisher: Pat Coryell
Development Editor: Kellie Cardone
Editorial Associate: Peter Mooney
Associate Project Editor: Lisa C. Sullivan
Senior Manufacturing Coordinator: Marie Barnes
Marketing Manager: Annamarie Rice
Marketing Assistant: Laura Hemrika

Cover image: © James Genus Jr./Stock Illustration Source

Selection 1: "Jackie Robinson" by Henry Aaron, from TIME, June 14, 1999.
© 1999 Time, Inc. Reprinted by permission.   Selection 2: "Vietnamese: A
Lifetime Commitment" by Ta Thuc Phu, M.D. from ORLANDO SENTINEL,
May 2, 1998. Reprinted by permission of the author.   Selection 3: "Qurán
Lesson: Exalt Moms, Dads" by Dr. Yasmeen Qadri, ORLANDO SENTINEL,
May 2, 1998. Reprinted by permission of author. *Acknowledgments continue
on p. 391.*

Copyright © 2005 by Houghton Mifflin Company. All rights reserved.

No part of this work may be reproduced or transformed in any form or
by any means, electronic or mechanical, including photocopying and
recording, or by any information storage or retrieval system without
the prior written permission of the copyright owner unless such copy-
ing is expressly permitted by copyright law. With the exception of non-
profit transcription in Braille, Houghton Mifflin is not authorized to
grant permission for further uses of copyrighted selections reprinted
in this text without the permission of their owners. Permission must
be obtained from the individual copyright owners as identified herein.
Address requests for permission to make copies of Houghton Mifflin
material to College Permissions, Houghton Mifflin Company, 222
Berkeley Street, Boston, MA 02116-3764.

Printed in the U.S.A.

Library of Congress Catalog Card Number: 2003110177

Student's edition ISBN: 0-618-42672-8
Instructor's edition ISBN: 0-618-42674-4

23456789-QUF-08 07 06 05 04

CONTENTS

❧

PART ONE
Americans in Transition

PART TWO

Rumblings in the Culture

PART THREE

Against All Odds

PART FOUR

Hard Questions

PART FIVE

America at Work

Contents

PREFACE

The essays and apparatus that make up *The Reader's Corner,* Second Edition, are based on the following premises. First, reading is an essential skill that is vital to success in college, work, and life. Reading is the foundation of most courses, a source for ideas, and a springboard to critical thought and action. Being able to read efficiently and critically will help students stay current in their chosen careers or professions, navigate the Internet, and update their knowledge and skills in a world that is exploding with rapidly changing information and new technology. On a personal level, reading is the vehicle that propels students into inner space, challenging their opinions, arousing new interests, and facilitating their intellectual growth. Most importantly, reading gives students ideas to think about, write about, and talk about, so that they can assume their rightful places in any discourse community.

NEW IN THE SECOND EDITION

- Each part of the book contains one or more new reading selections.
- One or more selections in each part are excerpted from textbooks. For convenience, look for the icon in the table of contents that designates a reading selection as a textbook excerpt.
- A new Part 5, America at Work, has been added. The Part 5 selections have a career focus.

- To provide more thematic focus, part openers explain the themes that unite the reading selections and include questions to guide the reading.
- For instructors who want to provide additional skills practice for students, an ancillary with supplementary exercises has been developed to accompany the text.

In addition, *The Reader's Corner* can help students build and sustain their reading skills in several ways:

- *The Reader's Corner* is a collection of fifty reading selections thematically organized into five parts that promote critical thinking and self-examination.
- Reading selections are written by a culturally diverse group of writers on a variety of thought-provoking topics that entertain, inform, and challenge students.
- *The Reader's Corner* favors a holistic approach to reading that encourages both the discovery of the reading process and the development of literal and critical reading skills.
- A carefully constructed apparatus following every selection leads students through the stages of the reading process, from prereading, through careful reading, to postreading and review.
- A combination of both objective and open-ended questions encourages students to read and think both analytically and critically.
- Questions for discussion and writing invite students to examine their ideas and share what they have learned, making knowledge their own.

SPECIAL FEATURES OF THE TEXT

Each reading selection is framed by a six-part apparatus that includes prereading and postreading activities designed to lead students logically through the processes of analytical reading and critical thinking. The following six features form the apparatus of *The Reader's Corner:*

- **First Thoughts** consists of three questions that help students preview the selection and access their prior knowledge on the author's topic.
- The **headnote** that precedes each selection contains information about the author or the selection and is designed to provoke interest and provide a background for the reading.

- **Word Alert** is a vocabulary feature that lists, defines, and locates by paragraph number words that may be unfamiliar to students or that may have special meanings that are essential to an understanding of the reading selection.
- **Comprehension Check** consists of ten multiple-choice questions that help students build and practice skill in finding the author's topic, purpose, and main idea; identifying stated details; and making inferences. These thought-provoking questions focus students' attention on what is both stated and unstated, leading them to read analytically and think critically.
- **Working with Words** is an exercise in deriving meaning from context. Students are given a group of sentences to complete, using words from the Word Alert feature. This exercise tests students' understanding of a word's meaning and their ability to recognize it in a different context.
- **Thinking Deeper** consists of four open-ended questions that encourage students to determine a reading's significance. The first two questions are designed to accomplish one or more purposes: to help students think critically about the author's ideas, examine the way a selection is structured, or apply concepts in practical contexts. The third question relates the selection to the unit theme. The fourth question is a writing prompt or other activity, although any one of the questions could be used either for writing or for discussion.

These features frame the reading selections with prereading and postreading activities that encourage students to prepare for reading, to engage actively in the process of reading, and to reflect on what they have learned after reading.

ANCILLARIES

An Instructor's Edition with answers is available. Additional exercises and teaching materials are available in a supplement to the text.

ACKNOWLEDGMENTS

A textbook is a combined effort among author, editors, and others who played a role in its conception, execution, and production. I am grateful to all those at Houghton Mifflin who played a part in bringing this book into being, especially Pat Coryell, who made it possible;

Peter Mooney, who oversaw its development, providing counsel and encouragement; Lisa C. Sullivan, who directed its production; and Annamarie Rice for her enthusiastic support of my work. I am grateful to the many others whom I do not know by name but whose work behind the scenes made this book possible. I thank my husband, Steve Kanar, for the way he encourages me and champions all my efforts, my friends and colleagues who shared their ideas, and the students whose needs, interests, and aspirations shaped my writing of the apparatus and my choice of the reading selections.

   Finally, I am grateful for the many excellent suggestions I received from colleagues who helped me develop this new edition of *The Reader's Corner* into its current form:

   Kathleen Smith Britton, *Florence-Darlington Technical College*
   Leslie Capiello, *Collin County Community College*
   Susann B. Deason, *Aiken Technical College*
   Terry Ray Parrish, *Hinds Community College*
   Robert Scattergood, Professor Emeritus, *Belmont Technical College*

The Reader's Corner

STARTING POINTS

WOULDN'T IT BE WONDERFUL if you could open a book or turn to the first page of an article with the confidence that not only would you understand what you read, but you would be able to remember the essential information? Wouldn't it be great if you could prepare yourself for the reading so that you could dive right in, without procrastinating?

You can.

Two facts about reading will serve as starting points. First of all, reading requires at least two people: you and the author. Think of reading as a conversation with another person. When you have a conversation, you listen to someone else's ideas, you think about them, and you offer your own opinion. Sometimes you agree; sometimes you disagree. When you do not understand some part of the conversation, you ask questions. Throughout the conversation, in the back of your mind, you may be relating what you are hearing to what you already know about the topic. Reading is like that. Although you cannot see or hear the author, you have his or her words on the page in front of you. The conversation takes place in your mind, as you read. For example, you may find yourself thinking, "What does this word mean?" or "Why does the author have this opinion?" In the back of your mind, you may also be thinking about experiences of your own that are similar to those you are reading about.

Second, reading is a process. When you read, your brain takes in information and either discards it or stores it for later use. What you may not realize is that *you can control this process.* You can improve your understanding and your memory by doing certain things before, during, and after reading.

Remember that reading is a conversation between you and the author. To control the reading process, become actively involved in the conversation. We call this *active reading,* and it can make all the difference in your ability to understand, remember, and enjoy reading.

The next three sections tell you more about the readings in this book and how to read them actively.

THE READINGS

This book takes you on a journey through the contemporary human mind. The authors are from different cultural, national, and ethnic backgrounds, and they write on a variety of topics and issues that are of general interest. The readings come from books, magazines, newspapers, and other sources. They range in length from short pieces to longer selections. The readings are arranged in five thematic units: *Part 1: Americans in Transition, Part 2: Rumblings in the Culture, Part 3: Against All Odds, Part 4: Hard Questions,* and *Part 5: America at Work.* Each unit opens with an explanation of the theme that is addressed in the ten readings that follow. The third discussion question following each selection addresses the unit themes.

The purpose of this collection is to provide you with a varied reading experience and a chance to develop your own reading process. Reading, like any other skill, takes time and practice. The readings in this collection and the exercises that accompany the readings will help you hone your existing skills and perhaps develop some new ones as well.

THE READING PROCESS

Reading is the process of taking in, sorting, and storing information. If you are reading passively—not paying attention, allowing yourself to become distracted, letting your mind wander—you are not in control of the process. As a result, you will not remember what you read. If you are reading actively—concentrating, ignoring distractions, thinking about the author's ideas—you are in control. As a result, you are more likely to understand and remember what you read. This section explains how the reading process works and what actions you can take before, during, and after reading that will put you in control.

Before Reading

At any given time, you are bombarded with all kinds of information: *It's hot. I'm tired. The phone is ringing. I have to be at work at 3:00 P.M. What was I supposed to study for the test?* These thoughts and others like them are going through your mind when you sit down to read. Therefore, unless you focus your attention on the reading, your other thoughts will dominate and will have a negative effect on your comprehension.

To focus your attention, find out what you can about the author. Then preview the selection by doing the following: First, read the title to determine the author's topic, and take a few minutes to explore what you already know about it. Your prior knowledge may serve as a context for the author's ideas and expand your understanding. If you have no prior knowledge of the topic, then ask questions such as these to help you build context:

- What can I find out about the topic?
- How does the topic relate to what we are studying in class?
- Have I read or heard anything related to the topic?

Next, read the first and last paragraph. One of these may contain a stated purpose, a main idea, or a strong clue to one or the other. Finally, read any other information that may be available, such as questions before or after the reading, or a list of vocabulary words and definitions. If the selection is divided into sections with headings, read them. Headings tell you the major divisions of the author's topic and may provide a strong clue to the author's main idea or purpose.

As you can see, the reading process actually begins *before* you read. Take an active step to clear your mind and set the stage for reading.

During Reading

Reading rarely proceeds smoothly from first word to last. College reading especially introduces new ideas, unfamiliar words or terms, and different styles of writing and methods of organization. Thus you may get off to a good start, then find yourself backtracking, stopping to look up the meaning of a word, or taking a few moments to think about what you have read. This is as it should be.

What happens during the reading process is that your brain is sorting the incoming information—separating the important from the nonessential, relating what is new to what is already known, and searching for the meanings of difficult words and sentences. If you are not paying attention, not actively engaging yourself in a conversation with the author, you are interrupting this natural process.

Active reading strategies to use during reading include the following: Read one paragraph at a time. Jot down in the margin or in a notebook thoughts or questions that occur to you as you read. Pay attention to the author's choice of words. What do they tell you about the author's attitude or feeling toward the topic? If you did not identify a purpose or main idea before reading, try to identify it during reading. Pay attention to how the ideas are organized. Is the author making comparisons, explaining steps in a process, narrating a series of events, describing a place or a person? If you are able to identify a main idea, find and mark the details that support or expand it. Ask yourself which of these details are the most significant. Think about the ideas and how they relate to what you already know or need to find out about the author's topic.

As you can see, the key to reading actively is to read for ideas and to discover which ideas are more important than others. When all else fails, keep going back to the title and first paragraph. Often these are your strongest clues to the author's overall topic or main idea.

After Reading

As soon as you finish reading, you begin to forget. The more time passes, the less you remember—unless you take active steps to prevent forgetting. Like a computer, your brain can store only what you tell it to save. This is why review is so important.

Review is the key to remembering. Review immediately after reading, while the ideas are still fresh in your mind. If you know you will be tested on the information, review frequently thereafter to refresh your memory. This will prevent you from spending the night before a test cramming, or from drawing a blank during class discussions.

A good way to review is to try this three-step strategy: **think, write, discuss.** First, *think* deeply about what you have learned and how you can use the information or apply it in your everyday life. Second, *write* a summary of the information. (A summary is a few sentences, in your own words, that express an author's main idea and significant details.) Third, *discuss* the reading with a study partner or group. By sharing your thoughts with others, you may get new insights or fill in gaps in your understanding. In addition, writing and discussing create new sensory pathways into your memory.

Table 1 summarizes the reading process and active reading strategies explained in this section.

TABLE 1 The Reading Process and Strategies for Active Reading

Stages of the Process	Active-Reading Strategies to Use Anytime
BEFORE READING	Read title and first and last paragraphs. Determine topic, main idea, purpose, and pattern. Access prior knowledge about topic. Read any headings for clues. Ask questions to guide thinking.
DURING READING	Read one paragraph at a time. Jot notes in margin. Ask questions to guide reading. Affirm or rethink the author's topic, main idea, purpose, and pattern. Mark significant details. Think about the author's ideas and relate them to what you know.
AFTER READING	Review immediately after reading, then frequently thereafter. Think about what you have learned and how you can use the information. Summarize what you have read in writing, and talk about it with a study group.

PRACTICAL STRATEGIES FOR THE READINGS

The exercises and information that accompany each reading are designed to help you apply active-reading strategies before, during, and after reading. Through consistent use of these strategies, you will develop a reading process that will lead to successful outcomes in all your reading.

For a brief overview, Table 2 breaks down the reading process as it applies to the readings in this book and lists the exercises to do or information to read at each stage.

Before You Read

First Thoughts is an exercise that helps you build a context for the reading. By answering the questions, you will find out what you already know about the author's topic. Your first thoughts should raise questions in your mind that enable you to enter into a mental conversation with the author.

The headnote at the beginning of each reading may provide information about the author, the reading, or both. This information, along with the definitions in *Word Alert*, a vocabulary feature, provides additional ideas for you to think about before reading.

TABLE 2 How to Read Each Reading Selection

Stages of Reading	What to Do at Each Stage of the Process
BEFORE READING	Do *First Thoughts* to build background and preview the reading. Read *Word Alert* so that you will know what words to watch for.
DURING READING	Read the selection. Refer to *Word Alert* as needed for definitions of boldfaced words. Use margin for note taking. Think about the author's ideas and ask questions as you read. Then look for answers.
AFTER READING	Do *Comprehension Check* to test yourself and practice reading skills. Do *Working with Words* to add new words to your vocabulary. Do *Thinking Deeper* as part of your review.

One more thing you can do before reading is to look up the reading selection in the Table of Contents and read the brief summary following the title. The summary may arouse your interest and provide additional clues to the author's purpose or main idea.

These prereading activities focus your attention on the reading, create a context for the author's ideas, and put you in a receptive frame of mind. Do the activities on your own or with a partner or group.

During Reading

As you think about the author's ideas during the process of reading, you can decide whether they expand or challenge your existing knowledge of the topic. Important details may stand out or questions may occur to you. If so, make notes in the margin or in a notebook. Pay attention to vocabulary and the way ideas are organized. These activities help you read actively, keep your attention focused, and encourage a mental conversation with the author.

After You Read

Reading occurs on two levels: *the literal level* (what an author says) and *the critical level* (what an author means). The questions in *Comprehension Check* are carefully structured to help you apply several essential reading skills to unlock the author's meaning on both these levels. *Working with Words* helps you apply another essential skill: using context clues to determine the meaning of an unfamiliar word. The next section provides a brief review of these essential skills.

Another exercise that follows each reading is *Thinking Deeper*, which consists of several suggestions for discussion and a writing activity. This exercise helps you review what you have learned so that you can integrate new ideas within your existing framework of knowledge and access them, if needed, at a later time.

ESSENTIAL READING SKILLS

To comprehend what you read, look ahead. Anticipate what comes next and predict a discussion's outcome. Effective anticipation and prediction depend on your being able to follow an author's ideas, separating essential from nonessential information. Fortunately, anyone can improve comprehension. Reading actively is one way. Developing your reading skills is another.

Reading involves a number of skills applied simultaneously. To understand these skills, it helps to consider them separately. This section explains several reading skills that will not only help you answer the comprehension check questions successfully, but also help you analyze, or think through, *any* reading selection for its literal and critical meaning:

- Find the author's topic and main idea.
- Identify the details that support the main idea.
- Determine the author's purpose.
- Look for an organizational pattern.
- Make inferences from stated details.
- Use context clues to define unfamiliar words.

Find the Topic and Main Idea

Reading is not just about words; it is about ideas. Some ideas are more important than others. The *main idea* is the most important idea in a selection. Everything else in the selection—every example, every other detail—supports the main idea. In a longer selection, the main idea is sometimes called the *central idea* to distinguish it from the main idea of a paragraph.

The main idea of a paragraph is often stated in a *topic sentence*. The topic sentence can appear anywhere in a paragraph, but it is usually the first sentence. To find the topic sentence, ask yourself these two questions:

- What is the author's topic?
- What does the author say about the topic?

The *topic* is what the whole paragraph is about. After reading a paragraph, you should be able to state the topic in one word or a short phrase. For example, "This paragraph is about *birth-control methods*" or "This paragraph is about *condoms*." When you have identified the topic, ask questions like these to determine the author's opinion: What does the author say about condoms? Which birth-control methods does the author discuss? Finally, look for a sentence that expresses both topic and opinion. This is the topic sentence. In the following example, the topic sentence is underlined:

> <u>Some contraceptives are more effective than others.</u> Birth-control pills have the highest effectiveness rate. Diaphragms and condoms are also effective, especially when used with a spermicidal cream or jelly. Creams and jellies alone are not as effective. Natural methods such as the rhythm method and coitus interruptus (withdrawing the penis before ejaculation) are the least effective. But even the best methods can lose their effectiveness if they are not used consistently.

In this paragraph, the topic sentence comes first. The author's topic is *contraceptives,* and the author's opinion is that *some are more effective than others.* Which methods are the most effective? Which are the least effective? Each of the remaining sentences in the paragraph contains a detail that answers these questions.

Notice too that the topic sentence is a broad, *general* statement. It summarizes what the whole paragraph is about. Each of the other sentences is a narrow, or *specific,* idea that supports or explains the main idea. A good rule to keep in mind is that main ideas are general ideas, and details are specific ideas. Now read the next example, in which the topic sentence is underlined:

> Birth-control pills contain hormones that cause changes in a woman's menstrual cycle so that ovulation does not take place. Diaphragms block the cervix, preventing sperm from entering the uterus. Spermicidal creams and jellies kill sperm. Natural methods try to circumvent the union of sperm and egg through timing. <u>Contraceptive methods work in different ways.</u>

In this paragraph, the topic sentence comes last. Notice that the topic sentence is a general statement that contraceptive methods work differently. Also notice that each of the preceding sentences contains a specific detail about a contraceptive method and how it works.

Now read the following example, in which the topic sentence is underlined:

> A variety of birth-control methods are available to couples today. Some of these methods are more effective than others. <u>The choice of a contraceptive depends on several considerations.</u> The effectiveness of the contraceptive is an important consideration. The couple must decide who will be responsible for birth control. Couples must also consider risks and side effects associated with contraceptives. Religious values may also be a factor in determining which contraceptive to choose or whether to use contraceptives at all.

In this paragraph, the topic sentence is the third sentence. The first two sentences introduce the topic. The fourth through sixth sentences provide the details that support the main idea.

Every paragraph has a main idea, but some paragraphs do not have a topic sentence. When there is no topic sentence, you must *infer,* or guess, the main idea. When you cannot find a main idea, try these tips for inferring the main idea: First, read the whole paragraph. Look for key words or repeated terms that help you determine the author's topic. Try to state the topic in one word or a short phrase. Next, read each sentence. Try to determine what all the ideas expressed in each sentence add up to. What one idea do they all seem to support? Once you are sure what the topic is, ask yourself, "What is the author's opinion about the topic?" Look for details in the paragraph that answer your question. These steps should enable you to form in your own mind a sentence that expresses the author's main idea. Now read the following paragraph, which does not have a topic sentence. What is the main idea?

> Some people believe that schools should be responsible for providing sex education to students. They believe that since students are going to have sex anyway, they should have enough information to be able to practice safe sex. Others believe that students should postpone sex until marriage. According to these people, sex education classes should advocate abstinence and teach the dangers of AIDS, other sexually transmitted diseases, and early pregnancy. Still others are opposed to sex education classes of any kind. These people think sex education should be left to parents.

First of all, *sex education* is repeated three times. Key words and phrases related to sex education are *sex, safe sex,* and *sexually transmitted diseases.* Therefore, the topic must be *sex education.* What does the author say about the topic? The details in the paragraph state the different beliefs that people have about sex education. Some think the schools should be responsible for sex education, but some do not. Some think we should give students the information they need if they are to have safe sex; others think we should tell them to abstain. You can infer from these details that the author's main idea is *people's views on sex education differ.* This is only one possible statement of the main idea. Any main idea statement will do as long as it says about the same thing as this one.

To find the central idea of a longer selection, such as the readings in this book, first ask yourself these questions:

- What is the topic of the entire selection?
- What is the author's opinion about the topic?

To find the topic, read the title, which may provide a strong clue. Then read the first paragraph or two. Look for a sentence in the opening paragraphs that states the author's topic and opinion. This sentence is the central idea. If you do not find such a sentence, then read the last paragraph, which may be a summary paragraph that states the central idea. Of course, the central idea of a selection can appear anywhere in the selection. Or it may be unstated. If reading the title and the first and last paragraphs does not help, look for clues in the details. Look for repeated words that may suggest the author's topic or opinion. Look for examples or reasons and ask yourself, "What do these details mean?" "What central idea do they all seem to support?"

Now read the following introductory paragraphs to a longer selection, in which the central idea is underlined.

GOOD KIDS ARE NOT HARD TO FIND

Although teen pregnancy is on the decline, it still interrupts the lives 1 of far too many young girls. Although smoking in the United States is declining overall, more teenage girls and young women are taking up the habit. We hear reports of widespread drug and alcohol abuse among high school students and binge drinking among college students. But most alarming are the kids who kill. The school shootings of 1998 and 1999 and more recent events have caused parents, educators—everyone—to ask "Why?"

These dire reports paint a frightening picture of American 2 youth, but they do not tell the whole story. Far more young people do not drink, take drugs, get pregnant, or kill their peers. <u>Most of the kids in every school, college, and community are busy studying, working, and preparing for a future filled with hope and pride.</u> Who are these young people, and what can we learn from them?

The topic, *Good Kids,* is stated in the title. The clues are *teen, young girls, teenage girls, young women, high school students, college students, kids, American youth,* and *young people.* The author's opinion is that good kids are working to achieve worthwhile goals. Topic and opinion are expressed in slightly different words in the third sentence, second paragraph. The last sentence states the author's purpose: to find out who the good kids are and what we can learn from them. As a reader, you can expect the author's details to answer the question posed in the last sentence.

Identify the Supporting Details

A *detail* is a fact, reason, or example that supports a main idea. Remember that the main idea is a *general* statement. The details that support it are *specific* ideas. Following is a topic sentence (main idea) and a list of details that support it.

> Edson Arantes do Nascimento, generally known as Pélé, dominated soccer for two decades.
>
> 1. In 1956, Pélé joined the Santos Football Club.
> 2. In 1958, he played in the World Cup for the first time, leading Brazil to victory.
> 3. In 1970, in another victory for Brazil, Pélé played his final World Cup.
> 4. In 1974, Pélé retired, then came out of retirement to play for the New York Cosmos in 1975.
> 5. In 1977, Pélé retired from the Cosmos.
> 6. In 1994, he was appointed Brazil's Minister of Sports.

The topic sentence tells you that *Pélé* (topic) *dominated soccer for two decades* (author's opinion). Each detail lists one of Pélé's achievements. These details are facts that support the main idea. Notice that each sentence in the list begins with a date. These dates serve two purposes: They let you know that important facts follow, and they help you follow a sequence of events.

Facts include dates, names of people and places, historical events, information that is part of the public record—anything that can be verified either by direct observation or by consulting an authoritative source. For example, President John F. Kennedy was assassinated in 1963—this is a fact that no one disputes. However, opinions differ as to whether there was one shot or two and whether Lee Harvey Oswald, the killer, was working alone.

As a reader, you should be able to distinguish facts from opinions. When in doubt about a detail, ask yourself, "Where could I go to find out whether this information is factual?" Pélé's achievements in the list above can be verified from a number of sources. For example, a biographical index would have this information. You could also find these facts in books, magazines, newspaper articles, or Internet sources that contain information about Pélé.

Some authors support their main ideas with reasons. A *reason* is an explanation that answers the question *why?* or *how?* Following is a topic sentence and a list of reasons that support it.

Jackie Robinson is an athlete I admire.

1. For one reason, he broke the color line in baseball.
2. Also, when faced with prejudice and discrimination, he refused to let these disappointments affect his game.
3. Another reason I admire Robinson is that he tried to convince others to hire blacks as coaches and managers.
4. One more reason I admire Robinson is that he was a gentleman who treated his fans with respect.

The topic sentence tells you that the author admires Robinson. Why? The details that follow provide the reasons. Each reason in the list above is introduced with a transition: *for one reason, also, another reason,* and *one more reason.* A *transition* is a word or phrase that connects ideas. Watch for transitions that help you find and follow an author's important details.

Examples are another type of detail that authors use to support main ideas. An *example* is an illustration or explanation that appeals to your senses or makes a comparison. Following is a topic sentence and a list of examples that support it.

Female athletes in most major sports have proved that they can compete successfully with male athletes.

1. For example, in the seventies, Billie Jean King defeated Bobby Riggs in the "Battle of the Sexes" tennis tournament at the Houston Astrodome.
2. Also, Manon Rheaume made history as the first woman to play in an NHL preseason game.
3. Katie Hnida, the first woman to play in a Division 1-A football game, showed that women can compete with men in this tough sport.

4. Most recently, Annika Sorenstam, the first female golfer in 58 years to be invited to play in a PGA tour event, didn't make the cut but played admirably.

The topic sentence tells you that *female athletes* (topic) *have proved that they can compete with male athletes* (opinion). What are the signs of this ability? The details that follow provide several examples. Transitions in each detail sentence signal that an example follows: *for example, also, showed,* and *most recently.*

Now read the following short passage and identify the author's overall main, or central, idea and the significant details that support it.

HOW THE CIVIL RIGHTS MOVEMENT BEGAN

It started with a seamstress from Montgomery, Alabama, who refused 1
to give up her seat on a city bus. Her name was Rosa Parks. Every morning, she got on the bus and sat in the back, as black people were required to do. But December 1, 1955, was different. On that day, Parks got on the bus as usual and took her seat in the back. When a white passenger was unable to find a seat in the front of the bus, the driver told Parks to give up her seat. She refused.

Parks was arrested for breaking the law; she was tried on Decem- 2
ber 5 and found guilty. Supporters of equal rights for black people, led by Martin Luther King, Jr., rallied around Parks and staged a boycott of the city bus system that lasted a little more than a year. The Supreme Court's decision to end segregation on public transportation ended the boycott.

The boycott was only the first in a series of nonviolent demon- 3
strations that reached a high point in 1963. King led the march on Washington, D.C., where he told those assembled, "I have a dream." King's dream was of an America where all people could live in peace and racial harmony. The movement's persistence led to the enactment of the Civil Rights Act in 1964, which outlawed segregation in public facilities and in hiring practices. Two other important pieces of legislation followed: the Voting Rights Act of 1965 and the Fair Housing Act of 1968.

From one woman's stand against the Montgomery city bus sys- 4
tem in 1955 to the enactment of anti-discriminatory laws in the 1960s had been a long ride. Following these legislative victories, the movement and its supporters turned their attention to improving education and eradicating racial prejudice.

The central idea of the entire passage is stated in the first sentence, first paragraph. The movement started with one woman who refused to give up her seat. The details in the rest of the selection tell you not only what happened to Rosa Parks, but also what the far-reaching consequences of her actions were. Following is a list of the significant details that support the central idea.

1. On December 1, 1955, Parks refused to give up her seat in the back of the bus to a white passenger (paragraph 1).
2. Parks was arrested for breaking the law (paragraph 2).
3. She was tried on December 5 and found guilty (paragraph 2).
4. A boycott of the city bus system led by Martin Luther King, Jr., lasted for over a year (paragraph 2).
5. In 1963, King led the march on Washington, the high point of the civil rights movement (paragraph 3).
6. The Civil Rights Act of 1964 outlawed segregation (paragraph 3).
7. Other important legislation, the Voting Rights Act of 1965 and the Fair Housing Act of 1968, was passed (paragraph 3).
8. After 1968, the movement focused on improving education and ending racial prejudice (paragraph 4).

These details are historical facts. They include the significant dates and key events of the civil rights movement that began with Rosa Parks's protest.

As you can see, identifying important details is an essential part of your reading process. Details support or explain an author's main idea. Details provide the facts, reasons, and examples that help you follow the development of an idea from an author's first sentence to the last.

Determine an Author's Purpose

An author's *purpose* is his or her reason for writing. Sometimes the purpose is stated, sometimes not. More often, you must determine the purpose by learning what you can from the topic, main idea, and details. The language (choice of words) and overall mood or feeling (tone) may also provide clues.

Three types of purposes motivate most writing: to *inform*, to *persuade*, to *entertain*. The informing purpose is a teaching purpose. The author wants you to know, understand, or be able to do something. The following paragraph is written to inform.

> Dr. Beatrice Hahn of the University of Alabama at Birmingham is credited with the discovery of the origins of HIV-1, the virus responsible for AIDS. Her findings were published in the journal *Nature* in February

1999. Hahn traced the virus to an African primate, a subspecies of the chimpanzee. Hahn and her colleagues were able to trace the chimps to the same region where humans were first known to have been infected with AIDS. How did humans get the virus? Hahn speculates that since the chimps were hunted for food, blood from the animals may have entered the human body through a wound.

The topic is *the discovery of HIV-1,* and the main idea is stated in the first sentence. The author's purpose is to inform readers about the discovery, who was responsible, and how it was done.

The goal of persuasive writing is to influence the way you think or feel about an issue. The author who wants to persuade has a strong opinion and may hope that you either already agree or are willing to change your mind. The following paragraph is written to persuade.

Opinion is divided on who should teach kids about sex. Some say it is the parents' responsibility. Others believe that the schools should take the lead. They're both wrong. Sex education is everyone's responsibility. If even one girl gets pregnant, if even one boy dies from AIDS, we have fallen down on the job. As parents, we need to talk to our children. As educators, we must find better ways to reach more kids. As citizens, we must demand that the media—songwriters and filmmakers—take responsibility for the unwholesome images they project to young people.

In this paragraph, the main idea is stated in the third sentence, and the purpose is to persuade readers that sex education is each person's responsibility. The phrases *we need* and *we must* suggest that this author's purpose is to influence our opinions about sex education.

Writing that entertains may provoke an emotional response, such as laughter or sadness, or it may express an idea, using images that appeal to your senses. The following paragraph is written to entertain readers.

For a couple of weeks my husband and I had been watching the nest that a bird had made on top of our back porch light. We were certain that she had laid her eggs, and we were eager for them to hatch. The nest was right under our bedroom window, and each day we would listen for the baby birds. Days passed and we heard nothing. We had decided that the mother bird had abandoned her nest, probably because of so much activity around our house. One day we decided to take a peek at the nest. We got within about ten feet of it, and five heads shot up. Then with a flurry of wings, five small chickadees flew out of the nest and went in separate directions. Was this their first flight? I guess we'll never know.

In this paragraph, the main idea is implied: Two people watch a bird's nest, hoping to see the baby birds. The author's purpose is to entertain readers with a story about the birds. Descriptive details help you visualize the scene.

The key to determining an author's purpose is to ask yourself, "What does this author expect of me, the reader?" Read the title and the first and last paragraphs. If you still cannot determine the purpose, keep reading. Find the central idea, which may contain a clue to the author's purpose. For example, the title "How the Civil Rights Movement Began" is a clue that the author's purpose is to *inform* readers about who or what started the movement. The central idea of the short passage about Rosa Parks on page 13 is stated in the first paragraph: *It started with a seamstress from Montgomery, Alabama, who refused to give up her seat on a city bus.* Based on this central idea, what does the author expect you to know? The author wants you to know what happened. The purpose is to inform you about the event that started the civil rights movement.

Suppose that after reading the title and the first and last paragraph and finding the central idea, you still cannot tell what the purpose is. Then let your response be a guide. Read the entire passage. Then ask questions to determine how you have responded to the reading. Your answers may lead you to the author's purpose. Questions to ask are these: "Did the author teach me something?" (inform); "Did the author try to influence me or change my point of view?" (persuade); "Did the author make me laugh or arouse another feeling, or create images in my mind?" (entertain).

Table 3 lists purposes, details that may help you identify them, and responses that authors expect from readers. Please note that Table 3 makes a general comparison only. As you become a more experienced reader, you will find that purposes overlap. For example, an author may first need to inform readers with facts about an issue before trying to persuade them to form an opinion. But even when more than one purpose is apparent, one purpose will dominate.

Look for an Organizational Pattern

Ideas expressed in English follow certain patterns. For example, it is common to say *the clock chimes at ten,* or *at ten the clock chimes,* but not *chimes clock ten at the.* Why? Because in English, as in any language, certain established sentence patterns dictate the placement of subjects, verbs, articles, and modifying phrases and clauses. Para-

TABLE 3   Understanding an Author's Purpose

Author's Purpose	Supporting Details	Expected Readers' Response
INFORM (to teach or explain)	Facts, examples, and other kinds of information	To understand or be able to apply information gained from reading
PERSUADE (to influence or convince)	Facts or other details chosen for their persuasive value or effect	To be convinced or moved to take action
ENTERTAIN (to express, arouse feeling, excite imagination)	Descriptive details and facts chosen for their entertainment value	To experience pleasure, both emotionally and intellectually

graphs, too, as well as longer selections, follow certain organizational patterns. By recognizing an author's chosen pattern, you can more easily anticipate what is to come. What are these patterns, and what are the signs by which you can recognize them?

Organizational patterns represent ways in which people think. For example, it is natural in conversation to make comparisons, define terms, explain how something works, list steps or stages in a process, or trace a sequence of events. Authors use patterns as handy ways to organize their ideas. The choice of a pattern is directly influenced by an author's purpose. For example, after Princess Diana died in 1997, authors whose purpose was to re-create the last day of her life used the *sequence* pattern to describe what she and her companion did every hour of that day. The following list briefly explains six common organizational patterns.

Generalization, Then Example. A general statement or idea is supported by one or more examples that explain and clarify the idea.

Sequence/Process. Sequences explain *when* and *in what order* events occur. Sequences are traced through dates, times, or numbers. Processes explain *how* things happen and the steps or stages that are involved. Sequence and process often occur together.

Comparison/Contrast. Objects or ideas are analyzed either according to their similarities (comparison) or according to their differences (contrast). Usually similarities *and* differences are considered.

Division/Classification. *Division* explains how parts relate to a whole. For example, to understand how an automobile works, you need to know how each part functions in relation to the whole engine. *Classification* establishes categories into which items can be sorted according to shared characteristics. For example, the cards in a deck can be sorted into clubs, spades, hearts, and diamonds. Division and classification sometimes occur together.

Cause/Effect. This pattern explains *why* things happen (the reasons or causes) and their consequences (results or effects). Causes and effects usually occur together.

Definition. This pattern provides either a brief explanation or an in-depth analysis of the meaning of a word, term, or idea.

Authors often mix patterns. For example, in a long essay that defines a term like *success* or *character,* an author may use examples or make comparisons even though the overall pattern is definition.

Questioning can help you discover an author's organizational pattern. For example, suppose you open the morning paper and read this headline: *Roof Collapses, Damages Sought.* Questions you could ask are: Why did the roof collapse? Whose fault was it? Did anyone get hurt? How much were the damages? Who will pay? Answers to the first two questions will tell you the *reasons* the accident happened. Answers to the last three questions will tell you the *results* or *consequences* of the accident. These questions and answers should help you determine that the author's pattern is *cause and effect.* Now you can anticipate what comes next: a detailed explanation of what caused the roof to collapse and what happened as a result.

Here is another example. You have been assigned to read an article titled *What Is Self-Esteem?* You might ask yourself the same question. The answer you come up with would be based on your prior knowledge. But without reading the article, do you know what the author means by self-esteem? Can you guess what organizational pattern the author follows? Since the answer to the question posed by the title would be a definition of self-esteem, you can guess that the pattern is *definition.* Now you have something to anticipate: What *is* the author's definition, and does it add to or contradict yours?

Another way to identify an author's pattern is to look for *transitions:* signal words and phrases that reveal the relationship of one idea to another. For example, the words *first, next,* and *then* can signal either a sequence of events or the steps of a process. Table 4 lists six organizational patterns and the transitions that may help you identify them.

TABLE 4   Organizational Patterns and Transitions That Signal Them

Patterns	Transitions
GENERALIZATION, THEN EXAMPLE	for example, for instance, such as, to illustrate, specifically, also, in addition, another, moreover, furthermore, to clarify
SEQUENCE/PROCESS	first, next, then, now, before, after, later, following, step, stage, method, procedure, how to, trace, numbers: 1, 2, 3, etc.
COMPARISON/CONTRAST	like, unlike, similar, different, as, as if, however, but, yet, although, on the other hand, on the contrary, to compare, to contrast, conversely
DIVISION/CLASSIFICATION	part, member, branch, section, segment, group, kind, type, class, category, division, to classify
CAUSE/EFFECT	reason, result, cause, effect, because, thus, since, therefore, consequently, due to
DEFINITION	for example, to illustrate, such as, means, to define, stands for

The following example passages illustrate six common organizational patterns. In each passage, the transitions that signal the author's pattern are underlined.

1.   Generalization, Then Example

The days of the week were named after the gods and goddesses of ancient times. <u>For example,</u> Sunday, then as now, was the first day of the week and was "the day of the sun." Monday was "the day of the moon." Ancient people of many cultures worshiped the sun and moon, believing that these celestial bodies were gods. Tuesday gets its name from *Tiw,* later called Mars, the god of war. Wednesday was named for *Woden,* "the furious one," a Germanic god. Thursday takes its name from *Thor,* the old Norse god of thunder. *Frig,* a goddess and the wife of Woden, gave her name to Friday. Saturday comes from *Saturn,* the Roman god of agriculture.

In this paragraph, days of the week and the origins of their names are the examples that explain the generalization made in the first sentence.

2.   Sequence/Process

What happens during the nine months of pregnancy? During the <u>first</u> three months, cells divide to become an embryo. The embryo becomes a fetus. At this stage, there is little increase in size but much differentiation of tissue. The <u>next</u> three months show more activity. The fetus becomes larger; it has a heartbeat, and its first movements occur. In the <u>last</u> three months of pregnancy, the fetus continues to grow. Its movements increase as it prepares for birth.

This paragraph traces the events that occur during the three stages of pregnancy. It describes both a sequence and a process.

3. Comparison/Contrast

When recent high school graduates arrive on college campuses, they soon learn that college <u>differs</u> from high school in several ways. First of all, high school teachers have close relationships with students and are likely to interact with them outside the classroom in sports and club activities. In college, <u>however</u>, the relationships are less close. Although some professors do get involved in extracurricular activities, many do not. Second, the workload in college differs from that in high school. College students have more reading to do, the reading is more diffi-cult, and most professors assign homework every time class meets. But in high school, most of the work is done in class, with students having homework only one or two nights a week on the average. A third <u>difference</u> is that students have more freedom in college. What students do between classes is their business. When they do not have a class scheduled, they neither have to be on campus nor have to ac-count for their whereabouts. <u>On the contrary</u>, high school students, with few exceptions, must remain on campus during school hours.

This paragraph explains three ways in which college differs from high school: relationships with teachers, workload, and the amount of freedom students have.

4. Division/Classification

The student body of Fairview Community College is <u>composed of</u> 35 percent recent high school graduates, 55 percent adult learners, and 10 percent seniors.

Students in these categories have the following <u>characteristics</u>. Recent high school graduates are seventeen to nineteen years old and are attending college for the first time. Most of them plan to transfer to a four-year college when they graduate. Adult learners, the largest <u>category</u>, are in their twenties and thirties. Some are at-tending college for the first time, while others are returning students who dropped out of college earlier in life to work, to raise families, or for some other reason. Most of them are in college to improve their skills and thus their job prospects. The senior learners are in their forties or older. Students in this category have come to retrain, to make career changes, or to find self-fulfillment.

The first paragraph *divides* Fairview's student body into three groups based on what percentage of the whole student population they represent. The second paragraph *classifies* the students in each category on the basis of their ages and reasons for coming to college.

5.   Cause/Effect

Yesterday my instructor returned my algebra test, and I was disappointed with my grade. I barely passed the test. Fortunately, I know the <u>reasons</u>. To begin with, I went into the test unprepared. I had put off my review until the night before the test. Then I spent only an hour studying, which was not enough time to review all the concepts and rules that were covered. The <u>second reason</u> is that I got nervous as a result of knowing that I was not prepared. My anxiety caused my mind to go blank, and I was unable to recall what I *had* studied. The <u>most important reason</u> is that I made some careless errors. Had I taken the time to proofread my paper before handing it in, I might have corrected my errors and earned a better grade. All things considered, I'm not surprised that I did so poorly.

This paragraph explains the causes and effects of being unprepared for a test.

6.   Definition

Recent scandals involving government officials at every level have left voters wondering whether any candidate's character can stand up to public scrutiny. Some have forgotten the <u>definition</u> of the term itself. *Character,* now as always, <u>describes</u> a set of personal qualities that we used to call virtues. These virtues include honesty, dependability, trustworthiness, fairness, modesty, and temperance. If we demanded these qualities of those who run for public office, how many would be eligible? Perhaps, like the marines, voters should insist on "a few good men" and women of character to serve the public.

This paragraph defines *character* as the possession of certain personal qualities.

Make Inferences from Stated Details

An *inference* is an educated guess about something you do not know based on what you *do* know. Inferences can be valid or invalid. A *valid* inference has sufficient knowledge and experience to back it up. An *invalid* inference does not.

Everyone makes inferences. For example, your decision to attend college was influenced by the inferences you made about your financial status (Can I afford the tuition?), your record of achievement (Will I be successful?), and your self-knowledge (Can I handle the workload?). Physicians make inferences about your health based on your symptoms and examination results. Using information gained from a résumé or interview, an employer makes inferences about an applicant's job qualifications. Buying an affordable home requires you to make valid inferences about your potential income and your ability to make mortgage payments. In each case, the inferences you make are based on the facts at hand. So it is with reading. To understand what an author *means,* consider what he or she *says.* In addition, your knowledge about the author's topic and your experience will also help you make valid inferences.

Read the following short paragraph followed by four inferences. Decide which inference is valid.

> A woman gets out of her car carrying a poodle. She enters a building. The sign on the building says Hawthorne Veterinary Clinic.
>
> 1. The woman owns the clinic.
> 2. The dog was injured in a car accident.
> 3. The woman is probably taking her dog to see the vet.
> 4. The woman wants to use the telephone.

First of all, consider the facts that are given: A woman carrying a dog into a building and the sign on the building that identifies it as a veterinary clinic. Second, what do you know from experience? People take their dogs to a veterinarian either because the dog needs care or because they need to board the dog. Taking facts and experience into account, the first inference is invalid because there are no facts in the paragraph to suggest that the woman owns the clinic. The second inference is invalid for the same reason: Nothing in the paragraph indicates that the dog is injured or that there was an accident. Facts and experience make the fourth inference invalid also. First of all, people usually do not go to veterinary clinics to use the telephone. Second, most people would probably leave the dog in the car while they made a phone call. Third, the facts in the paragraph do not indicate that the woman even wants to make a call. The third inference is a valid inference because the facts support it. The word *probably* also helps to make this inference valid. Even though experience suggests that the woman is taking the dog to the vet, you cannot say for certain what her purpose is without more information.

The most important thing to remember about inferences is that they are *guesses* about what is reasonable or probable based on whatever information is available. Therefore, get in the habit of questioning what you read and asking of the author, "How do you know?" and "Who says so?"

The following question is based on "How the Civil Rights Movement Began" on page 13. Read the question and the list of inferences that follows it. Which inference is valid?

> Why was the Supreme Court's decision to end all segregation on public transportation important to Rosa Parks and the demonstrators?
>
> 1. It meant that Parks could not be arrested again.
> 2. It put an end to racial discrimination.
> 3. It guaranteed that blacks would be treated fairly in court.
> 4. It showed that blacks could achieve their goals through nonviolent protest.

The first inference is invalid because the court decision was based solely on Parks's refusal to give up her seat, not on any other alleged crime. The second inference is invalid because racial discrimination has continued, as history and experience have shown. The third inference is invalid because some blacks have continued to receive unfair treatment in court—in the selection of juries, for example. Only the fourth inference is valid. The boycott had worked. African Americans could therefore assume that additional goals might be achieved through nonviolent forms of protest, such as boycotting businesses.

One or two comprehension questions following each reading selection in *The Reader's Corner* ask you to make inferences. When answering these questions, rely on your experience and the author's stated details.

Use Context Clues to Define Unfamiliar Words

Often in your reading you may encounter an unfamiliar word. Of course you can use your dictionary to determine the word's meaning, but before you do that, look for clues in the context that may help you define the word. Then use your dictionary to verify the meaning if you are still uncertain. By identifying and using four types of clues, you can improve your ability to define words in context.

Context refers to the sentence in which an unfamiliar word appears. If the sentence contains no clues, enlarge the context by looking for clues in the sentences just before and after the one that contains the word you are trying to define. The four types of clues are *definition, example, contrast,* and *experience.*

The *definition clue* consists of either punctuation marks that set off a synonym or longer definition or key words that signal the reader to look for a definition. In the following examples, words to be defined are in bold type.

> Jane **commiserated,** or sympathized, with a friend whose dog was lost. (A synonym is set off by commas.)

> **Cognition** (the study of how people think and learn) attracts many psychology majors as a field of specialization. (The definition is set off by parentheses.)

> To **harass** someone means to annoy him or her repeatedly. (The word *means* signals that a definition follows.)

The *example clue* is an illustration or explanation that defines an unfamiliar word either by creating familiar images in your mind or by recalling familiar objects, ideas, or situations. The following sentences contain example clues and a boldfaced word to be defined.

> Headaches, minor coughs and colds, and muscular aches and pains illustrate a few of the common **ailments** that are usually not serious unless they persist. (The examples of headaches, minor coughs and colds, and muscular aches and pains are clues that some ailments are minor illnesses.)

> Humans have **physiological needs** such as those for safety, food, and sex. (The examples of safety, food, and sex are clues that physiological needs are those needed to sustain life.)

The *contrast clue* is an antonym, or a word having an opposite meaning to that of the word you are trying to define. The following sentences contain antonyms to help you define the boldfaced words.

> Although we first thought that the painting was a **forgery,** it turned out to be genuine. (*Genuine* is an antonym of *forgery. Genuine* means real or authentic, so *forgery* means fake.)

> Drinking water should be clear, but the water coming out of my faucet looks **murky.** (*Clear* is an antonym of *murky.* Therefore, *murky* means unclear or clouded.)

The *experience clue* is one that you bring to the reading along with your skill of making an inference. By using the information an author

TABLE 5 Questions for Active Readers

Strategy	Questions to Ask
FIND THE MAIN IDEA	What is the author's topic? What is the author's opinion?
IDENTIFY THE DETAILS	What are the stated facts, reasons, or examples? What do the facts, reasons, or examples explain? What transitions can I find?
DETERMINE THE PURPOSE	Why did the author write this? What does the author expect of me? What do the title and the main idea tell me?
LOOK FOR PATTERNS	What are the author's main idea and purpose? How are the details related? What do the transitions tell me?
MAKE INFERENCES	What do I already know? What are the stated details? What do the details mean?
DEFINE WORDS IN CONTEXT	What are the author's clues? What signal words can I find? What does my experience tell me?

has provided in a sentence and by using what you have learned from experience in similar situations, you may be able to determine the meaning of an unfamiliar word. What clues can you find in the following sentences to help you define the boldfaced words?

> Some carry a rabbit's foot, but my **talisman** is a four-leaf clover. (If you know that a rabbit's foot and a four-leaf clover are good luck charms, then you can guess that a talisman is also a good luck charm.)

> The bookstore manager was **irate** when the student demanded a refund for a book that was dirty and filled with marginal notes. (How would you feel if someone to whom you had loaned a book returned it dirty and marked? You probably would be very angry, or irate, as was the bookstore manager.)

Remember that self-questioning keeps you focused and reading actively. As a review, Table 5 above lists the essential reading skills and questions to ask that will help you to identify an author's main idea, details, purpose, and pattern; to make inferences from your reading; and to use context clues to define words.

PART ONE

Americans in Transition

❧

As reflected in the latest census report, the face of America is becoming less white. Latinos will soon outnumber African Americans as the largest minority population in the United States. Asian immigrants are a widening slice of the American demographic pie. An immigrant culture from its beginnings, America is experiencing a new wave of people and ideas from all parts of the world. As our schools, communities, and workplaces grow more diverse, we must rethink what it means to be an American man or woman.

The selections in Part 1 are about individuals, past and present, who are struggling to preserve their identities and working to achieve their dreams. As you read and think about the selections, ask yourself these questions: Who am I? What do I value? What do I want?

FIRST THOUGHTS

To prepare yourself for the reading selection, answer the following questions, either on your own or in a group discussion.

1. Who was Jackie Robinson, and what do you know about him?
2. What do you know about the game of baseball, the National League, or the sport's most famous players?
3. Preview the title, headnote, and first one or two paragraphs. What do you think will follow?

WORD ALERT

barnstorming (1) traveling around the country, making speeches or performing
gawk (1) to stare stupidly
mocked (3) ridiculed, scorned, made fun of
vile (4) unpleasant or objectionable
forbearance (4) patience, restraint
suppress (5) to check or inhibit the expression of an impulse, to deliberately
hold back
rattling (7) unnerving, upsetting
reverence (8) a feeling of awe and respect and often love
mission (9) a special assignment given to a person or group
appalled (12) upset, dismayed

ૐ Jackie Robinson

HENRY AARON

*Henry ("Hank") Aaron holds the major league home run
record (755) and works for the Atlanta Braves organization.
In this article, he explains how baseball great Jackie Robinson influenced his career and what Robinson's life has
meant to the sport of baseball and to the nation.*

I WAS 14 YEARS OLD when I first saw Jackie Robinson. It was the spring 1
of 1948, the year after Jackie changed my life by breaking baseball's

color line. His team, the Brooklyn Dodgers, made a stop in my home-town of Mobile, Alabama, while **barnstorming** its way north to start the season, and while he was there, Jackie spoke to a big crowd of black folks over on Davis Avenue. I think he talked about segregation, but I didn't hear a word that came out of his mouth. Jackie Robinson was such a hero to me that I couldn't do anything but **gawk** at him.

They say certain people are bigger than life, but Jackie Robinson is   2 the only man I've known who truly was. In 1947 life in America—at least my America, and Jackie's—was segregation. It was two worlds that were afraid of each other. There were separate schools for blacks and whites, separate restaurants, separate hotels, separate drinking fountains and separate baseball leagues. Life was unkind to black people who tried to bring those worlds together. It could be hateful. But Jackie Robinson, God bless him, was bigger than all of that.

Jackie Robinson had to be bigger than life. He had to be bigger   3 than the Brooklyn teammates who got up a petition to keep him off the ball club, bigger than the pitchers who threw at him or the base runners who dug their spikes into his shin, bigger than the bench jockeys who hollered for him to carry their bags and shine their shoes, bigger than the so-called fans who **mocked** him with mops on their heads and wrote him death threats.

When Branch Rickey first met with Jackie about joining the   4 Dodgers, he told him that for three years he would have to turn the other cheek and silently suffer all the **vile** things that would come his way. Believe me, it wasn't Jackie's nature to do that. He was a fighter, the proudest and most competitive person I've ever seen. This was a man who, as a lieutenant in the Army, risked a court-martial by refus-ing to sit in the back of a military bus. But when Rickey read to him from *The Life of Christ,* Jackie understood the wisdom and the neces-sity of **forbearance.**

To this day, I don't know how he withstood the things he did with-   5 out lashing back. I've been through a lot in my time, and I consider myself to be a patient man, but I know I couldn't have done what Jackie did. I don't think anybody else could have done it. Somehow, though, Jackie had the strength to **suppress** his instincts, to sacrifice his pride for his people's. It was an incredible act of selflessness that brought the races closer together than ever before and shaped the dreams of an entire generation.

Before Jackie Robinson broke the color line, I wasn't permitted   6 even to think about being a professional baseball player. I once men-tioned something to my father about it, and he said, "Ain't no colored ballplayers." There were the Negro Leagues of course, where the Dodgers discovered Jackie, but my mother, like most, would rather her son be a schoolteacher than a Negro Leaguer. All that changed when Jackie put on No. 42 and started stealing bases in a Brooklyn uniform.

Jackie's character was much more important than his batting av- 7 erage, but it certainly helped that he was a great ball player, a .311 career hitter whose trademark was **rattling** pitchers and fielders with his daring base running. He wasn't the best Negro League talent at the time he was chosen, and baseball wasn't really his best sport—he had been a football and track star at UCLA—but he played the game with a ferocious creativity that gave the country a good idea of what it had been missing all those years. With Jackie in the infield, the Dodgers won six National League pennants.

I believe every black person in America had a piece of those pen- 8 nants. There's never been another ball player who touched people as Jackie did. The only comparable athlete, in my experience, was Joe Louis.[1] The difference was that Louis competed against white men; Jackie competed with them as well. He was taking us over segregation's threshold into a new land whose scenery made every black person stop and stare in **reverence.** We were all with Jackie. We slid into every base that he swiped, ducked at every fastball that hurtled toward his head. The circulation of the Pittsburgh *Courier,* the leading black newspaper, increased by 100,000 when it began reporting on him regularly. All over the country, black preachers would call together their congregations just to pray for Jackie and urge them to demonstrate the same forbearance that he did.

Later in his career, when the "Great Experiment" had proved to be 9 successful and other black players had joined him, Jackie allowed his instincts to take over in issues of race. He began striking back and speaking out. And when Jackie Robinson spoke, every black player got the message. He made it clear to us that we weren't playing just for ourselves or for our teams; we were playing for our people. I don't think it's a coincidence that the black players of the late '50s and '60s—me, Roy Campanella, Monte Irvin, Willie Mays, Ernie Banks, Frank Robinson, Bob Gibson and others—dominated the National League. If we played as if we were on a **mission,** it was because Jackie Robinson had sent us out on one.

---

[1] Born in 1914, Joe Louis was an American prizefighter. He held the world heavyweight title from 1937 to 1949. He successfully defended this title 25 times. He died in 1981.

Even after he retired in 1956 and was elected to the Hall of Fame   10
in 1962, Jackie continued to chop along the path that was still a long
way from being cleared. He campaigned for baseball to hire a black
third-base coach, then a black manager. In 1969 he refused an invita-
tion to play in an old-timers' game at Yankee Stadium to protest the
lack of progress along those lines.

One of the great players from my generation, Frank Robinson   11
(who was related to Jackie only in spirit), finally became the first black
manager, in 1975. Jackie was gone by then. His last public appearance
was at the 1972 World Series, where he showed up with white hair, carrying a cane and going blind from diabetes. He died nine days later.

Most of the black players from Jackie's day were at the funeral, but   12
I was **appalled** by how few of the younger players showed up to pay
him tribute. At the time, I was 41 home runs short of Babe Ruth's
career record, and when Jackie died, I really felt that it was up to me
to keep his dream alive. I was inspired to dedicate my home-run record to the same great cause to which Jackie dedicated his life. I'm still
inspired by Jackie Robinson. Hardly a day goes by that I don't think
of him.

COMPREHENSION CHECK

Purpose and Main Idea

1. What is the author's topic?
   a. sports
   b. baseball
   c. Jackie Robinson
   d. African American athletes

2. What is the author's central idea?
   a. African Americans have made significant contributions to the
      field of sports.
   b. Baseball is one of America's best-loved sports.
   c. Many African Americans have achieved fame in baseball.
   d. Jackie Robinson broke the color line and changed baseball
      forever.

3. The author's primary purpose is to
   a. express his ideas about Robinson's influence on his own life
      and our national life.
   b. inform readers about what life for minorities was like in 1947.
   c. persuade readers to take more of an interest in team sports.

    d. entertain us with amusing stories about the life of Jackie
       Robinson.

Details

4. In the author's opinion, the only athlete comparable to Jackie
   Robinson was
   a. Willie Mays.
   b. Roy Campanella.
   c. Joe Louis.
   d. Ernie Banks.

5. According to the author, in what other sports did Jackie Robinson
   excel?
   a. golf and tennis
   b. basketball and hockey
   c. football and track
   d. soccer and swimming

6. According to the author, Jackie's _____ was more important
   than his batting average.
   a. race
   b. daring
   c. talent
   d. character

7. Jackie Robinson accomplished all of the following *except* which one?
   a. He became a .311 career hitter.
   b. He was elected to the Hall of Fame.
   c. He played in an old-timers' game at Yankee Stadium in 1969.
   d. He helped his team win six National League pennants.

8. What is the author's dominant organizational pattern?
   a. Sequence: The author traces the development of Robinson's
     career.
   b. Comparison/contrast: The author compares baseball players
     to other athletes.
   c. Cause/effect: The author explains the reasons behind Robin-
     son's success.
   d. Definition: The author defines sportsmanship in baseball.

Inferences

9. In the first sentence of paragraph 9, what does the author mean
   by "Great Experiment"?
   a. The Brooklyn Dodgers hired its first black player.
   b. In 1947, baseball leagues were segregated.

    c. As a lieutenant in the Army, Robinson refused to sit in the back of a military bus.

    d. Robinson campaigned for baseball to hire a black third-base coach and a black manager.

10. According to the author, Robinson "understood the wisdom and the necessity of forbearance." Therefore, Robinson probably would have most admired which one of these 1960s civil rights advocates?

    a. Stokely Carmichael, an activist for the Black Power movement

    b. Bobby Seale, a prominent member of the Black Panthers, a militant group

    c. Martin Luther King, Jr., a preacher and advocate of nonviolent protest

    d. Malcolm X, a political leader of the Black Muslims

WORKING WITH WORDS

Complete the sentences below with these words from Word Alert:

barnstorming	rattling	reverence	mission	gawk
forbearance	suppress	appalled	mocked	vile

1. When the algebra instructor accidently punched a hole in his pocket with his pen, the students could not _____ their laughter.

2. Athletes who have become celebrities can expect people to _____ at them whenever they appear in public.

3. Raymond took a big gulp of his soda and immediately spit it out because it tasted _____ .

4. The instructor said to the students, "I am _____ that you would think I do not treat everyone fairly."

5. When someone shouts at you in anger, do you have the _____ not to shout back?

6. Michael Jordan's fans treat him with a respect that amounts to _____ .

7. "It is my _____ ," said the instructor, "to make sure that everyone develops the skills needed to pass this course."

8. Because the other students were _____ her by talking about the test and all the information she had not studied, Ramona became increasingly anxious.

9. The rock group Anorexia performed to sold-out audiences while _____ their way from Anchorage, Alaska, to Key West, Florida.

10. The fifth graders _____ their teacher by making faces and drawing unflattering pictures.

THINKING DEEPER

Ideas for discussion and writing:

1. The author says Jackie Robinson is the only man he knew who truly was bigger than life. Discuss what you think the author means by "bigger than life." Then give an example of someone you know or have read about who is bigger than life.

2. The author says that Jackie Robinson's sacrifice and selflessness "brought the races closer together than ever before and shaped the dreams of an entire nation." Discuss people you know or have read about whose efforts or accomplishments have brought people closer together.

3. Discuss how Jackie Robinson's life and career illustrate the Part 1 theme, *Americans in Transition*. For example, how had Americans' attitudes about African American athletes changed between the time Robinson first played for the Dodgers in 1947 and his retirement in 1956? Do race issues trouble national or college athletic teams today? If so, how are athletes and their fans dealing with these issues?

4. In this selection, the author writes about a man he admires, a man who both influenced his career and served as a role model. Write about someone you admire and respect, someone who has had a positive influence on your choices and behavior.

FIRST THOUGHTS

To prepare yourself for the reading selection, answer the following questions, either on your own or in a group discussion.

1. What do you know about Vietnamese family values?

2. What is one of your own family values?

3. Preview the title, headnote, and first one or two paragraphs. What do you think will follow?

WORD ALERT

perpetuate (3) prolong, extend
embodiment (4) representation
cornerstone (5) a fundamental basis
solicitude (5) concerned, attentive attitude
solemn (8) deeply serious, ceremonial
subversive (9) intending to undermine, corrupt, or ruin
exodus (10) a mass departure

❧ Vietnamese: A Lifetime Commitment

TA THUC PHU

The author is a resident of Winter Park, Florida. He served as a colonel in the Army of the Republic of Vietnam. His essay is a response to a question The Orlando Sentinel *asked readers: "How do you deal with your parents as they get older?"*

A VIETNAMESE SAYING GOES: "The father's creative work is as great as the Thai Son mountain; the mother's love is as large as the river flowing out to sea. Respect and love your parents from the bottom of your hearts. Achieve your duty of filial piety as a proper standard of well-behaved children." 1

I was pleased to see "Saturday Special" ask the question, "How do 2 you deal with your parents as they get older?" I want to relate some characteristics of the Vietnamese culture. You see, living together with elderly parents under the same roof is one of our national traditions. In fact, I am honored to have my 92-year-old mother-in-law living with me and my wife.

The family is the basic institution with which to **perpetuate** soci- 3 ety and provide protection to individuals. Generally speaking, the family structure in Southeastern Asia is more complex than the American family structure.

In Vietnamese society, the father is the head of the family. How- 4 ever, the father shares with his wife and children collective responsibilities—legally, morally and spiritually—and these responsibilities continue, even after children are grown up and married. Always, the mother has the same status as the father. In addition, she is the **embodiment** of love and the spirit of self-denial and sacrifice.

Vietnamese parents consider the parent-child relationship their 5 most important responsibility, and they train their children for a lifetime. In effect, the family is the small school where children learn to follow rules of behavior and speaking. The **cornerstone** of the children's behavior in the family is filial piety. Filial piety consists of loving, respecting and obeying one's parents. As a result, the obligation to obey parents does not end with the coming of age or marriage. Filial piety means **solicitude** and support of one's parents, chiefly in their old age. Vietnamese elders never live by themselves or in nursing homes. Instead, they live with one of their children, usually the eldest son. This is a family custom practiced in all Vietnamese homes.

We do not want to live far apart from our parents, regardless of 6 whether they are young or old, healthy or infirm, because we want to take care of them at any time until their deaths. That is our concept of gratitude to our parents for their hard work and sacrifice throughout the years.

I recall that, when I was growing up, my mother was severely crip- 7 pled. When we walked together, she held on to my arm for balance. It was difficult to coordinate our steps. My wife and I took turns holding my mother when she cried, and we helped her to walk two hours a day to exercise her body.

By living with our aging parents under the same roof, we also have 8 many occasions to demonstrate our respect for them in the **solemn** days of the lunar year, such as New Year's Day (Tet), and to celebrate their anniversaries. Our children would present New Year's wishes and symbols of good luck, such as bright red ribbons, to their grandparents to represent prosperity and longevity.

Most important in the Vietnamese value system is undoubtedly 9 our belief that children ought to be grateful to parents for the debt of birth, rearing and education. Children are taught to think of parents first, even at their own expense, to make sacrifices for their parents' sake, to love and care for them in their old age. Unfortunately, that practice is denied now by the communist regime in Vietnam. Children have been taught to spy on their parents and report to the Communist Party any **subversive** talk or irregular behavior.

Above all, since April 30, 1975, after the collapse of Saigon with the 10 communist takeover of South Vietnam and the tragic **exodus** of more than 2 million refugees to all parts of the world in search of freedom and a better future, Vietnamese families still practice the custom of living with the parents under the same roof. Deep feelings for families and ties to elders are still strong. These feelings and ties will endure despite these times of change. Even when our parents have been gone many years, we still think of them as living with us.

COMPREHENSION CHECK

Purpose and Main Idea

1. What is the author's topic?
   a. the war in Vietnam
   b. child-rearing practices in Vietnam
   c. holidays and celebrations in Vietnam
   d. how the Vietnamese deal with parents
2. What is the author's central idea?
   a. "I want to relate. . . ." paragraph 2, sentence 2
   b. "Vietnamese parents. . . . paragraph 5, first sentence
   c. "The cornerstone. . . ." paragraph 5, sentence 3
   d. "Most important. . . ." paragraph 9, first sentence
3. The author's primary purpose is to
   a. persuade readers that Vietnamese values are superior to others.
   b. inform readers about some characteristics of Vietnamese culture.
   c. express his feelings about the treatment of parents in other societies.
   d. entertain readers with stories about his parents' childhood.

Details

4. According to the author's details, which one of the following statements about the Vietnamese family is true?
   a. The father has the most status.
   b. The mother has more status than the father.
   c. Mother and father have equal status.
   d. Children have more status than either of the parents.

5. In Vietnamese culture, which institution perpetuates society and provides protection to individuals?
   a. family
   b. marriage
   c. the educational system
   d. the Communist Party

6. Which duty is the cornerstone of children's behavior within the family?
   a. dependability
   b. filial piety
   c. self-denial
   d. gratitude

7. Most important in the Vietnamese value system is
   a. parents' sacrifices.
   b. society's needs.
   c. children's gratitude toward parents.
   d. obedience to the government.

8. In which paragraph is *definition* the dominant pattern?
   a. paragraph 1
   b. paragraph 2
   c. paragraph 5
   d. paragraph 9

Inferences

9. Based on the context in which it is used, the word *infirm* in paragraph 6 means
   a. tired.
   b. aged.
   c. fit.
   d. ill.

10. Based on the author's details, which one of the following would be an example of filial piety?

a. moving far away from an elderly parent
b. suggesting that parents buy or rent their own home
c. doing what you want without regard to parents' approval
d. seeking a parent's advice about a job or relationship

WORKING WITH WORDS

Complete the sentences below with these words from Word Alert:

perpetuate　　cornerstone　　subversive　　exodus
solicitude　　embodiment　　solemn

1. Students would rather an instructor show _____ than a lack of concern.
2. Do not stand in the doorway when class is over or you might be trampled in the _____ .
3. A belief in a higher power is the _____ of many religions.
4. The crowd was _____ during the flag raising and the singing of the national anthem.
5. People who celebrate New Year's Eve hope to see the last of the old year's troubles and to _____ their successes.
6. Only a few people, such as Elizabeth Taylor or Marilyn Monroe, are the _____ of what it means to be a movie star.
7. Many believe that violent song lyrics and racist websites are a _____ influence on today's youth.

THINKING DEEPER

Ideas for discussion and writing:

1. According to the author, the duty of filial piety is important to Vietnamese families. How important is this concept in your culture, or to people of other cultures? What examples of filial piety have you seen in your life or that of others?
2. Read again the Vietnamese saying in paragraph 1 of the selection. Discuss this saying with a small group of your classmates. What does the saying mean? Do you and the members of your group have similar or different feelings about the roles and duties of mothers, fathers, and children? Write a saying of your own that

expresses your ideas. Then share your saying with the rest of the class.

3. Discuss how the Vietnamese attitudes toward the elderly that are explained in this selection illustrate the Part 1 theme, *Americans in Transition*. For example, what similarities and differences do you see between the values and attitudes expressed in this selection and your own? What can Vietnamese Americans and other Americans learn from each other? What changes in customs, traditions, and values might or might not occur when people leave their countries of origin to live in another country?

4. In this selection, the author says that the Vietnamese value the sacrifices that parents make for their children. Write about someone you know who sacrificed his or her own needs or desires for those of a child.

FIRST THOUGHTS

To prepare yourself for the reading selection, answer the following questions, either on your own or in a group discussion.

1. What do you know of the Qurán and its teachings about parents?
2. What are your views about caring for aging parents?
3. Preview the title, headnote, and first one or two paragraphs. What do you think will follow?

WORD ALERT

caliber (3) degree of worth or quality
perseverance (3) persistence, steadfastness
turbulent (3) restless, disturbed, chaotic
fragile (4) lacking physical or emotional strength
sacred (6) worthy of respect
dependent (8) relying on or requiring someone's support

ᴕ Qurán Lesson: Exalt Moms, Dads

YASMEEN QADRI

The author teaches in the College of Education at the University of Central Florida. She is the principal at the Muslim Academy in Goldenrod, Florida. This selection is another response to the question posed by The Orlando Sentinel: *"How do you deal with your parents as they get older?"*

THE MOST MISERABLE days of my life were when I was living in a dif- 1
ferent country, thousands of miles away from my parents.

Then, 20 years ago, my parents moved from India to the United 2
States to live with my sister. My father now is 82, my mother 68.

In India, my father was an ordinary man, but he worked very hard 3
to provide his children with the best education. Because public
schools in our city were not of a high **caliber,** he worked two jobs to

pay our tuition to a private school. Mom, with patience and **persever-ance,** walked me through the **turbulent** teenage years.

Those days when my parents fulfilled their responsibility are 4 gone. Now it is our turn to return love to our parents, to "handle with care" parents who are sometimes insecure and **fragile.**

My father, with his macho personality, still wants to maintain the 5 leadership role. This makes it challenging for us to make his American-born and reared grandchildren show him the same level of respect that we do. Despite a few challenges, we are fortunate to have our parents near us.

No doubt that lifestyles have changed today, not just in the United 6 States but throughout the world. For many families, respect, obedience and responsibility toward parents have become more of a fantasy than reality. Yet, no matter how much times change, parent-child relationships should and will remain strong. My faith has taught me that parents hold a **sacred** position. These verses from my religious book, the Qurán, further strengthen my belief:

"Treat your parents with great consideration; if either or both of 7 them live with you in their old age, do not say even 'fie' to them; nor rebuke them, but speak kind words to them; treat them with humility and tenderness and pray: 'Lord, be merciful to them just as they brought me up with kindness and affection.'"

I repeat these prayers daily, hoping that my parents never go 8 through the pain of being helpless or handicapped. Today, when both spouses work, it is a great challenge to take care of old, **dependent** parents. Although my parents live most of the time with my older sister, there are four siblings, and we share the responsibilities. My sister takes care of most of the finances, and I, for the most part, act as a counselor, listening to them and providing comfort and tender care.

The key to all this care is our faith. We strongly believe that we owe a 9 lot to our parents and will have rewards in the hereafter if we keep them happy. The Qurán mentions several times about parents' rights over those of their children. For example, it states "And we have enjoined upon man to do good to his parents. His mother bears him with trouble and she brings him forth in pain. And the bearing of him and the weaning of him." It also states, "Paradise lies under the feet of the mother."

We need to pass these values on to our children, so that we may 10 have a better life in our old age. Parents are the real strength and roots of a healthy family tree. As children, we need to strive to save these trees so that we can be under their shade. Without our parents, we could not have survived.

COMPREHENSION CHECK

Purpose and Main Idea

1. What is the author's topic?
    a. the history of the Qurán
    b. child rearing in India
    c. family relationships in India
    d. a lesson on respect for parents

2. Which sentence from the selection states the author's central idea?
    a. "Now it is our turn. . . ." paragraph 4, sentence 2
    b. "Despite a few challenges. . . ." paragraph 5, last sentence
    c. "My faith has taught me. . . ." paragraph 6, fourth sentence
    d. "We need to pass. . . ." paragraph 10, first sentence

3. The author's primary purpose is to
    a. express how her religious faith influences the way she treats her parents.
    b. inform readers about the traditions and culture of Indian Muslims.
    c. persuade readers to seek guidance from sacred texts.
    d. entertain readers with memories of her childhood.

Details

4. According to the author, all but which one of the following values have become more of a fantasy than a reality in the United States?
    a. obedience
    b. duty
    c. respect
    d. responsibility

5. The author says that the key to taking care of parents is
    a. tradition.
    b. love.
    c. faith.
    d. desire.

6. According to the author, the Qurán emphasizes
    a. parents' rights over children's rights.
    b. children's rights over parents' rights.
    c. equal rights for parents and children.
    d. limited rights for parents and children.

7. The author says that taking care of parents is a challenge when
    a. couples lack money.
    b. families are large.

    c. both spouses work.

    d. the parents are old.

8. What is the author's dominant organizational pattern?

    a. Sequence: The author traces the development of her religious faith.

    b. Comparison/contrast: The author compares the Qurán to other religious texts.

    c. Generalization then example: Examples from the Qurán explain the parents' sacred position in the family.

    d. Definition: The author defines the meaning of the word *macho.*

Inferences

9. If parents are the "strength and roots" of a healthy family tree (paragraph 10), then children are the

    a. leaves.

    b. water.

    c. soil.

    d. fruit.

10. Based on their views about parents and children, the authors of Selections 2 and 3 would be most likely to agree with which of the following sayings?

    a. Like mother, like daughter.

    b. Honor the father and the mother.

    c. The sins of the fathers are visited on the sons.

    d. Spare the rod and spoil the child.

WORKING WITH WORDS

Complete the sentences below with these words from Word Alert:

perseverance   turbulent   sacred
dependent   fragile   caliber

1. After a bout of pneumonia, a person's health may be so _____ that a relapse can occur.

2. During the _____ sixties, social unrest was the order of the day.

3. The _____ of civil rights activists and their supporters led to the enactment of antidiscrimination laws.

4. Because pets are _____ on their owners for food and shelter, owning a pet requires a commitment to its care.

5. To many, the American flag is a _____ symbol of democracy.
6. Joan chose to send her children to a private school because she
    thought the education they would receive there would be of a
    higher _____ than that in the public school.

THINKING DEEPER

Ideas for discussion and writing:

1. Religious teachings play a central role in the way the author and
    those of her culture treat parents. Do religious teachings play a
    role in your family life? What other teachings or beliefs influence
    the parent-child relationships in your culture?
2. Selections 2 and 3 discuss family values of two different cultures.
    What similarities and differences do you see in the Vietnamese
    and Indian family values as expressed in these selections? Which
    values and attitudes from one or both of these cultures do you
    also share?
3. Discuss how the attitudes toward parents explained in this selec-
    tion illustrate the Part 1 theme, *Americans in Transition.* For ex-
    ample, religious freedom is a cornerstone of democracy in the
    United States. Under the law, we are free to worship as we choose
    or to not worship if we so choose. Even so, people of different
    religions have not always been tolerant of one another. In the
    twenty-first century, how are we dealing with this problem? Do
    Americans seem more or less tolerant of differing religious views
    and practices? Does some discrimination still occur? What do
    you think?
4. Selections 2 and 3 were written in response to the question "How
    do you deal with your parents as they get older?" Write your own
    response to this question.

FIRST THOUGHTS

To prepare yourself for the reading selection, answer the following questions, either on your own or in a group discussion.

1. Where do we get names for children?
2. What does a name tell you about a person?
3. Preview the title, headnote, and first one or two paragraphs. What do you think will follow?

WORD ALERT

beckoned (2) signaled, motioned to
genealogist (11) one who studies or investigates family history
descent (11) ancestry, lineage
spawned (14) produced, gave rise to
shunning (20) avoiding, keeping away from
coin (21) to make, devise
Mosque (36) Islamic place of worship
deluged (45) overwhelmed
assimilation (58) absorption of a minority group into a prevailing culture

﷼ What's in a Name? Character, Identity, Ethnicity

DEBORAH P. WORK

What do names mean, and how do parents choose names for their children? In this selection the author, a writer from Fort Lauderdale, Florida, answers these questions.

L AFRANCES TROTTER WAS TALKING about how she came to name her 1
daughter.

She always knew a child of hers would be given a name that was 2
unique, a name no other child would answer to when the teacher
called roll or when a friend **beckoned** on a crowded street.

In her mind's eye, she had an image of a child who would be cul- 3
turally conscious and always aware of her heritage.

She turned to some friends from Nigeria, who helped name her 4
baby daughter, Akija. Akija Kalembre.

"I've studied African literature, and have always wanted to know 5
more about the culture, the food, and the different celebrations. It
seemed only natural that I would give my daughter an African name,"
says Trotter, who is African American.

But the name had to grow on her husband. "I don't like that," 6
he said.

To help the name take root in his heart and mind, she left it 7
around the house for him to see, spelled out in block letters on slips of
paper.

It worked. 8

"I was determined she would have a connection to her African 9
past," says Trotter, who lives in Sunrise, Florida. "It's like a present
from her ancestors."

Names are important. A parent's gift, they establish identity and 10
place, even if the name is too unusual to be found on a personalized
dime-store mug.

Dee Cattaneo, a Palm Beach County **genealogist,** says today's par- 11
ents have all but given up the traditional naming methods of the past.
For example, many families of European **descent** named their eldest
son after the husband's father. The next son took his maternal grandfather's name, with the same pattern used for girls. The children who
followed were given names that belonged to other relatives, so the
same names were recycled throughout families over and over.

"It would take ten children before a new name popped up," says 12
Cattaneo, a genealogist with Palm Beach Gardens Church of Latter
Day Saints.

But none of this is true today, she says. "The way parents name 13
their babies has changed drastically over the years. I feel sorry for
genealogists 100 years from now. They won't be able to figure anything out."

Unlike the sixties, which **spawned** a surge of children named for 14
social and environmental causes, like Harmony and Peace, the trend
today is toward names that reflect ethnic roots or economic status,
like Maxwell, Winthrop, and, what else, Rich.

And while the Bible still remains a popular place for parents of all 15
religions and nationalities to find a name, parents are also borrowing
names from their favorite TV characters or simply making them up.

Daisy Camacho, who is Puerto Rican, named her son Hector, four, 16
after his father. But her eight-year-old daughter, Christal, was named
after the star of a Hispanic soap opera.

Camacho, of Coral Springs, Florida, says her mother-in-law didn't 17
like the name at first because she was looking for something more traditionally Hispanic. But once she got hooked on the program, she
came to love the name.

"Everyone is out for the unusual," Cattaneo says. "We are seeing 18
more and more names that have no connection to family background
or history."

In African-American communities, for example, parents are com- 19
ing up with African-sounding names for their babies. Some are au-
thentic, some are not.

The trend began during the Civil Rights and black power move- 20
ments of the sixties, with black Americans choosing African or Islamic
names, **shunning** the names given to slaves by European masters.

Today, black parents are going one step further: they are using 21
their imaginations to **coin** new names.

This practice has been criticized for burdening children with awk- 22
ward names that are difficult to pronounce, while others see it as
positive.

Samida Jones, who works with teenage girls through a civic organ- 23
ization, has witnessed firsthand the movement toward non-European
names.

For every Helen and Sandra, there is a Saqauela and a Verlisha. 24
There is Zandra, Tamiya, Shenika, Zakia, Traveta, and Ashaunte. There
is even a Lakrishaw.

"I said, boy, times sure have changed. Where are the Marys and 25
Sues?" says Jones, whose own first name has Arabic roots. "Now it
seems people just make them up."

It's not difficult to understand black parents trying to forge a new 26
cultural identity for their children, Jones says. "The names have been
called weird, but they are just weird to people who expect European
names."

Still, made-up names lose something in the translation, she says. 27
"Parents should consider a name's true meaning, instead of merely
trying to be different."

Altan Erskin named her baby daughter Jamesha not because she 28
was searching for an identity, her roots, or anything remotely resem-
bling ethnicity.

She just likes the name's exotic sound.   29

"I knew I didn't want a plain name like Jane or Susan. And I wasn't 30 trying for anything that sounded African, either," says Erskin, twenty-one. "I just wanted something special. So I made her name up."

She liked the sound *mesha,* so she started at the beginning of the 31 alphabet: Amesha, Bamesha, Camesha.

"When I hit the letter *J,* I knew that was the one," Erskin says. "It 32 sounded just right."

Neither did Joni Sabri have any reservations when she named her 33 two sons. Since her husband Hassan Sabri is Palestinian, she gave her sons Muslim names.

"My husband gave me a book of Muslim names, complete with 34 meanings. I liked that they are many generations old; they go way back," says Sabri, who lives with her family in Pompano Beach.

Her four-year-old is Ali, "a famous Islamic name, very simple," 35 and the two-year-old is Khalid.

And Joni Sabri, raised Catholic but converted to Islam four years 36 ago, is Fatima at home and at the **Mosque.**

Muslims are encouraged to give their children certain names, says 37 Hassan Sabri, who has lived in this country for eight years.

For example, anything containing the verb *hamad,* which means 38 'to praise God,' is good.

"Mohammed is good for boys, and for girls Hamida is very popu- 39 lar," Hassan Sabri says.

One of a child's first rights is to be given a good name, Sabri 40 says. "Islam is a full way of life, and part of that way is naming your child."

Genealogist Cattaneo agrees that your name is your birthright, 41 and an important one because it follows you through life.

But the quest for the unforgettable name was not popular several 42 generations back, she says. And naming was as much about family as it was about that time in history.

"Back then, you didn't want to appear different or ethnic. Immi- 43 grants wanted to blend in; you wanted to be a part of where you lived," Cattaneo says.

"My husband's parents came over from Italy. They named him 44 Herbert, after Herbert Hoover. But they tucked in an Italian middle name—Mansuetto," she says. "Later on, they decided they didn't like (President) Hoover. So they call him Dick."

But today it's not as important to blend into the melting pot. Peo- 45 ple are looking for individuality. For example, libraries are being **del-**

uged with people looking for information to help them prove they have Native-American ancestry, Cattaneo says.

"The number of people tracing a Native heritage has increased 46 since the movie *Dances With Wolves,*" she says.

Virginia Osceola, who is a Seminole Indian, named her new baby 47 daughter Courtney. Her nine-year-old daughter Mercedes chose the name after hearing it in a local mall.

Osceola's other three youngsters are Tasha Kelly, Jo-Jo Dakota, and 48 Joseph Daniel.

Those, however, are their Anglo names, the names they use to at- 49 tend public school. But they also have Indian names.

What are they?   50

"They are only for Indians to know," Osceola says, taken aback 51 that someone would ask. "They are not to be given out."

Seminoles are not the only people who present their children with 52 two sets of names, one cultural.

In Franklin Tse's household, for example, his daughter Jennifer 53 might answer to Tse Ying Wah, which connotes elegance and gratitude.

"At a Chinese gathering, I would use that name," Tse says. "Most 54 parents, if they have hope and vision for their children, give them a name that will have impact. A dress you don't like you can throw away. But names always stick with you."

Many American Jews are turning back to traditional Hebrew 55 names like Ari and Rebecca.

Rochelle Liederman says there is no trick to naming Jewish ba- 56 bies, that it's really quite basic.

"You want to name your first child after a deceased loved one," 57 says Liederman.

Rochelle Liederman's experience illustrates how powerful a role 58 **assimilation** plays in naming a child.

Is trying to fit in always the answer? Maybe not, she says. 59

Her husband Lee Liederman recalls being in a fistfight every day 60 with public school kids who taunted those attending Hebrew school.

"It's difficult to retain your identity when there is prejudice. But it's 61 a hurtful thing to lose your name, knowing most of your family was killed during World War II," he says. "You wonder about who you are, you try to find out."

"And that's why I love this movement to identify your roots. Every- 62 one should push their children to name their offspring according to their ethnic background," says Rochelle Liederman.

COMPREHENSION CHECK

Purpose and Main Idea

1. What is the author's topic?
    a. European names
    b. African American names
    c. children's names
    d. family histories

2. Which sentence best states the author's central idea?
    a. In the past, parents named children after their ancestors.
    b. The trend today is toward names that reflect character, ethnicity, identity.
    c. In the sixties, naming children for social or environmental causes was a popular trend.
    d. Today, black parents coin imaginative new names for their children.

3. The author's primary purpose is to
    a. inform readers about trends in naming and what they mean.
    b. persuade readers to choose names for children that reflect their ethnic roots.
    c. entertain readers by mocking parents' weird choices of names.
    d. trace her heritage and the origin of her family name.

Details

4. Parents today choose children's names for all but which one of the following reasons, according to the author?
    a. to express individuality
    b. to honor ancestors
    c. to predict the child's future
    d. to reflect character or religious values

5. Of the author's examples below, which one is a made-up name— one that has no cultural or ancestral origins?
    a. Hamida
    b. Jamesha
    c. Mary
    d. Rebecca

6. According to the author, which of the following is *not* a popular source for finding a child's name today?
    a. the Bible
    b. TV characters
    c. the imagination
    d. family names

7. Which one of the paragraphs listed below is organized by generalization then example?
   a. paragraph 11
   b. paragraph 14
   c. paragraph 17
   d. paragraph 44

8. Which one of the paragraphs listed below is organized by com-
   parison/contrast?
   a. paragraph 11
   b. paragraph 14
   c. paragraph 17
   d. paragraph 44

Inferences

9. _____ and _____ agree that children have a right to a good
   name.
   a. Daisy Camacho and Virginia Osceola
   b. genealogist Cattaneo and Joni Sabri
   c. Altan Erskine and Samida Jones
   d. Tse Ying Wah and Rochelle Liederman

10. Cassius Clay, the American prizefighter, was named for Cassius
    Marcellus Clay (1810–1903), the American abolitionist who was
    minister to Russia. Clay later changed his name to Muhammad
    Ali. Using information from the selection, what is the probable
    meaning of this name?
    a. leader of the people
    b. simple man
    c. African father
    d. one who praises God

WORKING WITH WORDS

Complete the sentences below with these words from Word Alert:

genealogist	beckoned	deluged
assimilation	descent	Mosque
shunning	spawned	coin

1. Recent articles about the possible cloning of human organs in
   the future have _____ discussions about the ethics of genetic
   research.

2. The crew on the sailboat _____ to their friends on shore, invit-
    ing them to come aboard.

3. Whenever a new technological breakthrough occurs, someone
    must _____ a word or phrase to describe it.

4. Religious sites such as the reclining buddha or the Blue _____
    are popular tourist attractions.

5. When walking alone at night, stay on lighted walkways in heavily
    traveled areas, _____ dark alleys and out-of-the-way places.

6. If you want to trace your family history, a visit to a _____ may
    help.

7. Immigrants who seek _____ into their adopted cultures will
    learn the language and take part in the native people's customs
    and celebrations.

8. Lafrances Trotter named her daughter Akija Kalembre to cele-
    brate her African _____ .

9. Celebrities such as popular film stars and famous athletes
    are _____ with tons of mail and gifts from fans.

THINKING DEEPER

Ideas for discussion and writing:

1. Where do we get names, and why do we choose them? Discuss
    names of people you know that reflect the author's examples:
    biblical names, family names, made-up names, and so on.
    What reasons does the author give that motivate people's choice
    of a name? What additional origins of names or reasons for
    choosing a name can you think of that the author does not
    mention?

2. Working with a small group of students, research and discuss the
    origins and meanings of your names. Two possible sources to
    consider are a naming dictionary (available in your library's ref-
    erence section or online) and your parents. Ask them to explain
    the origin and meaning of your name and their reasons for
    choosing it. Then share your results with the rest of the class.

3. Discuss how this selection illustrates the Part 1 theme, *Americans
    in Transition.* For example, the author explains past and present
    trends in naming children and how these trends reflect their

times. What trends in naming have you observed in your lifetime? What social changes or developments can you forecast for the twenty-first century and what new trends in naming might occur as a result?

4. As explained in the selection, people have different reasons for naming their children and trends in naming change over time. Write about a name you would choose for a girl or boy and explain the reasons for your choice.

FIRST THOUGHTS

To prepare yourself for the reading selection, answer the following questions, either on your own or in a group discussion.

1. How many languages do you speak?
2. What is the value of knowing more than one language?
3. Preview the title, headnote, and first one or two paragraphs. What do you think will follow?

WORD ALERT

extolled (1) praised highly
immersed (5) deeply involved, absorbed
ironic (5) contrary to what is expected
scrutiny (7) close examination
enclaves (8) distinctly bounded areas enclosed within a larger unit; ethnic
  neighborhoods within a city
reproach (10) disapproval, criticism
facility (11) ease in doing

❧ My Spanish Standoff

GABRIELLA KUNTZ

*The author, a retired elementary-school teacher, lives in
Cape Girardeau, Missouri. In this selection, she explains her
reasons for insisting that her children learn English.*

ONCE AGAIN MY 17-year-old daughter comes home from a foreign-language fair at her high school and accusingly tells me about the pluses of being able to speak two languages. Speaker after speaker has **extolled** the virtues of becoming fluent in another language. My daughter is frustrated by the fact that I'm bilingual and have purposely declined to teach her to speak Spanish, my native tongue. She is not the only one who has wondered why my children don't speak Spanish. Over the years friends, acquaintances and family have asked me the

From *Newsweek*, 5/4/98 © 1998 Newsweek, Inc. All rights reserved. Reprinted by permission.

same question. Teachers have asked my children. My family, of course, has been more judgmental.

I was born in Lima, Peru, and came to the United States for the first 2 time in the early '50s, when I was 6 years old. At the parochial school my sister and I attended in Hollywood, Calif., there were only three Hispanic families at the time. I don't know when or how I learned English. I guess it was a matter of survival. My teacher spoke no Spanish. Neither did my classmates. All I can say is that at some point I no longer needed to translate. When I spoke in English I thought in English, and when I spoke in Spanish I thought in Spanish. I also learned about peanut-butter-and-jelly sandwiches, Halloween and Girl Scouts.

We went to a high school in Burbank. Again, there were few His- 3 panic students at the time. My sister and I spoke English without an "accent." This pleased my father no end. He would beam with pleasure when teachers, meeting him and my mother for the first time and hearing their labored English, would comment that they had no idea English was not our native tongue.

My brother was born in Los Angeles in 1959, and we would speak 4 both English and Spanish to him. When he began to talk, he would point to an object and say its name in both languages. He was, in effect, a walking, talking English-Spanish dictionary. I have often wondered how his English would have turned out, but circumstances beyond our control prevented it.

Because of political changes in Peru in the early '60s (my father 5 being a diplomat), we had to return to Peru. Although we had no formal schooling in Spanish, we were able to communicate in the language. I was thankful my parents had insisted that we speak Spanish at home. At first our relatives said that we spoke Spanish with a slight accent. But over time the accent disappeared, and we became **immersed** in the culture, our culture. My brother began his schooling in Peru, and even though he attended a school in which English was taught, he speaks the language with an accent. I find that **ironic** because he was the one born in the United States, and my sister and I are the naturalized citizens.

In 1972 I fell in love and married an American who had been living 6 in Peru for a number of years. Our first son was born there, but when he was 6 months old, we came back to the States. My husband was going to get his doctorate at a university in Texas.

It was in Texas that, for the first time, I lived in a community with 7 many Hispanics in the United States. I encountered them at the grocery store, the laundry, the mall, church. I also began to see how the Anglos in the community treated them. Of course, I don't mean all, but enough to make me feel uncomfortable. Because I'm dark and have dark eyes and hair, I personally experienced that look, that unspoken and spoken word expressing prejudice. If I entered a department store, one of two things was likely to happen. Either I was ignored, or I was followed closely by the salesperson. The garments I took into the changing room were carefully counted. My check at the grocery store took more **scrutiny** than an Anglo's. My children were complimented on how "clean" they were instead of how cute. Somehow, all Hispanics seemed to be lumped into the category of illegal immigrants, notwithstanding that many Hispanic families have lived for generations in Texas and other Southwestern states.

To be fair, I also noticed that the Latinos lived in their own **en-** 8 **claves,** attended their own churches, and many of them spoke English with an accent. And with their roots firmly established in the United States, their Spanish was not perfect either.

It was the fact that they spoke neither language well and the prej- 9 udice I experienced that prompted my husband and me to decide that English, and English only, would be spoken in our house. By this time my second dark-haired, dark-eyed son had been born, and we did not want to take a chance that if I spoke Spanish to them, somehow their English would be compromised. In other words, they would have an accent. I had learned to speak English without one, but I wasn't sure they would.

When our eldest daughter was born in 1980, we were living in 10 southeast Missouri. Again, we decided on an English-only policy. If our children were going to live in the United States, then their English should be beyond **reproach.** Of course, by eliminating Spanish we have also eliminated part of their heritage. Am I sorry? About the culture, yes; about the language, no. In the Missouri Legislature, there are bills pending for some sort of English-only law. I recently read an article in a national magazine about the Ozarks where some of the townspeople are concerned about the numbers of Hispanics who have come to work in poultry plants there. It seemed to me that their "concerns" were actually prejudice. There is a definite creeping in of anti-Hispanic sentiment in this country. Even my daughter, yes, the one who is upset over not being bilingual, admits to hearing "Hispanic jokes" said in front of her at school. You see, many don't realize despite her looks, that she's a minority. I want to believe that her flawless English is a contributing factor.

Last summer I took my 10-year-old daughter to visit my brother, 11 who is working in Mexico City. She picked up a few phrases and words with the **facility** that only the very young can. I just might teach her Spanish. You see, she is fair with light brown hair and blue eyes.

COMPREHENSION CHECK

Purpose and Main Idea

1. What is the author's topic?
    a. the difficulty of learning languages
    b. why her children don't speak Spanish
    c. her reasons in favor of bilingual education
    d. the benefits of speaking two languages

2. Which sentence from the selection states the author's central idea?
    a. "Speaker after speaker. . . . " paragraph 1, second sentence
    b. "My daughter is. . . ." paragraph 1, third sentence
    c. "It was the fact that. . . ." paragraph 9, first sentence
    d. "If our children. . . ." paragraph 10, third sentence

3. The author's primary purpose is to
    a. express her opinion about teaching only English to her children.
    b. persuade Hispanic parents to teach their children Spanish.
    c. entertain readers with stories about her life in a South American country.
    d. inform readers about the status of bilingual education in the United States.

Details

4. The author was born in
    a. California.
    b. Peru.
    c. Missouri.
    d. Texas.

5. In Texas, the author noticed all but which one of the following about Latinos?
    a. They spoke both English and Spanish well.
    b. They lived in their own enclaves.
    c. They all seemed to be regarded as illegal immigrants.
    d. They attended their own churches.

6. The author cites all but which one of the following as examples of unspoken prejudice?
    a. Garments she took into the changing room were counted.
    b. Her checks received extra scrutiny from clerks.
    c. She was ignored in department stores.
    d. Being fluent in two languages is seen as a virtue.

7. According to the author, what is one drawback of not teaching her children to speak Spanish?

a. Her daughter speaks English with no accent.
b. Part of their heritage has been eliminated.
c. Speaking English saves her children from prejudice.
d. People do not realize that her child is a minority.

8. What is the author's dominant organizational pattern?
    a. Sequence: She traces her development from childhood to the present.
    b. Process: She explains a method for teaching students to be bilingual.
    c. Comparison/contrast: She compares living in Peru with living in the United States.
    d. Cause and effect: She explains why she has chosen not to teach her children to speak Spanish.

Inferences

9. When the author says in paragraph 10, "There is a definite creeping in of anti-Hispanic sentiment in this country," she means:
    a. People have always shown prejudice toward Hispanics.
    b. There is no prejudice in the United States.
    c. Prejudice toward Hispanics is growing.
    d. Prejudice toward Hispanics is decreasing.

10. The author of this selection would most likely agree with which of the following statements?
    a. Few Hispanic children encounter prejudice.
    b. Latino culture has little influence in the United States.
    c. Latino culture and heritage should be preserved.
    d. Hispanic children should be taught English only.

WORKING WITH WORDS

Complete the sentences below with these words from Word Alert:

immersed	scrutiny	extolled	ironic
reproach	facility	enclaves	

1. Everyone was amazed by the _____ with which Yvonne picked up a few Spanish phrases on the trip to Mexico sponsored by the Humanities Department.

2. Many instructors have _____ the educational benefits of international travel, such as experiencing a culture firsthand and practicing the use of new language skills.

3. At the airport, incoming tourists and their luggage were under
   the _____ of customs officials, who were looking for
   contraband.

4. San Francisco's Chinatown is one of the largest _____ of Asian
   Americans in the United States.

5. When Rochelle visited Milan, she _____ herself in that city's
   culture, language, and history.

6. It seems _____ that some American tourists refuse to "go native" when they are abroad, preferring to stay in American hotels
   and eat American food.

7. When Jane was planning to spend her junior year abroad, her
   parents helped her find an apartment in a neighborhood that
   was beyond _____ in terms of safety.

THINKING DEEPER

Ideas for discussion and writing:

1. Is English a requirement for success in the United States? Does
   being bilingual have advantages? Discuss your views on language
   as they relate to this selection.

2. The author expresses concern that by eliminating Spanish at
   home, she has eliminated part of her children's heritage. Does
   not learning a second language necessarily rob children of their
   culture? Discuss whether it is possible for children to learn a different language and still maintain their heritage. What could
   parents do to reach this goal?

3. Discuss how this selection illustrates the Part 1 theme, *Americans
   in Transition.* For example, what *is* American culture? Who are
   today's Americans, and are they different from Americans of the
   past?

4. What aspect of your culture or history would you like to pass on
   to your children? What would you tell them about their family
   background and traditions? Write about one important thing that
   you would like them to know and remember.

FIRST THOUGHTS

To prepare yourself for the reading selection, answer the following questions, either on your own or in a group discussion.

1. What do you seek in a marriage partner, a career, a place to live and make your home?
2. Are your expectations in these areas the same as or different from those of your parents?
3. Preview the title, headnote, and first one or two paragraphs. What do you think will follow?

WORD ALERT

obeisance (2) respectful gesture or attitude
queries (5) questions
ransacked (6) searched thoroughly
mirthless (6) without cheer, unhappy
flippant (9) disrespectfully humorous or casual
rhapsodizing (12) expressing oneself in an overly enthusiastic way
compromise (14) a settlement of differences in which each side gives up
    something
indentured (15) bound into the service of another
vague (17) unclear
paradoxes (18) unexplainable or contradictory aspects

❧ The Good Daughter

CAROLINE HWANG

Caroline Hwang is the author of a novel, In Full Bloom, *published in 2003. In this selection she discusses how her dreams and plans for the future differ from those of her parents.*

THE MOMENT I WALKED into the dry-cleaning store, I knew the 1 woman behind the counter was from Korea, like my parents. To show her that we shared a heritage, and possibly get a fellow country-

From *Newsweek*, 9/21/98 © 1998 Newsweek, Inc. All rights reserved. Reprinted by permission.

man's discount, I tilted my head forward, in shy imitation of a traditional bow.

"Name?" she asked, not noticing my attempted **obeisance**.   2

"Hwang," I answered.   3

"Hwang? Are you Chinese?"   4

Her question caught me off-guard. I was used to hearing such   5
queries from non-Asians who think all Asians all look alike, but never
from one of my own people. Of course, the only Koreans I knew were
my parents and their friends, people who've never asked me where I
came from, since they knew better than I.

I **ransacked** my mind for the Korean words that would tell her who   6
I was. It's always struck me as funny (in a **mirthless** sort of way) that
I can more readily say "I am Korean" in Spanish, German and even
Latin than I can in the language of my ancestry. In the end, I told her
in English.

The dry-cleaning woman squinted as though trying to see past the   7
glare of my strangeness, repeating my surname under her breath. "Oh,
Fxuang," she said, doubling over with laughter. "You don't know how
to speak your name."

I flinched. Perhaps I was particularly sensitive at the time, having   8
just dropped out of graduate school. I had torn up my map for the future, the one that said not only where I was going but who I was. My
sense of identity was already disintegrating.

When I got home, I called my parents to ask why they had never   9
bothered to correct me. "Big deal," my mother said, sounding more **flippant** than I knew she intended. (Like many people who learn English
in a classroom, she uses idioms that don't always fit the occasion.) "So
what if you can't pronounce your name? You are American," she said.

Though I didn't challenge her explanation, it left me unsatisfied.   10
The fact is, my cultural identity is hardly that clear-cut.

My parents immigrated to this country 30 years ago, two years be-   11
fore I was born. They told me often, while I was growing up, that, if I
wanted to, I could be president someday, that here my grasp would be
as long as my reach.

To ensure that I reaped all the advantages of this country, my par-   12
ents saw to it that I became fully assimilated. So, like any American of
my generation, I whiled away my youth strolling malls and talking on
the phone, **rhapsodizing** over Andrew McCarthy's blue eyes or analyzing the meaning of a certain upper-classman's offer of a ride to the
Homecoming football game.

To my parents, I am all American, and the sacrifices they made   13
in leaving Korea—including my mispronounced name—pale in

comparison to the opportunities those sacrifices gave me. They do not see that I straddle two cultures, nor that I feel displaced in the only country I know. I identify with Americans, but Americans do not identify with me. I've never known what it's like to belong to a community—neither one at large, nor of an extended family. I know more about Europe than the continent my ancestors unmistakably come from. I sometimes wonder, as I did that day in the dry cleaner's, if I would be a happier person had my parents stayed in Korea.

I first began to consider this thought around the time I decided to   14
go to graduate school. It had been a **compromise:** my parents wanted me to go to law school; I wanted to skip the starched-collar track and be a writer—the hungrier the better. But after 20-some years of following their wishes and meeting all of their expectations, I couldn't bring myself to disobey or disappoint. A writing career is riskier than the law, I remember thinking. If I'm a failure and my life is a washout, then what does that make my parents' lives?

I know that many of my friends had to choose between pleasing   15
their parents and being true to themselves. But for the children of immigrants, the choice seems more complicated, a happy outcome impossible. By making the biggest move of their lives for me, my parents **indentured** me to the largest debt imaginable—I owe them the fulfillment of their hopes for me.

It tore me up inside to suppress my dream, but I went to school for   16
a Ph.D. in English literature, thinking I had found the perfect compromise. I would be able to write at least about books while pursuing a graduate degree. Predictably, it didn't work out. How could I labor for five years in a program I had no passion for? When I finally left school, my parents were disappointed, but since it wasn't what they wanted me to do, they weren't devastated. I, on the other hand, felt I was staring at the bottom of the abyss. I had seen the flaw in my life of halfwayness, in my planned life of compromises.

I hadn't thought about my love life, but I had a **vague** plan to make   17
concessions there, too. Though they raised me as an American, my parents expect me to marry someone Korean and give them grandchildren who look like them. This didn't seem like such a huge request when I was 14, but now I don't know what I'm going to do. I've never been in love with someone I dated, or dated someone I loved. (Since I can't bring myself even to entertain the thought of marrying the non-Korean men I'm attracted to, I've been dating only those I know I can stay clearheaded about.) And as I near that age when the question of marriage stalks every relationship, I can't help but wonder if my parents' expectations are responsible for the lack of passion in my life.

My parents didn't want their daughter to be Korean, but they don't 18
want her fully American, either. Children of immigrants are living
paradoxes. We are the first generation and the last. We are in this
country for its opportunities, yet filial duty binds us. When my parents
boarded the plane, they knew they were embarking on a rough trip. I
don't think they imagined the rocks in the path of their daughter who
can't even pronounce her own name.

COMPREHENSION CHECK

Purpose and Main Idea

1. What is the author's topic?
    a. the difficulty of being a good daughter
    b. Koreans' and Americans' cultural differences
    c. problems of adjustment for immigrants
    d. family values in the Korean community
2. What is the author's central idea?
    a. Children are happiest when they choose a career that their
        parents approve.
    b. Having to choose between your parents' dreams and your own
        makes being a good daughter difficult.
    c. Children of immigrants feel displaced because they have roots
        in two cultures.
    d. To reap the advantages of living in the United States, immi-
        grant children must become fully assimilated.
3. The author's primary purpose is to
    a. entertain readers with a story about a Korean family.
    b. inform readers about aspects of Korean culture.
    c. persuade readers to follow the wishes of their parents.
    d. explain why it is hard to be a good daughter.

Details

4. Among Koreans, the traditional gesture of respect is to
    a. shake hands.
    b. smile.
    c. bow.
    d. make a fist.
5. The author says that she speaks all but which one of the follow-
    ing languages?
    a. German
    b. Spanish

    c. Chinese

    d. English

6. It was the author's dream to become
    a. a writer.
    b. a lawyer.
    c. the owner of a dry-cleaning business.
    d. a Ph.D. in English literature.

7. The author says that her cultural identity is not clear-cut for all but which one of the following reasons?
    a. She knows more about Europe than about the country her ancestors came from.
    b. Her parents saw to it that she became fully assimilated.
    c. She has been able to maintain her Korean culture and language.
    d. She was born in the United States, but her parents were born in Korea.

8. The author's dominant pattern in this selection is
    a. definition.
    b. contrast.
    c. process.
    d. sequence.

Inferences

9. In what way has the author been "the good daughter," as the title suggests?
    a. She has done whatever her parents wanted without any self-examination.
    b. She has tried to live up to her parents' expectations, but it has not been easy.
    c. She has followed her own path, without considering her parents' wishes.
    d. She has sought counseling from people outside her family.

10. The author's statement from paragraph 16, "I had seen the flaw in my life of halfwayness, in my planned life of compromises," probably means:
    a. Immigrant children will never be satisfied.
    b. Her parents should not have left Korea.
    c. She should have chosen the career her parents wanted.
    d. To find happiness, she must be true to herself.

WORKING WITH WORDS

Complete the sentences below with these words from Word Alert:

rhapsodizing	obeisance	ransacked	flippant
compromise	mirthless	queries	
indentured	paradoxes	vague	

1. Although the moon is clear and bright at night, in daylight it is only a _____ shadow of itself.
2. To bow or curtsy before the Queen of England is an act of _____ .
3. Robbers _____ the house, looking for jewels or any items of value.
4. Although our guest speaker cannot stay to answer questions, the committee members will remain as long as necessary to field your _____ .
5. After all your _____ about this restaurant, I certainly hope the food is as good as you say.
6. Since we each want to go to a different movie, let's _____ by seeing one of them tonight and the other next week.
7. Why some parents drink and smoke in the home yet insist that their children abstain from these habits is one of life's _____ .
8. Having to fire employees because their jobs have been eliminated is a _____ task.
9. My boss's many acts of kindness made me feel _____ to him.
10. When the student's comment provoked disrespectful laughter from the class, the instructor scolded him for his _____ remark.

THINKING DEEPER

Ideas for discussion and writing:

1. The author says that she is torn between her parents' dreams and her own. Do you identify with this dilemma? How do you compromise between your parents' wishes and your own?
2. In paragraph 13, the author says, "I identify with Americans but Americans do not identify with me." What is your reaction to this statement? What do you think the author means?

3.   Discuss how this selection illustrates the Part 1 theme, *Americans in Transition*. One of our long-standing American values is that children should be free to choose their own mates, careers, and lifestyles. But immigrant parents from some cultures do not embrace this value, believing instead that parents should make these choices for their children. Thus conflicts result when the children of these immigrants demand more freedom of choice as an American right. What resolution do you see to these differences? In the future, do you see parents becoming more or less involved in their adult children's lives and choices?

4.   This selection begins with an anecdote (brief story) that illustrates how the author learned something important about herself: She did not know how to pronounce her name. Write about an incident in your past that taught you something important about yourself.

FIRST THOUGHTS

To prepare yourself for the reading selection, answer the following questions, either on your own or in a group discussion.

1. Where are you from?
2. Alex Haley is the author of *Roots,* a book about a man's search for his African ancestry. What are "roots"? What are *your* roots?
3. Preview the title, headnote, and first one or two paragraphs. What do you think will follow?

WORD ALERT

countered (1) responded
perky (1) cheerful and self-confident
intimate (4) personal, familiar
impostor (4) one who uses a false name or identity to deceive
garish (9) gaudy, loud, glaring, flashy
expectantly (14) eagerly anticipating, looking forward to

❧ No Place Like Home

JENNIFER J. CRISPIN

Jennifer J. Crispin is an author who lives near Ramstein Air Base in Germany. In this selection, she explains how the simple question "where are you from" can have a complex answer.

"WHERE ARE YOU from?" my new co-worker asked. I loaded her 1 brand-new, brand-name suitcase into the dark-blue air force van. "Where are *you* from?" I **countered** as I unlocked the passenger door for her. "Florida." She smiled brightly. The new enlistee was a tiny, cute blonde with a brand-new, brand-name suitcase and a hometown. Cute and tiny didn't bother me. Blonde and **perky** I could live with. What really made me jealous was that she knew where she was from.

From *Newsweek,* 5/26/97 © 1997 Newsweek, Inc. All rights reserved. Reprinted by permission.

"Are you excited to be here in Italy?" I asked as we headed for the 2
snack bar on base. This was her first air force assignment, and, as her
sponsor, I had to make sure she ate before I dropped her off at the dormitory. "Yeah," she said, bouncing a little in her seat like the teenager
she was. "You didn't answer my question. Where are you from?"

I know where my roots are. My mom and dad were both born in 3
the same South Jersey county. Mom "helped" Dad with his high-
school algebra homework. (She did it for him.) Unfortunately for
them, her mom was their algebra teacher. That sort of thing happens
when you're from somewhere. Though my mother lives in California
with her husband, she knows she's from New Jersey. My father and his
wife live in Las Vegas now, but he, too, knows he's from New Jersey.

I've spent a total of three years in New Jersey. I can't say I'm from 4
there, because that would imply an **intimate** knowledge of the area.
Someone else from New Jersey would know right away I'm an **impostor.**

Usually when I explain this, people give me a funny look and ask, 5
"Where were you born?" They insist that wherever you were born is
where you're from. I feel trapped, like they want to push me into a corner. I'm not from the state where I was born. Dad joined the air force
after he left college. He was in technical school at Keesler Air Force
Base in Mississippi when I was born. We lived in Mississippi for a few
more months, then Dad got an assignment to Florida. My brother was
born in Florida, but he's not from Florida any more than I'm from Mississippi.

We moved to bases in Nevada and California. Then Dad changed 6
air force jobs, and we went overseas. We lived in Greece and Portugal.
Whenever we moved, Dad would send us to live with his mother in
New Jersey until he got settled. The kids didn't like me because I wasn't
from there. Adults always said, "She's lived in Greece and Portugal. You
should be impressed." Kids don't take well to adults' telling them they
should be impressed. The kids reminded me that I wasn't from New
Jersey. Just like I wasn't from Greece or Portugal.

When I was 11, we moved to Rhein-Main Air Base in Germany. I 7
was a part of history there. The air force dedicated our school to two
pilot heroes of the Berlin airlift, and my band class played at the ceremony. I felt connected to Germany. But there were American kids who
were born there, who had been going to Halvorsen-Tunner school
their whole lives. They knew I wasn't from Germany.

Three years after arriving at Rhein-Main, we moved again, against 8
my very loud protests. I would hate Italy, I promised with every fiber of
my 14-year-old being. I would not like anything about it.

Italy lived up to my grim expectations, at first. Vicenza High 9
School depressed me, with its dimly lit hallways and **garish** red lock-
ers. As I despaired of ever making a true friend, Heather came into my
life. Heather was as rootless as I. She made it her mission to be my
friend. She worked backstage in plays I acted in and always talked to
me in computer class, even when I was rude and mean. I couldn't help
being friends with her. We're still best friends, and Vicenza is our history. It's as close as we can get to a place we're from. Although I didn't
like Vicenza at first, I grew to love it. But there are always people who
have lived there longer. Vicenza belongs to them. I can't really say I'm
from Vicenza.

Heather and I came up with an answer for people who asked, 10
"Where are you from?" Our addresses in Italy ended with APO NY because all the mail was processed through New York. We thought we finally had a clever way to respond. We could say we were from Apo, N.Y.

Not for long, though. The military postal system changed the ad- 11
dresses. The final line for Europe now reads APO AE for Area Europe.
Well, I can't say I'm from APO AE because that's not the address I had
growing up. Stumped again.

When I joined the air force at 18, my dad was stationed in Los An- 12
geles. According to the government, your hometown is wherever you
enlist. So for the $5\frac{1}{2}$ years I served, my records said I was from Los Angeles. I had lived in Los Angeles for about eight months, but for official
purposes, it was my hometown.

The government sent me to South Korea for a year and the Azores 13
for 15 months. My next assignment was Aviano Air Base in Italy. I was
returning to the country that felt most like home. I worked with a tal-
ented air force news producer who loved Italy as much as I did. We got
married a year and a half after we met. John is from Iowa. He went to
school two blocks from his home. His family has been there so long
that they're included in town-history books. When his folks asked me
where I was from, I didn't have an answer.

Just like I didn't have an answer for my air force co-worker. Her 14
bright face waited **expectantly** for an answer. I had to make up something on the spot because I didn't want to go through the speech
again. "I'm not from anywhere," I said.

I'm not from anywhere. But that's as much a part of my identity as 15
a hometown is for other people. I am a person who is not from anywhere, and after 26 years of mumbling, I can finally admit it with
pride. I am from nowhere, and I am from everywhere. That's the way I
like it.

COMPREHENSION CHECK

Purpose and Main Idea

1. What is the author's topic?
   a. historical places
   b. military life
   c. benefits of travel
   d. the meaning of home

2. Which one of the following sentences states the author's central idea?
   a. "What really made. . . ." paragraph 1, last sentence
   b. "I know where. . . ." paragraph 3, first sentence
   c. "According to the. . . ." paragraph 12, second sentence
   d. "I am a person who. . . ." paragraph 15, third sentence

3. The author's primary purpose is to
   a. persuade readers that home is where you were born.
   b. explain what home means to her.
   c. entertain readers with anecdotes about military life.
   d. inform readers of the benefits of travel.

Details

4. The author has lived in all but which one of the following countries?
   a. Italy
   b. Greece
   c. Australia
   d. Portugal

5. Where was the author born?
   a. Mississippi
   b. New Jersey
   c. Nevada
   d. California

6. According to the author, the government says that home is
   a. the place of your birth.
   b. wherever you enlist.
   c. your primary residence.
   d. where you are stationed.

7. The place that felt most like home was
   a. the United States.
   b. Germany.
   c. Italy.
   d. South Korea.

8. Of the patterns listed below, which one is the author's dominant pattern?
   a. Process: She explains the steps she followed in tracing her ancestry.
   b. Comparison: She explains the advantages and disadvantages of places she has lived.
   c. Definition: She defines what "home" or "being from somewhere" means to her.
   d. Sequence: She traces the events of her life in the air force.

Inferences

9. The author would probably agree that a place truly belongs to
   a. those whose parents or relatives live there.
   b. the people who were born there.
   c. anyone who declares residence there.
   d. those who have lived there the longest.

10. The author would most likely agree with which one of the following sayings?
    a. A rolling stone gathers no moss.
    b. Home is where the heart is.
    c. Everyone is from somewhere.
    d. There's no place like home.

WORKING WITH WORDS

Complete the sentences below with these words from Word Alert:

expectantly   impostor   garish
countered   intimate   perky

1. Have you ever heard of The Great _____ , a man who used disguise to assume several identities?
2. Ask Mary Jo for the names of some good restaurants in Boston because she has _____ knowledge of that city.
3. At our first sight of Las Vegas, we reeled at the dazzling lights and _____ casinos.
4. The students who knew they had done well waited _____ for their midterm exams to be returned.
5. Those who are happy and self-confident may not like being called _____ , even though the description fits.
6. When someone asked Clark his age, he _____ with "old enough."

THINKING DEEPER

Ideas for discussion and writing:

1. Discuss the meaning of this sentence: "Where are you from?"
    How many meanings of "home" or "being from somewhere" can
    you find in the selection? How would you be most likely to an-
    swer the question "Where are you from?"

2. The author says in paragraph 3, "I know where my roots are." In
    paragraph 15, she says, "I'm not from anywhere." Discuss the
    author's meaning in these two statements. How can she know
    where her roots are but not know where she's from?

3. Discuss how this selection illustrates the Part 1 theme, *Americans
    in Transition*. For example, is the growing number of people from
    different cultural, ethnic, and national groups in the United
    States changing our ideas of who we are and where we are from?
    How does Americans' tendency to move from town to town and
    job to job affect the idea of "home" or a "hometown"? What ef-
    fects do divorce, remarriage, or single parenthood—characteristics
    of our times—have on a person's identity or sense of place?

4. Think about your roots, where you were born, and all the places
    you have lived. Then write your definition of "home."

8

FIRST THOUGHTS

To prepare yourself for the reading selection, answer the following questions, either on your own or in a group discussion.

1. Speaking from your own experience, are boys and girls treated differently in school?

2. Do you think that men and women are best suited to different activities or occupations? Which ones are each sex suited for? Why?

3. Preview the title, headnote, and first one or two paragraphs. What do you think will follow?

WORD ALERT

plummet (1) to decline suddenly or steeply, plunge
rambunctious (2) boisterous and disorderly; noisy and undisciplined
mired (4) stuck, entangled, trapped
spate (6) a sudden flood, rush, or outpouring
rash (8) outbreak of events within a brief time
rhetoric (10) pretentious, insincere, intellectually vacant language
scoffs (10) ridicules, mocks
inclusiveness (11) the state of taking in all or everything in its scope
advocates (13) supporters of a cause

❧ Beyond the Gender Myths

MARGOT HORNBLOWER

In this selection from Time, *the author questions whether boys and girls have special needs and suggests a different focus for today's parents and educators.*

GIRLS TODAY ARE in trouble. They lose confidence in early adoles- 1
cence. Their grades **plummet,** and, following sexual stereotypes, their interest in math and science flags. They are plagued by eating disorders, suffer depression, get pregnant, attempt suicide. And it all

makes headlines, spawns research projects and prompts calls for single-sex education.

Boys today are in trouble too. They are locked into rigid classroom 2 routines before they are ready; their **rambunctious** behavior, once thought normal, is now labeled pathological, with such diagnoses as attention-deficit disorder and hyperactivity. They lose self-esteem and lag behind girls in reading and writing—erupting in violent behavior, killing themselves more often than girls. It all makes headlines, spawns research projects and prompts calls for remedial measures.

What's a parent to think?   3

Mired in the sociology, education theory and hype surrounding 4 "gender equity," we sometimes overlook the common humanity of children: what they share and how they differ, regardless of gender. "The focus on girls has translated into the notion that somehow if you help girls, you hurt boys," says Susan Bailey, executive director of the Wellesley Centers for Women. "People want a quick fix, but there is no one-size-fits-all solution for either girls or boys."

It was Bailey's 1992 report, *How Schools Shortchange Girls*, that 5 sparked a national hand-wringing epidemic over the plight of adolescent girls—especially their loss of interest in math and science. Financed by the American Association of University Women, the report surveyed a decade of research and concluded that teachers paid less attention to girls than boys, that textbooks reinforced sexual stereotypes and that college-entrance tests favored boys. A year later, another study documented widespread sexual harassment in schools.

A **spate** of books such as Peggy Orenstein's *Schoolgirls: Young 6 Women, Self-Esteem and the Confidence Gap* and Mary Pipher's *Reviving Ophelia,* which spent nearly three years on best-seller lists, triggered a surge of creative solutions. A corporate-sponsored program, Take Our Daughters to Work Day, spread across the U.S. in an effort to encourage girls to examine varied careers. In Lincoln, Neb., teacher Jane Edwards partners with a local architectural firm to challenge high school girls to use technology, math and science to solve design problems. In Aurora, Colo., middle school teacher Pam Schmidt has created Eocene Park, a paleontology field school that encourages girls to explore this traditionally male-dominated science.

More controversial has been a renewed interest in segregation. 7 Enrollment in private and religious schools for girls rose more than 15% between 1991 and 1997. New girls' schools were founded, including the public Young Women's Leadership Academy in New York City's

Harlem, which is currently under challenge as unconstitutional in a complaint lodged with the U.S. Department of Education. In California, Massachusetts, Virginia, Nebraska and Oklahoma, local school districts began experimenting with single-sex classrooms.

Predictably, the renewed attention to girls has sparked a backlash. 8 Parents are demanding that their sons be included in Take Our Daughters to Work Day. A surge of new books, such as Michael Gurian's *A Fine Young Man* and William Pollack's *Real Boys,* focuses on boys' emotional crises and academic problems in reading and writing. Researchers are exploring not just sexual harassment of girls but bullying and teasing of boys. A **rash** of school shootings by boys has brought calls to cut back on violent video games and provide more in-school counseling. And parents are objecting to certain excesses: "Is it really fair," wrote Kathleen Parker, a columnist for the Orlando *Sentinel,* "that one of [my son's] feminist teachers refuses even to use male pronouns, referring to all students as 'shes' and all work as 'hers'?"

Pollack, a clinical psychologist who teaches at Harvard Medical 9 School, says most schools are failing boys by forcing them into an "educational straitjacket." Elementary schools lack male teachers, "sending a message to boys that learning is primarily for girls." Young boys, he claims, learn at different tempos, and perhaps the cutoff birth month for starting school should be later for boys than for girls. Once there, boys should be allowed to move around more, taking short recesses when they are restless. They should be able to use computers rather than be forced to write by hand before their small-motor skills are developed. Noting that boys constitute 71% of school suspensions and are less likely to go to college than girls (58% vs. 67%), he says, "Boys' self-esteem as learners is more at risk than that of girls."

Are things as bad as some say? Or has the emotionally charged 10 **rhetoric** used by gender-equity theorists overstated the problem? A report last March found no evidence that girls improve their academic performance or their emotional health in single-sex settings. What helps girls is what helps boys: smaller classes, a demanding curriculum and encouragement regardless of gender. In the past decade, the gender gap for math and science, such as it was, has narrowed to the point of statistical irrelevance. Overall, males have somewhat higher standardized math and science test scores, while females have slightly higher school grades. Girls and boys are taking about the same math and science courses in high school, but boys are more likely to take advanced-placement courses in chemistry and physics. Girls are

slightly more likely to take AP biology. Patricia Campbell, an education researcher in Groton, Mass., **scoffs** at the notion of "opposite"
sexes with different learning styles. "When you just know somebody's
gender, you don't know anything about their academic skills or interests," she says. "The stereotypes of girls being collaborative and boys
competitive, of girls being into relationships and boys into numbers—
that's laughable."

Campbell researched the techniques of math and science teach- 11
ers in three states and found that those who were successful with both
boys and girls shared common traits:

- They allowed no disrespect: teachers did not put down students,
  and students did not make fun of one another.
- They used more than one instruction method—lectures, small-
  group work, diagrams, peer tutoring—so that kids who learn better with one strategy rather than another were not left behind.
- They divided their attention equally among students, refusing to
  let a small group monopolize discussion. "Research shows that
  unless specific action is taken, four to seven people tend to dominate any group," she says. "In a coed class, more of the attention
  getters may be boys, but a lot of boys, as well as girls, are left out. A
  single-sex class does not change the pattern—only deliberate **inclusiveness** works for everyone."

Gurian, a Spokane, Wash., therapist who has written two books on 12
boys, notes that four adolescent males drop out of school for every
one adolescent female. Among his prescriptions for helping our sons:
provide them with mentors; provide twice as much emotional nurturing—spending time with them, developing family rituals, giving them
new freedoms and responsibilities; restrict TV, video games and
movies. Strikingly, these recommendations are precisely what our
daughters need too.

Where boys' and girls' **advocates** generally agree is on the destruc- 13
tive nature of gender stereotyping. If girls are urged to catch up in
math and join ice-hockey teams, boys should be encouraged to write
poetry and take dance classes without being labeled sissies. Parents
can enhance gender-neutral self-esteem by suggesting that a daughter help fix a leaky pipe—or a son whip up an omelet. "A little girl who
says she wants to be a doctor gets a lot of support," says Bailey, whose
Wellesley Centers are devoting their next gender-equity conference to

boys. "But if a boy talks about wanting to be a nurse, the reaction is that it doesn't fit a masculine image. Parents and teachers need to foster an environment where sexual stereotypes don't shape education."

If that ever happens, headline writers and social scientists can 14 stop arguing about which sex is least favored, and teachers can concentrate on paying more nuanced attention to our children as individuals, for that is what they are.

COMPREHENSION CHECK

Purpose and Main Idea

1. What is the author's topic?
   a. education
   b. equal rights
   c. gender myths
   d. raising children
2. Which of the following statements best expresses the author's central idea?
   a. Boys and girls today are in trouble because of gender stereotyping.
   b. Educators have shown a renewed interest in segregation of boys and girls.
   c. Sociologists and others overlook the common humanity of children.
   d. A backlash has resulted from a renewed attention to girls.
3. The author's primary purpose is to
   a. inform readers of the various gender myths.
   b. entertain readers by exposing some of the mistakes researchers have made.
   c. explain how educators meet the needs of children.
   d. persuade readers that children should be treated as individuals.

Details

4. During early adolescence, girls are in trouble for all but which one of the following reasons, according to the author?
   a. They lose confidence in themselves.
   b. They are prone to violence and hyperactivity.
   c. Their interest in math and science flags.
   d. Their grades plummet.

5. Boys are in trouble for all but which one of the following reasons, according to the author?
    a. They lag behind girls in reading and writing.
    b. Their rambunctious behavior is labeled pathological.
    c. They are locked into rigid classroom routines before they are ready.
    d. They are plagued by eating disorders and suffer from depression.

6. Boys' and girls' advocates agree on which one of the following?
    a. Parents cannot enhance self-esteem.
    b. Gender stereotyping is destructive.
    c. Stereotypes should shape education.
    d. Nursing does not fit a masculine image.

7. According to the author, boys and girls are helped by all but which one of the following?
    a. encouragement regardless of gender
    b. segregated schools and classrooms
    c. smaller classes
    d. a demanding curriculum

8. What is the author's dominant pattern in this selection?
    a. The author explains a *process* for eliminating gender stereotyping.
    b. The term *gender myth* is *defined*.
    c. Theories about boys' and girls' characteristics and behaviors are *compared*.
    d. Students are *classified* by gender.

Inferences

9. Patricia Campbell, who scoffs at the notion of opposite-sex learning styles, would be most likely to support a classroom in which
    a. children's interests are encouraged regardless of gender.
    b. children are all of the same sex.
    c. the teacher calls on only those who volunteer.
    d. small-group work is the only instructional method being used.

10. With which one of the following statements do you think that the author would be most likely to agree?
    a. Boys will be boys.
    b. A woman needs a man like a fish needs a bicycle.
    c. Boys and girls are children first.
    d. Sugar and spice, that's what girls are made of.

WORKING WITH WORDS

Complete the sentences below with these words from Word Alert:

> inclusiveness   rhetoric   scoffs   mired
> rambunctious   advocates   plummet   spate   rash

1. I'd like to go to the party tonight, but I'm _____ so deep in as-signments that I have to get some studying done.
2. Medora liked the _____ of the student government organiza-tion, which encouraged all students to participate.
3. After watching his grades _____, Al decided to buckle down and crack the books.
4. Voters are tired of politicians' _____ and wish candidates would speak honestly and directly.
5. We've had a _____ of rain this week that has caused flooding in some areas.
6. _____ of free speech resist all attempts at censorship, whether of books, movies, or the Internet.
7. My friend, who does not believe I am serious about losing weight, _____ at my attempts to diet and exercise.
8. Police in my neighborhood have cracked down on speeders, following a _____ of accidents during the last two weeks.
9. Some children who are normally _____ may be mistakenly labeled hyperactive.

THINKING DEEPER

Ideas for discussion and writing:

1. Identify and discuss the gender myths that this author thinks we should get beyond. What are these myths, and what evidence of gender stereotyping have you seen, either in your early school years or in the present?
2. In paragraph 11, the author lists the traits that Campbell found successful teachers share. Discuss these traits. Do they seem characteristic of the good teachers you have known? What exam-ples or instances can you cite that illustrate the opposite behav-iors? What additional traits or techniques can you think of that

would help teachers encourage the best in every student, regardless of gender?

3. Discuss how this selection illustrates the Part 1 theme, *Americans
    in Transition*. For example, do you think that the gender myths
    explained in this selection will continue to influence the way
    boys and girls are treated in school? Do you expect sexual stereo-
    typing to continue, or do you think we are more likely to treat
    children as individuals as the twenty-first century develops? As a
    parent, how do you, or will you, want your boy or girl to be
    treated in school? What opportunities do you hope are available
    to him or her?

4. As a child in school, were you usually treated as an individual, or
    were certain skills or behaviors expected of you because of your
    gender? Were you ever encouraged to pursue or not to pursue a
    certain interest or activity because of your gender? Write about a
    time in your life when gender either did or did not hinder you
    from doing what you wanted to do.

FIRST THOUGHTS

To prepare yourself for the reading selection, answer the following questions, either on your own or in a group discussion.

1. What do you know, or what have you read, about Martin Luther King, Jr.?
2. What do you know, or what have you read, about the civil rights movement of the 1950s and 1960s?
3. Preview the title, headnote, and first one or two paragraphs. What do you think will follow?

WORD ALERT

seared (1) scorched, burned
manacles (2) handcuffs
languishing (2) neglected or unattended, existing in miserable conditions
defaulted (4) failed to fulfill an obligation
sweltering (5) oppressively hot
tranquility (5) calmness, serenity
ghetto (7) section of a city occupied by a minority group, often because of economic or social pressure
hew (19) cut, carve out
prodigious (21) great in size or force

❧ I Have a Dream

MARTIN LUTHER KING, JR.

Martin Luther King, Jr., was a minister and leader of the civil rights movement during the 1950s and 1960s. A martyr for his cause, King was assassinated on April 4, 1968, at the age of 39. The following selection is a speech King delivered on the occasion of the march on Washington, D.C., on August 28, 1963. This appeal for racial justice and equality still inspires readers.

FIVE SCORE YEARS AGO, a great American, in whose symbolic shadow 1
we stand, signed the Emancipation Proclamation. This momentous

decree came as a great beacon light of hope to millions of Negro slaves who had been **seared** in the flames of withering injustice. It came as a joyous daybreak to end the long night of captivity.

But one hundred years later, we must face the tragic fact that the 2 Negro is still not free. One hundred years later, the life of the Negro is still sadly crippled by the **manacles** of segregation and the chains of discrimination. One hundred years later, the Negro lives on a lonely island of poverty in the midst of a vast ocean of material prosperity. One hundred years later, the Negro is still **languishing** in the corners of American society and finds himself an exile in his own land. So we have come here today to dramatize an appalling condition.

In a sense we have come to our nation's capital to cash a check. 3 When the architects of our republic wrote the magnificent words of the Constitution and the Declaration of Independence, they were signing a promissory note to which every American was to fall heir. This note was a promise that all men—yes, black men as well as white men—would be guaranteed the unalienable rights of life, liberty, and the pursuit of happiness.

It is obvious today that America has **defaulted** on this promissory 4 note insofar as her citizens of color are concerned. Instead of honoring this sacred obligation, America has given the Negro people a bad check, a check which has come back marked "insufficient funds." But we refuse to believe that there are insufficient funds in the great vaults of opportunity of this nation. So we have come to cash this check—a check that will give us upon demand the riches of freedom and the security of justice. We have also come to this hallowed spot to remind America of the fierce urgency of *now*. This is no time to engage in the luxury of cooling off or to take the tranquilizing drugs of gradualism. *Now* is the time to make real the promises of Democracy. *Now* is the time to rise from the dark and desolate valley of segregation to the sunlit path of racial justice. *Now* is the time to open the doors of opportunity to all of God's children. *Now* is the time to lift our nation from the quicksands of racial injustice to the solid rock of brotherhood.

It would be fatal for the nation to overlook the urgency of the mo- 5 ment and to underestimate the determination of the Negro. This **sweltering** summer of the Negro's legitimate discontent will not pass until there is an invigorating autumn of freedom and equality; 1963 is not an end, but a beginning. Those who hope that the Negro needed to blow off steam and will now be content will have a rude awakening if the nation returns to business as usual. There will be neither rest nor **tranquility** in America until the Negro is granted his citizenship rights.

The whirlwinds of revolt will continue to shake the foundations of our nation until the bright day of justice emerges.

But there is something that I must say to my people who stand on 6 the warm threshold which leads into the palace of justice. In the process of gaining our rightful place we must not be guilty of wrongful deeds. Let us not seek to satisfy our thirst for freedom by drinking from the cup of bitterness and hatred. We must forever conduct our struggle on the high plane of dignity and discipline. We must not allow our creative protest to degenerate into physical violence. Again and again we must rise to the majestic heights of meeting physical force with soul force. The marvelous new militancy which has engulfed the Negro community must not lead us to a distrust of all white people, for many of our white brothers, as evidenced by their presence here to-day, have come to realize that their destiny is tied up with our destiny and their freedom is inextricably bound to our freedom. We cannot walk alone.

And as we walk, we must make the pledge that we shall march 7 ahead. We cannot turn back. There are those who are asking the devo-tees of civil rights, "When will you be satisfied?" We can never be satis-fied as long as the Negro is the victim of the unspeakable horrors of police brutality. We can never be satisfied as long as our bodies, heavy with the fatigue of travel, cannot gain lodging in the motels of the highways and the hotels of the cities. We cannot be satisfied as long as the Negro's basic mobility is from a smaller **ghetto** to a larger one. We can never be satisfied as long as a Negro in Mississippi cannot vote and a Negro in New York believes he has nothing for which to vote. No, no, we are not satisfied, and we will not be satisfied until justice rolls down like waters and righteousness like a mighty stream.

I am not unmindful that some of you have come here out of great 8 trials and tribulations. Some of you have come fresh from narrow jail cells. Some of you have come from areas where your quest for free-dom left you battered by the storms of persecution and staggered by the winds of police brutality. You have been the veterans of creative suffering. Continue to work with the faith that unearned suffering is redemptive.

Go back to Mississippi, go back to Alabama, go back to South Car- 9 olina, go back to Georgia, go back to Louisiana, go back to the slums and ghettos of our northern cities, knowing that somehow this situa-tion can and will be changed. Let us not wallow in the valley of despair.

I say to you today, my friends, that in spite of the difficulties and 10 frustrations of the moment I still have a dream. It is a dream deeply rooted in the American dream.

I have a dream that one day this nation will rise up and live out the 11
true meaning of its creed: "We hold these truths to be self-evident,
that all men are created equal."

I have a dream that one day on the red hills of Georgia the sons of 12
former slaves and the sons of former slaveowners will be able to sit
down together at the table of brotherhood.

I have a dream that one day even the state of Mississippi, a desert 13
state sweltering with the heat of injustice and oppression, will be
transformed into an oasis of freedom and justice.

I have a dream that my four little children will one day live in a na- 14
tion where they will not be judged by the color of their skin but by the
content of their character.

I have a dream today.   15

I have a dream that one day the state of Alabama, whose gover- 16
nor's lips are presently dripping with the words of interposition and
nullification, will be transformed into a situation where little black
boys and black girls will be able to join hands with little white boys and
white girls and walk together as sisters and brothers.

I have a dream today.   17

I have a dream that one day every valley shall be exalted, every hill 18
and mountain shall be made low, the rough places will be made plain,
and the crooked places will be made straight, and the glory of the Lord
shall be revealed, and all flesh shall see it together.[1]

This is our hope. This is the faith with which I return to the South. 19
With this faith we will be able to **hew** out of the mountain of despair a
stone of hope. With this faith we will be able to transform the jangling
discords of our nation into a beautiful symphony of brotherhood.
With this faith we will be able to work together, to pray together, to
struggle together, to go to jail together, to stand up for freedom together, knowing that we will be free one day.

This will be the day when all of God's children will be able to sing 20
with new meaning

> My country, 'tis of thee,
> Sweet land of liberty,
>   Of thee I sing:
> Land where my fathers died,
> Land of the pilgrims' pride,
> From every mountainside,
>   Let freedom ring.

---

[1] This paragraph paraphrases Isaiah 40:4–5.

So let freedom ring from the **prodigious** hilltops of New Hamp- 21
shire. Let freedom ring from the mighty mountains of New York. Let
freedom ring from the heightening Alleghenies of Pennsylvania. Let
freedom ring from the snowcapped Rockies of Colorado. Let freedom
ring from the curvaceous peaks of California.

But not only that. Let freedom ring from Stone Mountain of Geor- 22
gia. Let freedom ring from Lookout Mountain of Tennessee. Let freedom ring from every hill and molehill of Mississippi. From every
mountainside, let freedom ring.

When we let freedom ring, when we let it ring from every village 23
and every hamlet, from every state and every city, we will be able to
speed up that day when all of God's children, black men and white
men, Jews and Gentiles, Protestants and Catholics, will be able to join
hands and sing in the words of the old Negro spiritual, "Free at last!
Free at last! Thank God almighty, we are free at last!"

COMPREHENSION CHECK

Purpose and Main Idea

1. The author's topic is
    a. racial justice.
    b. freedom.
    c. democracy.
    d. segregation.
2. The central idea of this selection is stated in
    a. paragraph 1, first sentence: "Five score years. . . ."
    b. paragraph 2, first sentence: "But one hundred. . . ."
    c. paragraph 4, eighth sentence: "Now is the time to rise. . . ."
    d. paragraph 10, first sentence: "I say to you. . . ."
3. The author's *primary* purpose is to
    a. inform us that a problem exists.
    b. entertain us with his dreams for the future.
    c. express his anger and indignation.
    d. persuade us to put an end to racial injustice.

Details

4. Who is the "great American" referred to in paragraph 1?
    a. George Washington
    b. Abraham Lincoln
    c. Thomas Jefferson
    d. Alexander Hamilton

5. According to King, blacks were not free because of
   a. their inalienable rights.
   b. a constitutional amendment.
   c. segregation and discrimination.
   d. the Emancipation Proclamation.

6. In paragraph 6, King cautions his followers to avoid
   a. violence.
   b. peaceful demonstration.
   c. protest.
   d. all white people.

7. In paragraph 5, the author's pattern is
   a. comparison and contrast.
   b. cause and effect.
   c. generalization then example.
   d. definition.

8. In paragraphs 10–18, the author's pattern is
   a. comparison and contrast.
   b. cause and effect.
   c. generalization then example.
   d. definition.

Inferences

9. King's meaning in paragraph 5, first sentence is:
   a. The need for justice is not urgent.
   b. Blacks are not determined.
   c. The summer of revolt is now over.
   d. The fight for citizenship rights will continue.

10. In paragraph 7, "The Negro's basic mobility is from a smaller ghetto to a larger one" means that blacks at that time
    a. had economic opportunity.
    b. did not want to leave their neighborhoods.
    c. lacked freedom of mobility.
    d. prefered larger neighborhoods.

WORKING WITH WORDS

Complete the sentences below with these words from Word Alert:

tranquility	prodigious	seared
languishing	defaulted	ghetto
sweltering	manacles	hew

1. The prisoner was brought in _____ to the jail.
2. The student's books lay _____ in the corner, covered with dust from disuse.
3. Leaders of all races have said that education is the way out of the _____ and the key to economic and social mobility.
4. Looking out our window, we watched rain clouds form over the _____ hills beyond.
5. On a _____ summer day, it is a good idea to stay in the shade.
6. Because of having _____ on a loan, Chris's credit was ruined.
7. Before putting the roast in the oven, Grandma _____ it on all sides to seal in the juices.
8. A crater on the moon is called The Sea of _____ , probably because it looks so calm.
9. One who is accomplished at woodworking is able to _____ out of a block of wood an object of great beauty.

THINKING DEEPER

Ideas for discussion and writing:

1. King's speech enumerates the "promises of democracy," the cherished freedoms that are the rights of citizenship in the United States. Study the selection to find where these rights and freedoms are stated. Then discuss their importance, how they affect your life, and what life would be like without them.
2. Working with a partner or small group, go to your college's library or media center and watch a film of King's speech, which may be available on video or through the Internet. As you listen to the speech, pay attention to King's delivery: his emphasis on certain words and phrases. Notice too how the speech is organized. After listening, discuss the speech and its effect on you. Which parts seemed particularly moving or meaningful, and why? What did you notice about the speech after hearing it that you had not noticed while reading it? Discuss your thoughts about the organization and effectiveness of the speech with the rest of the class.
3. Discuss how this selection illustrates the Part 1 theme, *Americans in Transition*. First, read again and discuss paragraphs 10–18. How far have we come since King gave his speech in 1963? What parts of his dream have come to pass? What parts have yet to be realized?
4. Think about all the rights and freedoms that Americans enjoy. Then write about your most cherished right or freedom.

10

FIRST THOUGHTS

To prepare yourself for the reading selection, answer the following questions, either on your own or in a group discussion.

1. What is the difference between prejudice and stereotypes?

2. What causes some people to discriminate against others?

3. Preview the title, headnote, and the first one or two paragraphs. What do you think will follow?

WORD ALERT

In a textbook chapter, the words to watch may appear in boldface, in italics, or in a special color.

stereotypes (1) the perceptions, beliefs, and expectations a person has about members of a certain group

schemas (1) ideas about the world based on past experience and expectations

prejudice (3) a positive or negative attitude toward people in certain groups

discrimination (3) differential treatment of people in different groups

cognitive (7) relating to the mental processes underlying all aspects of human thought

contact hypothesis (9) the idea that stereotypes or prejudice toward a group will decrease as contact with the group increases

⅔ Prejudice and Stereotypes

DOUGLAS A. BERNSTEIN
AND PEGGY W. NASH

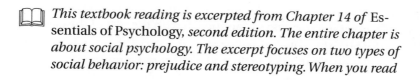

This textbook reading is excerpted from Chapter 14 of Es-sentials of Psychology, second edition. The entire chapter is about social psychology. The excerpt focuses on two types of social behavior: prejudice and stereotyping. When you read

Douglas A. Bernstein and Peggy W. Nash, *Essentials of Psychology*, 2nd ed. (Boston: Houghton Mifflin, 2002), pp. 496–499.

from textbooks, remember that headings may signal topics, main ideas, or important details.

A LL OF THE principles underlying impression formation, attribu- 1
tion, and attitudes come together in prejudice and stereotypes. **Stereotypes** are the perceptions, beliefs, and expectations a person has about members of some group. They are **schemas** about entire groups of people (S. T. Fiske, 1998). Typically, they involve the false assumption that all members of a group share the same characteristics. The characteristics that make up the stereotype may be positive, but more often they are negative. The most prevalent and powerful stereotypes focus on observable personal attributes, particularly ethnicity, gender, and age (Eberhardt & Fiske, 1998).

The stereotypes people hold can be so ingrained that their effects 2
on behavior are automatic and unconscious (Abreu, 1999). In one study, for example, white participants were shown pictures of black individuals (M. Chen & Bargh, 1997). The pictures were flashed so quickly, though, that the images were *subliminal*, meaning that the participants were not aware of seeing them (see Chapter 4). The images did have an effect, however. When these participants interacted with an African American man soon afterward, they behaved more negatively toward him and saw him as more hostile than did participants who had not been exposed to the pictures. The subliminally presented pictures had apparently activated the participants' negative stereotypes about blacks, thus altering their perceptions and behavior—all without their being aware of it.

Stereotyping often leads to **prejudice**, which is a positive or nega- 3
tive attitude toward an individual based simply on his or her membership in some group (Worchel et al., 2000). *Prejudice* means literally "to prejudge." Many theorists believe that prejudice, like other attitudes, has cognitive, affective, and behavioral components. Stereotyped thinking is the cognitive component of prejudicial attitudes. The hatred, admiration, anger, and other feelings people have about stereotyped groups constitute the affective component. The behavioral component of prejudice involves **discrimination,** which is differential treatment of individuals who belong to different groups.

THEORIES OF PREJUDICE AND STEREOTYPING

Not all prejudice and stereotyping occur for the same reason. Three 4
theories, each with supporting research, help to explain many instances of stereotyping and prejudice.

Motivational Theories

For some people, prejudice serves to meet certain needs and increases 5
their sense of security. This idea was first proposed by T. W. Adorno
and his associates fifty years ago (Adorno et al., 1950) and elaborated
more recently by Robert Altemeyer (1988, 1994). These researchers
suggest that prejudice is especially likely among people who display a
personality trait called *authoritarianism*. According to Altemeyer, authoritarianism is composed of three main elements: (1) acceptance of
very conventional or traditional values, (2) willingness to unquestion-
ingly follow the orders of authority figures, and (3) an inclination to
act aggressively toward individuals or groups identified by these authority figures as threats to the person's values or well-being. Indeed,
people with an authoritarian orientation tend to view the world as a
threatening place (Winter, 1996). One way to protect themselves from
the threats they perceive all around them is to strongly identify with
people like themselves—their *in-group*—and to reject, dislike, and
perhaps even punish people from groups that are different from their
own. Looking down on and discriminating against members of these
out-groups—such as people from other religious or ethnic groups, gay
men and lesbians, the elderly, or people with physical disabilities—
may help authoritarian people feel safer and better about themselves
(Haddock & Zanna, 1998b).
    Another motivational explanation of prejudice involves the con- 6
cept of social identity. Whether or not they display authoritarianism,
most people are motivated to identify with their in-group and tend to
see it as better than other groups (M. B. Brewer & Brown, 1998). As a
result, members of an in-group often see all members of out-groups
as less attractive and less socially appropriate than members of the in-
group and may thus treat them badly (Dovidio, Gaertner, & Validzic,
1998). In short, prejudice may result when people's motivation to enhance their self-esteem causes them to belittle other people.

Cognitive Theories

Stereotyping and prejudice may also result from the social-cognitive 7
processes that people use in dealing with the world. There are so many

other people, so many situations in which one meets them, and so many behaviors that others might display that one cannot possibly attend to and remember them all. Therefore, people must use schemas and other cognitive shortcuts to organize and make sense of their social world (Fiske, 1998). Often these **cognitive** processes provide accurate and useful summaries of other people, but sometimes they lead to inaccurate stereotypes. Instead of remembering every single detail about every person we meet, we often group people into social categories such as doctor, senior citizen, Republican, student, Italian, and the like (Rothbart & Lewis, 1994). To further simplify perception of these categories, we tend to see group members as being quite similar to one another. Thus, members of an ethnic group may find it harder to distinguish among specific faces in other ethnic groups than in their own (Anthony, Cooper, & Mullen, 1992). People also tend to assume that all members of a different group hold the same beliefs and values, and that those beliefs and values differ from their own (Dovidio, Gaertner, & Validzic, 1998). Finally, because particularly noticeable stimuli tend to draw a lot of attention, noticeably rude behavior by even a few members of an easily identified ethnic group may lead people to see an *illusory correlation* between rudeness and ethnicity (D. L. Hamilton & Sherman, 1994). As a result, they may incorrectly believe that all or most members of that group are rude.

Learning Theories

Like other attitudes, prejudice can be learned. Some prejudice is 8 learned as a result of conflicts between members of different groups, but people also develop negative attitudes toward groups with whom they have had little or no contact. Learning theories suggest that children can acquire prejudices just by watching and listening to the words and deeds of parents, peers, and others (Rohan & Zanna, 1996). Movies and television also portray ethnic or other groups in ways that teach stereotypes and prejudice (Liebert & Sprafkin, 1988). And as mentioned earlier, children may be directly reinforced for expressing prejudice. In fact, small children often know about the supposed negative characteristics of many groups long before they ever meet people in those groups (Quintana, 1998).

REDUCING PREJUDICE

One clear implication of the cognitive and learning theories of preju- 9 dice and stereotyping is that members of one group are often ignorant or misinformed about the characteristics of people in other groups. Before 1954, for example, most black and white schoolchildren in the United States knew very little about one another because they went to separate schools. Then the Supreme Court declared that segregated public schools should be prohibited. In doing so, the court provided a real-life test of the **contact hypothesis,** which states that stereotypes and prejudice toward a group will diminish as contact with the group increases (Pettigrew, 1997).

Did the school desegregation process of the 1960s and 1970s con- 10 firm the contact hypothesis? In a few schools, integration was followed by a decrease in prejudice, but in most places either no change occurred or prejudice actually increased (Oskamp & Schultz, 1998). However, these results did not necessarily disprove the contact hypothesis. In-depth studies of schools with successful desegregation suggested that contact alone was not enough—indeed, that integration reduced prejudice only when certain social conditions were created (M. B. Brewer & Brown, 1998). First, members of the two groups had to be of roughly equal social and economic status. Second, school authorities had to promote cooperation and interdependence between ethnic groups by having members of the two groups working together on projects that required reliance on one another to achieve success. Third, the contact between group members had to occur on a one-to-one basis. It was only when *individuals* got to know each other that the errors contained in stereotypes became apparent. Finally, the members of each group had to be seen as typical and not unusual in any significant way. When these four conditions were met, the children's attitudes toward one another became more positive.

Elliot Aronson (1995) describes a teaching strategy, called the *jig-* 11 *saw technique,* that helps create these conditions. Children from several ethnic groups must work together on a team to complete a task such as writing a report about a famous person in history. Each child learns, and provides the team with, a separate piece of information about this person, such as place of birth or greatest achievement (Aronson, 1990). Studies show that children from various ethnic groups who take part in the jigsaw technique and other cooperative learning experiences show substantial reductions in prejudice toward other groups (e.g., Aronson, Wilson, & Akert, 1999). The success reported in these studies has greatly increased the popularity of cooperative learning exercises in U.S. classrooms. Such exercises may not eliminate all aspects of ethnic prejudice in children, but they seem to be a step in the right direction.

Can friendly, cooperative, interdependent contact reduce the 12 more entrenched forms of prejudice seen in adults? It may. When equal-status adults from different ethnic groups work jointly toward a common goal, bias and distrust can be reduced. This is especially true if they come to see themselves as members of the same group rather than belonging to opposing groups (Dovidio & Gaertner, 1999; Gaertner, Dovidio, & Bachman, 1997). The challenge to be met in creating such cooperative experiences in the real world is that the participants must be of equal status—a challenge made more difficult in many countries by the sizable status differences that still exist between ethnic groups (Dovidio, Gaertner, & Validzic, 1998).

In the final analysis, contact can provide only part of the solution 13 to the problems of stereotyping, prejudice, and discrimination. To reduce ethnic prejudice, we must develop additional techniques to address the social cognitions and perceptions that lie at the core of bigotry and hatred toward people who are different from us (Monteith, Zuwerink, & Devine, 1994). Altering these mental processes will be difficult because, as we saw earlier, they can operate both consciously and unconsciously, causing even those who do not see themselves as prejudiced to discriminate against individuals who are different (Blair & Banaji, 1996; McPhail & Penner, 1995; Phelps et al., 2000).

COMPREHENSION CHECK

Purpose and Main Idea

1. What is the authors' topic?
    a. social psychology
    b. discrimination
    c. prejudice and stereotypes
    d. personality theories
2. What is the authors' central idea?
    a. Prejudice and stereotyping occur in many societies.
    b. Several theories explain prejudice and stereotyping.
    c. Prejudice and stereotypes are common research subjects.
    d. Some people experience prejudice or stereotyping more often than others.
3. The authors' primary purpose is to
    a. inform readers about the reasons behind prejudice and stereotypes.
    b. express their opinions on prejudice and stereotyping.

    c. entertain readers with examples of people who have overcome prejudice in their lives.

    d. persuade readers that discrimination is an ingrained behavior that cannot be changed.

Details

4. According to the authors, the most prevalent and powerful stereotypes focus on all but which one of the following?
    a. gender
    b. behavior
    c. age
    d. ethnicity

5. Which theories account for the fact that people can develop negative attitudes toward groups with whom they have had little or no contact?
    a. motivational theories
    b. behavioral theories
    c. cognitive theories
    d. learning theories

6. According to the authors, *authoritarianism is* characterized by all but which one of the following?
    a. aggressiveness toward those seen as threatening
    b. acceptance of traditional or conventional values
    c. identification with all members of society
    d. willingness to follow orders unquestioningly

7. According to the authors, which one of the following explains why people tend to attribute the behaviors of a few group members to the group as a whole?
    a. schemas
    b. authoritarianism
    c. the contact hypothesis
    d. an illusory correlation

8. What is the dominant pattern by which the ideas in the entire excerpt are organized?
    a. Cause and effect: The authors explain what causes prejudice and stereotyping.
    b. Definition: The authors define prejudice and stereotyping.
    c. Sequence: The authors explain how prejudice develops.
    d. Classification: The authors group common stereotypes into categories.

Inferences

9. Which one of the following *best* explains why cooperative learning experiences help reduce prejudice in children?
   a. They provide opportunities for children to get to know one another.
   b. They increase the number of in-group members versus out-group members.
   c. They place everyone in the group on an equal footing.
   d. They encourage positive interpersonal relationships.
10. Which one of the following is a real-world example of an *illusory correlation?*
   a. the belief that marriage laws should not be changed to allow gay and lesbian unions
   b. the opinion that female golfer Annika Sorenstam has no business competing with men in a PGA tournament
   c. the view that the United States should enter into war only with the support of the United Nations
   d. the belief held by some Americans following the September 11 attacks that all Muslims hold anti-American views

WORKING WITH WORDS

Complete the sentences below with these words from Word Alert:

contact hypothesis   cognitive   stereotypes
discrimination   prejudice   schemas

1. The National Organization of Women accused Augusta National of _____ because it does not allow women to be members.
2. Decision making, problem solving, and imagining are only three of the mental activities involved in _____ processing.
3. Children who fear dogs may have formed negative _____ about them based on past encounters.
4. People who think all the members of a certain ethnic group look alike or behave similarly are reacting to _____ .
5. According to the _____ , prejudice toward a group may decrease as interaction with members of that group increases.
6. A negative attitude toward someone based on his or her race is but one example of _____ .

THINKING DEEPER

Ideas for discussion and writing:

1. In paragraph 10, the authors explain that school integration reduced prejudice among children only when four conditions were met. What were these conditions? What instances can you recall from your own schooling in which similar conditions were created? What were the results?

2. The authors also say that stereotypes and prejudice can be reduced through friendly, cooperative, and interdependent contact. What examples can you provide of stereotypes or beliefs that you once held, but that have now changed as a result of your relationships with others?

3. Discuss how the theories of prejudice and stereotyping explained in this excerpt relate to the Part 1 theme, *Americans in Transition.* For example, what information gained from the excerpt increases your self-knowledge or your understanding of those from different cultures and backgrounds?

4. In a psychology course, you will study different theories of personality and behavior. To differentiate among these theories and make them easy to remember, try making a comparison chart like the one below. This chart is only partially filled in. Use information from the excerpt to complete the chart.

Type of Theory	Explanation	Text Examples	My Example
Motivational theories	For some people, prejudice may meet certain needs and increase their sense of security	The personality trait of authoritarianism; the concept of social identity	The Boy Scouts' rejection of gay troop leaders
Cognitive theories	Stereotyping and prejudice result from the mental processes people use to deal with the world		
Learning theories			

PART TWO

Rumblings in the Culture

❧

The culture *of a people consists of its behavior patterns, its arts, its beliefs, its institutions such as family and education, and all other products of human work and thought. Cultural change may happen gradually. For example, the traditional American college student (young, white, and male) of your grandparents' generation is no longer typical. Today's campuses are increasingly diverse: Women outnumber men, and a wide variety of races, ethnicities, and nationalities are represented. However, cultural change can also be swift. Following the tragic events of September 11, 2001, many Americans realized that their safety and freedoms could no longer be taken for granted. Some Americans left financially rewarding jobs to pursue more meaningful careers.*

Whenever change that affects our lives or alters the way we think about one another occurs, we hear rumblings in the culture. The selections in Part 2 are about cultural change and how people react to it. As you read and think about the selections, ask yourself these questions: What is the issue? Where is the conflict? How can it be resolved?

FIRST THOUGHTS

To prepare yourself for the reading selection, answer the following questions, either on your own or in a group discussion.

1. What fast-food restaurants are available in your area?
2. What are the restaurants' similarities and differences?
3. Preview the title, headnote, and first one or two paragraphs. What do you think will follow?

WORD ALERT

precursor (1) predecessor, forerunner; an indicator of something that is to come

conglomerate (1) group of businesses or companies under one central management

rubric (3) a rule or direction

reiterated (3) said or done again, repeated

cater (4) to provide food service, to attend to someone's needs

demeanour (5) behavior (American spelling: demeanor)

proprietor (5) owner

adheres (6) remains attached, follows devotedly

ramifications (6) developments, consequences

∂६ The Ritual of Fast Food

MARGARET VISSER

In this selection from The Rituals of Dinner, *the author explains the appeal of fast-food restaurants: why we like them and how they serve our needs.*

A N EARLY **PRECURSOR** of the restaurant meal was dinner served to 1
the public at fixed times and prices at an eating house or tavern.
Such a meal was called, because of its predetermined aspects, an "ordinary," and the place where it was eaten came to be called an "ordinary," too. When a huge modern business **conglomerate** offers fast

food to travellers on the highway, it knows that its customers are likely
to desire No Surprises. They are hungry, tired, and not in a celebratory
mood; they are happy to pay—provided that the price looks easily
manageable—for the safely predictable, the convenient, the fast and
ordinary.

Ornamental formalities are pruned away (tables and chairs are 2
bolted to the floor, for instance, and "cutlery" is either nonexistent or
not worth stealing); but rituals, in the sense of behaviour and expectations that conform to preordained rules, still inform the proceedings.
People who stop for a hamburger—at a Wendy's, a Hardee's, a McDonald's, or a Burger King—know exactly what the building that houses the
establishment should look like; architectural variations merely ring
changes on rigidly imposed themes. People want, perhaps even need,
to *recognize* their chain store, to feel that they know it and its food in
advance. Such an outlet is designed to be a "home away from home,"
on the highway, or anywhere in the city, or for Americans abroad.

Words and actions are officially laid down, learned by the staff 3
from handbooks and teaching sessions, and then picked up by customers in the course of regular visits. Things have to be called by their
correct names ("Big Mac," "large fries"); the McDonald's **rubric** in
1978 required servers to ask "Will that be with cheese, sir?" "Will there
be any fries today, sir?" and to close the transaction with "Have a nice
day." The staff wear distinctive garments; menus are always the same,
and even placed in the same spot in every outlet in the chain; prices
are low and predictable; and the theme of cleanliness is proclaimed
and tirelessly **reiterated.** The company attempts also to play the role
of a lovable host, kind and concerned, even parental: it knows that
blunt and direct confrontation with a huge faceless corporation
makes us suspicious, and even badly behaved. So it stresses its love of
children, its nostalgia for cosy warmth and for the past (cottage roofs,
warm earth tones), or its clean, brisk modernity (glass walls, smooth
surfaces, red trim). It responds to social concerns—when they are insistent enough, sufficiently widely held, and therefore "correct." Mc-
Donald's, for example, is at present busy showing how much it cares
about the environment.

Fast-food chains know that they are ordinary. They *want* to be or- 4
dinary, and for people to think of them as almost inseparable from the
idea of everyday food consumed outside the home. They are happy to
allow their customers time off for feasts—on Thanksgiving, Christmas, and so on—to which they do not **cater.** Even those comparatively

rare holiday times, however, are turned to a profit, because the companies know that their favourite customers—law-abiding families—
are at home together then, watching television, where carefully placed
commercials will spread the word concerning new fast-food products,
and re-imprint the image of the various chain stores for later, when
the long stretches of ordinary times return.

Families are the customers the fast-food chains want: solid citi-   5
zens in groups of several at a time, the adults hovering over their children, teaching them the goodness of hamburgers, anxious to bring
them up to behave typically and correctly. Customers usually maintain a clean, restrained, considerate, and competent **demeanour** as
they swiftly, gratefully, and informally eat. Fast-food operators have
recently faced the alarming realization that crack addicts, craving salt
and fat, have spread the word among their number that French fries
deliver these substances easily, ubiquitously, cheaply, and at all hours.
Dope addicts at family "ordinaries"! The unacceptability of such a
thought was neatly captured by a news story in *The Economist* (1990)
that spelled out the words a fast-foods **proprietor** can least afford to
hear from his faithful customers, the participants in his polite and
practiced rituals: the title of the story was "Come on Mabel, let's
leave." The plan to counter this threat included increasing the inten-
sity of the lighting in fast-food establishments—drug addicts, apparently, prefer to eat in the dark.

The formality of eating at a restaurant belonging to a fast-food   6
chain depends upon the fierce regularity of its product, its simple but
carefully observed rituals, and its environment. Supplying a hamburger
that **adheres** to perfect standards of shape, weight, temperature, and
consistency, together with selections from a pre-set list of trimmings,
to a customer with fiendishly precise expectations is an enormously
complex feat. The technology involved in performing it has been
learned through the expenditure of huge sums on research, and after
decades of experience—not to mention the vast political and economic
ramifications involved in maintaining the supplies of cheap beef and
cheap buns. But these costs and complexities are, with tremendous
care, hidden from view. We know of course that, say, a Big Mac is a cultural construct: the careful control expended upon it is one of the
things we are buying. But McDonald's manages—it must do so if it is to
succeed in being ordinary—to provide a "casual" eating experience.
Convenient, innocent simplicity is what the technology, the ruthless
politics, and the elaborate organization serve to the customer.

COMPREHENSION CHECK

Purpose and Main Idea

1. What is the author's topic?
   a. family meals
   b. food service
   c. restaurant management
   d. fast-food restaurants

2. What is the central idea of this selection?
   a. Wendy's, McDonald's, and Burger King are three examples of the typical fast-food restaurant.
   b. Consumers expect convenience, simplicity, and cleanliness from a fast-food restaurant.
   c. Fast-food chains meet consumers' expectations through an elaborate system of preordained rules and behaviors.
   d. No longer a purely American phenomenon, the fast-food restaurant has spread to other nations around the world.

3. The author's primary purpose is to
   a. express her viewpoint that fast-food restaurants need improvement.
   b. persuade readers that one fast-food restaurant is better than all the others.
   c. inform us about what we expect from fast-food chains and what they do to meet our expectations.
   d. entertain us with the variety of fast-food restaurants and menus that are available.

Details

4. In the author's opinion, consumers expect all but which one of the following from their favorite fast-food restaurant?
   a. simplicity
   b. convenience
   c. cleanliness
   d. variety

5. A conglomerate that offers fast food knows that travelers want
   a. unusual food.
   b. a place to celebrate.
   c. no surprises.
   d. a formal atmosphere.

6. According to the author, all but which one of the following are characteristic of the fast-food chains?

    a. They do not respond to social concerns.
    b. Menus and uniforms do not change.
    c. They want to be ordinary.
    d. They cater to families.

7. According to the author, fast-food operators responded to the threat of drug addicts as customers by changing the restaurants'
    a. hours.
    b. menu.
    c. lighting.
    d. atmosphere.

8. What is the author's dominant organizational pattern?
    a. Sequence: She traces the development of the fast-food restaurant in the United States.
    b. Comparison: She compares two fast-food restaurants.
    c. Cause and effect: She explains the reasons we like to eat in fast-food restaurants.
    d. Definition: She defines the term *fast-food restaurant*

Inferences

9. The author uses the word *ordinary* to mean all but which one of the following?
    a. everyday
    b. a type of restaurant
    c. simple
    d. innovative

10. Which answer best explains why fast-food restaurants did not want drug addicts as customers?
    a. Restaurant managers are prejudiced.
    b. The restaurants had an image to protect.
    c. The staff was concerned about crime.
    d. Drug addicts have no money to spend.

WORKING WITH WORDS

Complete the sentences below with these words from Word Alert:

ramifications	precursor	demeanour
conglomerate	proprietor	rubric
reiterated	adheres	cater

1. Finding a husband or wife may be difficult for a person who ex-
    pects someone to _____ to his or her every need.
2. Before you make a decision, think ahead to its possible _____
    and whether you can live with them.
3. "No, I won't accept your paper tomorrow," said the instructor.
    "How many times have I _____ today's deadline?"
4. Today's race car could be the _____ of tomorrow's sports sedan.
5. As the _____ of this store, I am the one who establishes busi-
    ness hours and the rules of operation.
6. "I don't like your _____ today," said the instructor to the chil-
    dren, who were talking and not paying attention.
7. Under the _____ of faculty responsibilities, instructors must
    meet all classes at their scheduled times or make prior arrange-
    ments.
8. Students appreciate an instructor who _____ to posted office
    hours and is, therefore, available to answer questions.
9. Ours is only one of many companies that have become a
    huge _____ of businesses, offering diverse services to
    consumers.

THINKING DEEPER

Ideas for discussion and writing

1. In paragraph 2, the author defines *rituals* in context as "behavior
    and expectations that conform to preordained rules." According
    to this definition, what does the author mean by the "ritual" of
    fast food?
2. What do you expect from a fast-food restaurant? In what way do
    the interior and exterior design, the words and actions of em-
    ployees, the restaurant's image, and the food offered meet your
    needs? Do your experiences reflect the author's analysis of what
    customers want and how the fast-food chains serve them? What
    else can you add about fast-food restaurants and their customers
    that the author did not mention?
3. Discuss how this selection illustrates the Part 2 theme,
    Rumblings in the Culture. In the past, the morning or evening
    meal at home was for most American families a ritual that en-
    couraged feelings of closeness. But many of today's families eat

fewer meals together and eat more meals out. Is this a positive or negative cultural development, and why?

4. Write about your favorite restaurant and why you like it. Some points to consider are the restaurant's design, atmosphere or theme, price, food offerings, and image.

FIRST THOUGHTS

To prepare yourself for the reading selection, answer the following questions, either on your own or in a group discussion.

1. What do you recall of the school shootings that occurred in several states in the late 1990s?
2. Why do you think some children become violent and murderous?
3. Preview the title, headnote, and first one or two paragraphs. What do you think will follow?

WORD ALERT

ideologies (3) beliefs or doctrines that are the bases of a political, economic, or other system

agendas (3) lists or programs of things to be done or considered

rampage (6) violent, frenzied action or behavior

attribute (16) to relate to a cause or a source

rapport (21) a relationship, especially one of mutual trust

reticent (26) inclined to keep one's feelings and personal affairs to oneself, restrained or reserved

reluctant (26) unwilling, resistant

❧ Children Want Parents' Attention

JEFF KUNERTH

On May 20, 1999, a 15-year-old boy was charged with shooting and wounding six classmates at Heritage High School in Conyers, Georgia. Jeff Kunerth, a staff writer for The Orlando Sentinel, *suggests that we should look beyond guns and the Internet for the causes of this shooting and other incidents of school violence. The article appeared in the* Sentinel *in May 1999.*

S CHOOL SHOOTINGS HAVE become the universal inkblot test for 1 Americans. We see whatever we're looking for in the causes behind children shooting classmates.

It's guns. It's the Internet. It's music, movies and video games. It's 2 parents without time and teachers without authority. It's a lack of God. It's too much freedom.

It's a lot of adults with **ideologies** and **agendas** looking for some- 3 one, something, somewhere to blame.

But when you talk to the children whose lives are threatened by 4 this epidemic of violence, they say pretty much the same thing regardless of race and income.

The message is: Shut up and listen.   5

"Parents don't pay attention. They don't pay attention because 6 they really don't want to hear," said Jennifer O'Connor, a 15-year-old freshman at Heritage High School, where a boy her age is charged with wounding six fellow students in a shooting **rampage** Thursday.

What the kids of Conyers want adults to hear is that the world they 7 live in bears little resemblance to that of their parents' days in high school. They are tired of hearing from adults, over and over, that it wasn't like this when they were growing up.

"The world they lived in is gone. It's not like that any more. They 8 have no idea what going to high school is like even for one day," said Stephanie Patterson, 18, who will be graduating from nearby Salem High School on Friday.

These are kids raised to fear strangers, stay away from drugs and 9 not catch AIDS. They've come home to empty houses since they left grade school. They've endured more than their fair share of divorce.

One girl said that when her parents divorced nine years ago, "That 10 was the only time in my whole life when I felt lonely."

They know fear, even if they haven't met violence.   11

"I'm afraid I'll die a slow and painful death like if somebody shoots 12 me and I bleed to death," said 13-year-old Lawren McCord, a middle school student.

They want to feel safe at school, but they don't think more police 13 officers in the hall, more surveillance cameras or bans on backpacks and trench coats will protect them. They don't think restrictions on guns, movies, music, video games will help. They don't expect society to save them or teachers to raise them.

"They want more security in the schools, but if someone wants to do 14 anything like that [kill students], they can't stop it," said Ken Wilson, 14.

Kids aren't into the blame game, but they see what's going on and 15 know who is responsible: It's the kids themselves and the parents who raised them.

They see in some of their classmates a lack of discipline, and they 16 **attribute** that to a lack of caring or involvement by parents.

"Most of the kids I know with problems say their parents don't care 17 about them," said Melissa Dawkins, 15, a sophomore at Heritage High. "They never see their parents. They never talk to their parents. They say, 'I can come home whenever I want because my parents don't care.'"

Kids know classmates who control the family, whose parents are 18 afraid to discipline or punish them. And when they see that, they are not surprised that those students have no respect for adults, no feelings for others. Kids see the signs of trouble adults either fail to recognize, ignore or deny.

"They see what they see, but they push it away as if nothing is 19 wrong," Patterson said.

They know from their own lives that trust, respect and communi- 20 cation between parent and child begins early. If parents wait until the trouble starts to begin paying attention to their children, it's already too late.

Melissa Dawkins said the **rapport** she has with her parents is rein- 21 forced with every meal. In her house, everyone is required to eat supper together on weeknights. That's where conversation starts and communication takes place.

"Even if we don't want to eat, we have to sit down and talk. It really 22 helps. They know what's going on in your life," Melissa said. "Most kids I know, everybody eats when they want to. It's not like that at my house."

Ask kids what kind of parents they will be when they grow up, and 23 you'll hear what kind of parents they want.

"I'm just going to make sure I spend plenty of time with them and 24 talk to them and be a major part of their lives," said Becca Watson, a 15-year-old sophomore at Heritage High.

Although times have changed, some things do not. Kids still want 25 parents who are involved in their lives, who know their children well enough to sense when something is wrong and who are there to listen when they have something to say.

And if teenagers seem **reticent** and **reluctant** to talk, sometimes 26 they see adults react the same way. Communication, they say, goes both ways.

"Parents don't share their feelings either," Patterson said.   27

She said her father was so disgusted and angry about the Heritage   28
shootings that he refused to talk about it. He opened up and expressed
his feelings only when the family's church brought teens and parents
together to talk about what happened.

At that meeting, adults and children shared their emotions—how   29
frightened and worried the parents were for their children's safety, and
how grateful the children were for their parents' presence. Children
said they didn't know their parents cared that much, and parents said
they didn't know their children needed more attention.

"It's kind of sad," Patterson said, "that something like this had to   30
happen to bring us together."

COMPREHENSION CHECK

Purpose and Main Idea

1. What is the author's topic?
    a. what parents want from schools
    b. what children want from parents
    c. why schools cannot stop violence
    d. what causes school violence

2. What is the central idea of this selection?
    a. Schools cannot stop violence because children are violent by
        nature.
    b. Children want parents who will leave them alone and let them
        do what they want to do.
    c. The kids themselves and the parents who raised them are
        responsible for school violence.
    d. Parents want school administrators to improve the security on
        school campuses.

3. The author's primary purpose is to
    a. entertain us with a vivid description of the shooting at Her-
        itage High School.
    b. express the opinion that parents are not to blame for their
        children's actions.
    c. persuade readers that parents ought to listen to their children.
    d. inform us about the number of school shootings that have
        occurred in recent years.

Details

4. According to the author, who or what is to blame for school
    violence?
    a. guns
    b. too much freedom
    c. music, movies, and video games
    d. kids and their parents

5. Children want parents to
    a. tell them about the past.
    b. listen and pay attention to them.
    c. stay out of their lives.
    d. keep their feelings to themselves.

6. According to the author, children today live in a different world
    from that of their parents for all of the following reasons except
    which one?
    a. Today's children are raised to fear strangers.
    b. They come home to empty houses.
    c. They feel safe and secure at school.
    d. Drugs, AIDS, and violence threaten their lives.

7. According to the author, children and parents are alike in what
    respect?
    a. They both like the same kinds of music and TV shows.
    b. Neither parents nor children care about each other.
    c. They grew up under similar circumstances.
    d. Both are reluctant to share their feelings.

8. What is the author's dominant organizational pattern?
    a. Process: He offers a program for stopping school violence.
    b. Comparison and contrast: He discusses similarities and differ-
        ences among various incidents of school violence.
    c. Cause and effect: He discusses the causes of school violence
        and its effects on children.
    d. Sequence: He traces the events that led to the Heritage High
        School shootings.

Inferences

9. Jeff Kunerth and the author of Selection 11 would probably both
    agree that
    a. shared meals reinforce positive feelings among parents and
        children.

    b. parents and children need to be more open with each other.
    c. television, movies, and the Internet are to blame for violence in the schools.
    d. parents and children have certain expectations about ways to behave in restaurants.

10. With which one of the following sayings would the author be most likely to agree?
    a. Spare the rod and spoil the child.
    b. Children should be seen and not heard.
    c. Communication is a two-way street.
    d. The child is father of the man.

WORKING WITH WORDS

Complete the sentences below with these words from Word Alert:

attribute	reluctant	agendas	rampage
ideologies	reticent	rapport	

1. Trey was _____ to make purchases over the Internet because he was worried about credit card security.

2. An instructor who has good _____ with students treats them with respect and takes their questions seriously.

3. Last week a tornado went on a _____ through several southern states, leaving many families homeless.

4. We are all tired of hearing from politicians whose _____ do not address the issues we care about.

5. Self-motivated students _____ their grades to the kind and amount of studying that they do.

6. Instructors should stick to teaching their subjects instead of using their classrooms as forums for their own _____.

7. Outgoing people have no trouble talking about themselves, but those who are _____ will steer the conversation in another direction.

THINKING DEEPER

Ideas for discussion and writing

1. The author of this selection sees a lack of communication be-
    tween parents and children. Do you agree? What, if anything, do
    the ages of parents and children have to do with their ability to
    share their thoughts and feelings with one another?

2. Much has been said and written about school violence. What do
    you think are its causes? What can be done about it? For example,
    do we need tighter security on campus or more gun control, or
    do you agree with Jeff Kunerth that the answer lies within
    ourselves?

3. Discuss how this selection illustrates the Part 2 theme,
    Rumblings in the Culture. For example, there is what we call a
    high school "culture": ways of dressing, speaking, and behaving.
    As part of this culture, students form groups, or cliques, and
    there is little interaction among them. What was the prevailing
    culture at your high school? What objections to it, if any, did stu-
    dents voice? Compare your high school culture to that of your
    parents. What are the similarities and differences?

4. Write about an aspect of your high school culture that was either
    harmful or beneficial. What were its effects on students?

FIRST THOUGHTS

To prepare yourself for the reading selection, answer the following questions, either on your own or in a group discussion.

1. What does the word *conscience* mean to you?

2. As a parent or future parent, what can you do to teach your children right from wrong?

3. Preview the title, headnote, and first one or two paragraphs. What do you think will follow?

WORD ALERT

intact (9) whole, unbroken, unimpaired
therapeutic (9) having healing powers
disquieting (10) troubling, disturbing
wanton (15) immoral, undisciplined, unrestrained
superficial (16) trivial, insignificant, lacking depth
intrinsic (17) inherent, of or relating to the essential nature of a thing
void (22) emptiness
didactic (24) instructive in an overly moralistic way
conscience (27) sense of right and wrong, a preference for right over
   wrong

❧ Killings Show Moral Void That Psychology Cannot Fill

BARBARA LERNER

Barbara Lerner, a Chicago-based freelance writer, has a doctoral degree in psychology. She wrote this article for The Orlando Sentinel, *and a version of it has run in* National Review *and the* Detroit News. *In the article, Lerner answers some of the questions raised by the shooting spree at Columbine High School in Littleton, Colorado, in 1999.*

T HE QUESTIONS WON'T go away. The Colorado shooting spree—the 1
eighth in two years—forces us to face them again.

Why all these wanton killings by schoolboys, this senseless spiral 2
of schoolhouse slaughter?

Who are these kids? Why are they doing it? What can we do?   3

In the 1990s, most parents look to psychology for answers. But 4
psychology doesn't have one set of answers; it has two: pre-'60s answers and post-'60s answers. And they conflict.

Every American knows the post-'60s answers. Turn on the televi- 5
sion and you hear them from all the talking heads. Not just establishment experts but mainstream teachers, preachers, politicians and
journalists, too. All subscribe to the conventional wisdom of the '90s:
All kids who kill are in great distress; they've been neglected, rejected
and abused; their self-esteem is low; they are crying out for help.

Kids who kill need more love and understanding, more communi- 6
cation and parental attention, more early intervention, professional
counseling and anger-management training. And the reason we have
more of these kids today is that we have more absent parents, more
entertainment media violence, more guns.

Will the Colorado killers fit this profile? Were they the abused off- 7
spring of harsh, uncaring parents and a cold, indifferent community?
Were they desperately unhappy kids with nowhere to turn for help?

So far, it doesn't look like it.   8

Eric Harris and Dylan Klebold both came from **intact** middle- 9
income families variously described by neighbors as "solid," "sensible"
and "utterly normal." Both already had been through the **therapeutic**
mill. Each boy had received individual counseling. Harris got anger-
management training, as well. Both finished their therapy in February,
two months before the crime, and both got glowing reports from their
counselors.

Maybe, when the facts are known, they will turn out to be a lot 10
more like Kip Kinkel, the 15-year-old Oregon shooter who vanished
from the news as soon as his **disquieting** life story began to emerge,
because it didn't fit the profile at all.

Kinkel was a problem for the conventional wisdom because he 11
had it all, everything 1990s experts recommend.

His parents were popular teachers, one of them was always there 12
for him when he came home from school, and both did their best to
make him happy, spending time with him, taking him on family vacations, helping him get whatever he wanted, even when the things he
wanted unnerved them.

They made few demands, rejected firm discipline as too harsh, 13
and sought professional help, early and often.

They were in counseling, along with Kip in May 1998, when he 14
shot them both dead, killed two of his many school friends, and
wounded 18 others.

Looking at cases like this, psychologists in the 1950s and earlier 15
had a set of answers you don't hear much any more. Here's an updated
sample: We have more **wanton** schoolboy killers today because we
have more narcissists, and the step from being a narcissist to being a
wanton killer is a short one, especially in adolescence.

A narcissist is a person who never progressed beyond the self- 16
love of infancy, one who learned **superficial** social skills—narcissists
are often charming—but never learned to truly love another, and,
through love, to view others as separate persons with a worth and
value equal to their own.

To the narcissist, other people have no **intrinsic** worth; their value 17
is purely instrumental. They are useful when they satisfy his desires
and enhance his self-esteem; disposable as bottle caps when they
don't. Only he matters, and because his sense of self-importance is so
grossly inflated, his feelings are easily hurt.

When they are, when others thwart him or fail to give him the ex- 18
cessive, unearned respect he demands, he reacts with rage and seeks
revenge, the more dramatic the better.

Take guns away from kids like these, and many won't settle for 19
knives and baseball bats; they'll turn to deadlier weapons—to explo-
sives, as that overgrown schoolboy, Ted Kaczynski did, or to environmental poisons, as the young subway saboteurs of Japan's Aum Shinri
Kyo did.

Kip was on his way—police found five bombs at his house. And 20
the Colorado killers upped the ante; they made more than 30 bombs
and used shrapnel, as well as bullets, to blow away their victims.

Will more counseling and anger-management classes help?   21

At best, they are palliatives in cases such as these. They can put a 22
patch over the hole at the core of these kids, the moral **void,** but they
cannot fill the hole.

No brand of psychology can, and earlier brands—Freud's espe- 23
cially—had the humility to recognize that. He saw the hole for what it
is, a moral hole that only moral training can fill.

Not just calm, rational, smiley-face, **didactic** lessons, but the kind 24
of intense, gut-level experiences children have when their parents
draw a sharp moral line and demonstrate a willingness to go all out to

defend it. It is the kind of experiences that make it clear to their kids early on that there are limits to what can be accepted, actions so morally wrong that they cannot and will not be tolerated.

Through experiences like these, normal children learn that the 25 unconditional parental love they could take for granted as infants and toddlers can no longer be taken for granted. It is no longer uncondi- tional; it can be withdrawn.

And to avoid that frightening outcome, the child learns to see his 26 parents as more than human piñatas, full of goodies he has only to hit away at to get.

He learns to see them as moral beings with standards and values 27 that are more important than his own immature wishes, and he be- gins to internalize those standards and values, making them his own, developing a **conscience** in the process.

Many 1990s experts don't understand this process. They focus 28 only on self-esteem, not on esteem for others, asking only if the child is loved, not whether the child has learned to love and respect others.

The experts of this decade also obsess about the methods parents 29 use to teach their kids, ignoring the content, the moral lessons they are trying to teach, insisting that any physical punishment, however infrequently and judiciously applied, is child abuse.

These experts have no real solutions to offer, when the problem is 30 overindulgence rather than abuse, as it so often is in the 1990s.

They are part of the problem, and the sooner we recognize that, 31 the better off we will be.

COMPREHENSION CHECK

Purpose and Main Idea

1. What is the author's topic?
   a. counseling and anger management
   b. school killings and what we can do about them
   c. psychologists and their methods
   d. the parents of Harris and Klebold

2. What is the central idea of this selection?
   a. Only moral training at an early age, not psychology, can pre- vent children from becoming killers.
   b. A lack of self-esteem is what causes students to lash out vio- lently against their classmates.
   c. Most parents look to psychology for a solution to the problem of school violence.

    d. The Colorado killings have forced us to face some difficult questions.

3. The author's primary purpose is to
    a. express her opinion on the causes of school violence.
    b. entertain us with a description of psychologists and their methods.
    c. inform readers of the questions that the eruption in school violence has raised.
    d. persuade readers to ignore the experts and provide moral training for their children.

Details

4. The author says that in the 1990s, most parents seek answers from
    a. themselves.
    b. religious leaders.
    c. psychologists.
    d. teachers.

5. According to the author, the conventional wisdom about kids who kill consists of all but which one of the following?
    a. They are in great distress.
    b. They've been neglected and abused.
    c. Their self-esteem is low.
    d. They lack a moral center.

6. According to the author, Kip Kinkel's parents did all of the following except
    a. make few demands on him.
    b. withhold what he wanted if it unnerved them.
    c. reject firm discipline as too harsh.
    d. seek professional help early.

7. According to the author, moral training can best be accomplished by
    a. the use of didactic lessons.
    b. psychologists and other experts.
    c. experiences that set limits for behavior.
    d. focusing only on self-esteem.

8. What is the author's dominant organizational pattern in paragraphs 15 through 17?
    a. sequence
    b. process
    c. definition
    d. classification

Inferences

9. The author would probably agree that children who resort to violence are most lacking in
    a. counseling.
    b. parental love.
    c. a conscience.
    d. social skills.

10. Read again paragraphs 21 and 22. In these paragraphs, the author says that counseling and anger-management classes are palliatives. Based on the example stated in the second sentence of paragraph 22, you can infer that *palliative* means
    a. bandages or other sterile wrappings.
    b. something that relieves but does not cure.
    c. prescription drugs.
    d. soothing words.

WORKING WITH WORDS

Complete the sentences below with these words from Word Alert:

> disquieting   therapeutic   intrinsic   wanton   void
> superficial   conscience   didactic   intact

1. The judge called the children who had blown up Ms. Blackburn's boxwoods with cherry bombs reckless and _____ .

2. The _____ sound of sirens in the hours before dawn can unnerve anyone.

3. The reviewers' comments were _____ , indicating that they had not understood the author's meaning.

4. Many people believe that it is _____ for people who have a cold to eat chicken soup.

5. Winona's _____ would not allow her friend Ben to take the blame for her mistakes.

6. Some instructors provide hands-on experiences, while others resort to the more _____ techniques of lecturing.

7. Resolving a marital problem is hard if one person wants a divorce but the other one wants to keep the family _____ .

8. Although their _____ worth may be little, some objects mean a lot to us because of their sentimental value.

9. Lisa leaned over the edge of the old well and stared into
    the _____ , seeing nothing.

THINKING DEEPER

Ideas for discussion and writing

1. Do you believe that people are more or less accountable for their
    actions today than they were in the past? On what do you base
    this belief?

2. Compare and contrast the views of Barbara Lerner and Jeff
    Kunerth, the author of Selection 12. Discuss how each author
    answers the questions: "Why do schoolboys kill?" and "What can
    we do about it?" What is each author's solution to the problem?
    With which author do you agree and why?

3. Discuss how this selection illustrates the Part 2 theme,
    Rumblings in the Culture. For example, the author speaks of a
    cultural shift from pre-sixties psychology, which placed the
    blame for bad behavior on the individual, to post-sixties psychol-
    ogy, which places the blame on parents, society—everyone but
    the individual. What have been the effects of this shift?

4. Write about a time in your life when you did something that you
    knew was wrong. What happened? How did you feel? How did
    others react to what you had done? If you had to do it over, what
    would you do differently?

FIRST THOUGHTS

To prepare yourself for the reading selection, answer the following questions, either on your own or in a group discussion.

1. What do you know about military-base schools?

2. What do you think should be done to improve public schools?

3. Preview the title, headnote, and first one or two paragraphs. What do you think will follow?

WORD ALERT

earnestly (1) sincerely, seriously
vouchers (2) written authorizations exchangeable for cash or credit
incompetence (3) lack of qualifications or skills
refutation (5) proving to be false, denying the truth of
secular (5) worldly rather than spiritual, not bound by a religion
exemplary (5) worthy of imitation, serving as a model
proficiency (8) having skill or competence
pedagogical (10) relating to teaching or instruction
predisposed (14) inclined, made to do something in advance
haphazardly (14) by chance, casually

❧ Why Do Students at U.S. Military-Base Schools Excel?

WILLIAM RASPBERRY

William Raspberry, a syndicated columnist, is a member of the Washington Post Writers Group. In this article, which ran in The Orlando Sentinel *in December 1999, he challenges readers to examine the reasons for the success of military-base schools as they seek public-school reform.*

"Why Do Students at U.S. Military-Base Schools Excel?" by William Raspberry. © **1999, The Washington Post Writers Group. Reprinted with permission.**

S OMETIMES I THINK that there are just two kinds of people in the world: 1
those who know easily and precisely why so many of our schools
aren't working very well and those who, no matter how **earnestly** they
struggle with the question, can't quite manage to figure it out.

The first group is by no means of one mind. Their dead-certain 2
answers involve everything from phonics to teachers colleges to direct
instruction; from poverty and racism to prayer and **vouchers** and cor-
poral punishment.

The second group, of which I am decidedly a member, will grant 3
that portions of the dead-certain answers frequently make sense but
will insist that they don't explain enough. Nor do we (some of us, anyway) accept the notion that indifference and **incompetence** on the
part of teachers is the main ingredient of failure.

I have stated—and still believe—that the inability of some parents to 4
get their children ready for school learning is a huge part of the problem. Still, I keep probing for some more comprehensive explanation.

And for good reason. Every explanation will find its **refutation** some- 5
where. A touchy-feely approach, a **secular** outlook, a penny-pinching
budget—will, somewhere, sometime, produce **exemplary** results.

How—to take the question that really sparked this column—does 6
one explain the unusual success of some of the schools on America's
military bases? Eighth-graders in these 71 schools as a group were out-
performed in writing by only one state—Connecticut—on the 1998
National Assessment of Educational Progress. They tied for fourth
place in reading.

According to *The Wall Street Journal's* Daniel Golden, it isn't just 7
test scores that make these schools special. Eighty percent of the graduates of these military-base schools go on to college—even though
many of them switch from one school to another several times during
their school years, meaning that they have to catch on to new teachers
and make new friends again and again.

Poverty? Half the 34,000 students in these schools qualify for free 8
or reduced-price lunches—an accepted measure of poverty—because
their parents are in the bottom pay ranks. Two out of five are either
black or Hispanic, but they achieve at or above **proficiency** at rates far
exceeding those of the civilian world.

How do these schools succeed where their nonmilitary counter- 9
parts so often fail?

Several possibilities come to mind—some of them **pedagogical,** 10
some relating to the involved presence of parents, particularly fathers—
but here, for want of knowledge to the contrary, is my first choice:

These children have parents who believe that their own efforts— 11
not race, not special gifts, not breaks—are the chief determinant of
their success. It's a point that researchers who examine the American
military keep coming to: Service members believe that the military,
for all its shortcomings, is fairer than the civilian world, believe that
the requirements for advancement are clear, attainable and (usually)
fairly administered.

If they didn't believe these things, of course, they would hardly 12
stay in military careers. Their nonservice counterparts, just as obviously, cannot quit the civilian life just because they think it's unfair.

My guess—and that's all it is—is that people who believe that they 13
can achieve based on their own efforts tend to rear children who share
that belief. Military children, I am suggesting, may have an unusual
degree of academic success because they hold to an unusual degree
the empowering belief that they are in control of their destinies.

Too many poor and minority children in the civilian world are 14
predisposed to harbor the disempowering view that life is unfair,
that breaks are **haphazardly** distributed and that race is a near-
insuperable barrier to success.

There are other possible explanations for the disproportionate 15
achievement of military schools, and some of them—the presence of
fathers who are both self-disciplined and accepting of military discipline, for instance—are quite attractive.

Which are the correct explanations? 16

I don't know, but I can tell you this: If I were running a failing 17
school system, I would surely try to find out.

COMPREHENSION CHECK

Purpose and Main Idea

1. What is the author's topic?
   a. public school reform
   b. the success of military-base schools
   c. public schools vs. private schools
   d. education in the United States

2. Which one of the following sentences best states the author's
   central idea?
   a. There are two opposing views as to why our public schools are
      failing.

    b. Parents' inability to get their children ready for learning is the cause of school failure.

    c. Race, special gifts, and breaks are not the chief reasons for students' success in school.

    d. One reason for the success of military-base schools is that military children believe that they can succeed on their own.

3. The author's primary purpose is to
    a. entertain readers by describing his experiences in military-base schools.
    b. inform readers that public schools are in need of reform.
    c. express what he thinks is the reason that military-base schools have been successful.
    d. persuade readers to send their children to military-base schools.

Details

4. Raspberry says that sometimes he thinks there are just two groups of people. The first group's dead-certain answers, he says, involve all but which one of the following?
    a. phonics
    b. teachers colleges
    c. poverty and racism
    d. class size

5. As a member of the second group, Raspberry agrees that the first group's answers
    a. are on the wrong track.
    b. explain his own views exactly.
    c. often make sense but don't explain enough.
    d. have not been well researched or proven.

6. According to Daniel Golden, military-base schools are special for all of the following reasons but which one?
    a. Their students achieve consistently higher test scores than students in most public schools.
    b. Eighty percent of their graduates go on to college.
    c. Fifty percent of the students' parents are in the top pay ranks.
    d. Minority students' achievement is higher than that of civilians.

7. Raspberry says that military-base children may have an unusual degree of academic success because

    a. they believe that they are in control of their own destinies.

    b. they are the victims of poverty and racism.

    c. their parents are not involved in their learning.

    d. service members believe that the military is unfair.

8. What is the dominant organizational pattern of this selection?

    a. Sequence: The author traces the development of the public-school reform movement.

    b. Definition: The author defines what it means to be a military-base school student.

    c. Cause and effect: The author explains reasons for military-base schools' success.

    d. Comparison and contrast: The author compares public schools and military-base schools.

Inferences

9. The author would probably agree that, more often than not, a minority student's poor grade on a test is the result of

    a. poverty or lack of opportunity.

    b. incompetent or indifferent teaching.

    c. racial prejudice and discrimination.

    d. insufficient study or lack of effort.

10. The word *empowering* in paragraph 13 and the word *disempowering* in paragraph 14 have what relationship?

    a. The words are synonyms: Their meanings are similar.

    b. They are antonyms, or opposites in meaning.

    c. The two terms are unrelated.

    d. Both words are slang expressions.

WORKING WITH WORDS

Complete the sentences below with these words from Word Alert:

> incompetence pedagogical proficiency earnestly vouchers
> haphazardly predisposed refutation exemplary secular

1. The detective walked around the crime scene, _____ looking at objects here and there in no apparent order.

2. Speaking _____ to the students, the instructor reminded them of the upcoming test and how much she hoped that they would succeed.

3. Parents in some states receive _____ that allow them to use tax dollars to send their children to private schools.

4. College students whose placement test scores are low may be required to take courses to improve their _____ in their areas of weakness.

5. The newspaper cited our town's high school as _____ because 70 percent of its graduates go on to college.

6. Some parents who send their children to a private school may choose a _____ school rather than a religious one.

7. Phonics instruction and whole-language instruction are but two of the elementary teacher's _____ tools.

8. Employees who do not know how to do some tasks may be accused of _____ when all they need is instruction.

9. After reading a positive film review, you might be _____ to enjoy the movie.

10. The candidate's _____ of his opponent's false and uncalled-for charges was both loud and angry.

THINKING DEEPER

Ideas for discussion and writing

1. In paragraph 11, the author says that military children "have parents who believe that their own efforts—not race, not special gifts, not breaks—are the chief determinant of their success." Do you agree that success is mainly the result of effort? Explain your reasons in a class discussion.

2. Read again paragraphs 13 and 14. Discuss what the author means by empowering and disempowering beliefs. Do you agree with the author that our beliefs can act as springboards or barriers to success? Explain your reasons, using examples from your own life or others' lives.

3. Discuss how this selection illustrates the Part 2 theme, *Rumblings in the Culture.* For example, the public school is an American institution, a hallmark of American democracy and culture. But as more and more parents become dissatisfied with public schools, they are seeking alternatives. Those who can afford it have sent their children to private schools. Others have called for public-school reform, looking to private schools and

military-base schools as examples for public schools to follow. What do you know of the school reform debate? What do you see as the future of American public schools?

4. Write about an empowering or disempowering belief that you grew up with and how it has affected your performance in school or another aspect of your life.

FIRST THOUGHTS

To prepare yourself for the reading selection, answer the following questions, either on your own or in a group discussion.

1. What role does religion or spirituality play in your life?
2. What needs does religion or spirituality fulfill?
3. Preview the title, headnote, and first one or two paragraphs. What do you think will follow?

WORD ALERT

clarity (2) clearness of thought, lucidity
lilt (3) a cheerful or lively manner of speaking
reveling (6) enjoying, taking pleasure or delight
unfettered (6) unrestrained, freed
tremulous (10) quivering or shaking, fearful or timid
onslaught (10) a violent attack
sustaining (15) maintaining, supporting, encouraging
zealots (15) fanatics
wary (19) cautious, on guard
tangible (19) able to be touched, understood, or treated as fact
gratification (19) pleasure, satisfaction
transfixed (22) awe-inspired

ॐ Seeking Spirituality in a Time of Tragedy

DONNA BRITT

Donna Britt is a member of the Washington Post Writers Group. In this article, which ran in The Orlando Sentinel *in May 1999, she explains her own struggle with spirituality and offers a message of hope for readers.*

© 1999, The Washington Post Writers Group. Reprinted with permission.

"T HIS DO IN REMEMBRANCE of me."   1
   The familiar phrase, one of many offered in a sermon by a min- 2
ister I hadn't seen in weeks, settled over me like a veil. Staring at my
tiny church's altar, I felt one of those rare moments of sweet **clarity**
wash over me.

In remembrance of me. The words—mingled with the sun splash- 3
ing through sanctuary windows, the piercing melodies of birds outside,
the minister's passionate **lilt**—blended into something like perfection.

Pulling me back.   4

I hadn't been to church in a while because I was angry at God for 5
letting a loved one die after I had specifically asked Him to forbid it.
After confessing my disillusionment to my minister, I was surprised
when he suggested that I take a church break. "You may find you're not
as mad at God as you think," he said.

So for a string of Sundays, I stayed away—shopping, reading the 6
newspaper, **reveling** in the suddenly **unfettered** hours I would normally spend preparing for and worshiping in church.

Eight weeks later,I had to go back. I wasn't sure why, though a 7
world with no communal, public sharing of spirituality felt . . . wobbly.

Then Littleton happened.   8

Suddenly, God's name was on countless lips. Suddenly, the spirit- 9
non-grata so seldom mentioned in mainstream news media was the
center of discussion.

Tremulous teens described praying to God as they hid under 10
desks from the **onslaught.** Stricken parents spoke of the Lord helping
them heal. In a shattering interview, Craig Scott—whose sister, Rachel,
died at Columbine High—clutched the hand of Michael Shoels, father
of the slain student Isaiah, saying, "I really trust God's hand over this."

Somehow the ease with which these victims spoke of their faith 11
seemed odd. It was strange, hearing so much public discussion of God
after so much near-silence.

Writing about teen violence afterward, I blamed news-media im- 12
ages, parental disconnection, easy gun access and drugs—without
thinking to mention America's spiritual drift, until hours after deadline.

Why was that? Why, when increasingly it appears Dylan Klebold 13
was a once-normal kid sucked into Eric Harris' bloody fantasies? I've
heard nothing about either boy's religious training. But kids grounded
in God often have more spiritual weapons with which to fight darkness, whether or not they use them.

And there is so much darkness to fight.   14

We have become frighteningly independent of our ancestors' 15
sustaining spirituality. If not for athletes who give thanks after sports
victories—or **zealots,** whose slaying of abortionists mock religion—
we would rarely hear mention of the God in whom most Americans
believe. Somehow, the country described by its pledge of allegiance as
"one nation under God" and whose currency is stamped IN GOD WE
TRUST, seems terribly secular.

And not terribly bothered by it.   16

Today, it takes the unspeakable—like a girl being shot dead after 17
telling a gun-wielding classmate that she's a believer—to make people
speak of the deity who informed our forebears' every move. In fact,
God—as well as Allah, Buddha and others—remains central to millions. Yet their beliefs get news-media attention only when awfulness
is done in His name.

As a nation, I suspect, we're a bit mad at God. Or at least deeply 18
suspicious of Him.

We're **wary** of anything that might make us look gullible or unso- 19
phisticated, that advocates such outmoded concepts as submission
and sacrifice, that can be so easily misused—as scandal-smeared
politicians who wallow in prayer, and Christians who would "cleanse"
Yugoslavia of its Muslim citizens illustrate. Yet the same "sophisti-
cates" who grumble about religion's lack of **tangible** guarantees spend
millions on products whose ads promise **gratification** in a finger-snap
and invest in scientific solutions that also may fail.

Anyway, who has the time? Spirituality looks like the worst kind of 20
hard work: the kind that can, despite one's best efforts, disappoint.

Yet like all hard work, it delivers payoffs that the quick-and-easy 21
seldom can—or so our grandparents and great-grandparents insisted.
They knew even if they never found it, the strenuous search for God's
love within themselves was a worthy distraction from the rage, petti-
ness and bitterness that might otherwise consume them. Hard work is
the *point.*

Transfixed in church that day, I knew why I had been pulled back. 22
For a few moments each week, everything makes sense. For a few moments each week, I push myself to forgive the unforgivable, to embrace those I would scorn, to locate a better, more generous me.

In that perfect moment, I realized that my departed loved one—all 23
the departed loved ones who honored God, publicly and often, in the face
of tremendous difficulty—would rather have me there than anywhere.

I was there, in good measure, in remembrance of them.   24

COMPREHENSION CHECK

Purpose and Main Idea

1. What is the author's topic?
    a. the author's search for spirituality
    b. ways to handle tragedy
    c. the decline of morality
    d. the importance of belief systems

2. Which one of the following sentences best states the author's central idea?
    a. In the mainstream media, God's name is seldom the center of discussion.
    b. The search for spirituality brings comfort, self-understanding, and relief in times of tragedy.
    c. Religious beliefs are central to millions of people throughout the world.
    d. Public displays of religious faith make us look gullible and unsophisticated.

3. The author's primary purpose is to
    a. persuade readers to worship at the church of their choice.
    b. entertain readers by describing a typical service at her church.
    c. inform readers that church attendance is declining.
    d. express what her spiritual search has meant to her.

Details

4. According to the author, why had she stopped going to church?
    a. Her minister told her to take a break.
    b. She was angry at God for letting a loved one die.
    c. She thought church attendance was an outmoded practice.
    d. Her family did not approve of her form of worship.

5. In her writing after the Littleton shootings, the author blamed teen violence on all of the following but
    a. news-media images.
    b. parental disconnection.
    c. access to guns and drugs.
    d. America's spiritual drift.

6. Which of the following lost a son in the Littleton shootings?
    a. Rachel Scott
    b. Craig Scott
    c. Eric Harris
    d. Michael Shoels

7. The author explains the generalization "there is so much dark-
    ness to fight," using all of the following examples except which
    one?
    a. independence from our ancestors' spirituality
    b. athletes who give thanks after victories
    c. the slaying of abortionists
    d. a nation that seems terribly secular

8. What is the organizational pattern in paragraphs 5–8?
    a. cause and effect
    b. comparison and contrast
    c. process
    d. sequence

Inferences

9. What does the author mean by "America's spiritual drift" in para-
    graph 12?
    a. the number of religious groups in America
    b. our tendency to turn to God in times of trouble
    c. the lack of public sharing of spirituality
    d. a growing interest in non-Christian religions

10. Which of the following sayings is closest to the author's meaning
    of "Hard work is the *point*" (paragraph 21)?
    a. No pain, no gain.
    b. Getting there is half the fun.
    c. Winning doesn't matter; it's how you play the game.
    d. Anything worth getting is worth waiting for.

WORKING WITH WORDS

Complete the sentences below with these words from Word Alert:

gratification	sustaining	reveling	clarity
unfettered	tremulous	tangible	wary
transfixed	onslaught	zealots	lilt

1. After the game, the fans of the winning team ran onto the field,
    cheering and _____ in their victory.

2. If it were not for our _____ members and their contributions,
    our museum could not survive.

3. For some people, heartfelt thanks are not enough; instead, they
    want _____ rewards, such as gifts or money.

4. Small buildings and mobile homes could not stand the _____ of the hurricane's high winds.

5. In a moment of _____ , the student finally understood what had seemed unclear.

6. The children were _____ as they sat in the darkened theater waiting for the horror film to begin.

7. Be _____ of any supposedly free offers, as they may have hidden costs.

8. The morning was filled with sunshine, the fragrance of spring flowers, and the _____ of birdsong.

9. I can't wait for my vacation: two _____ weeks in the sun with no phones ringing, no appointments to keep.

10. In the 1960s, airports were filled with _____ passing out leaflets proclaiming stop this or end that.

11. We were _____ as we stood before Dali's painting "The Crucifixion."

12. Some people spend all they earn buying things they want now, while others postpone _____ and save for the future.

THINKING DEEPER

Ideas for discussion and writing

1. Discuss Donna Britt's statement, "kids grounded in God often have more spiritual weapons with which to fight darkness." Do you agree or disagree? What do you think she means by "spiritual weapons" and by "darkness"? What darkness do adults fight, and what are their spiritual weapons? Finally, what role do you think spirituality does or should play in our lives and why?

2. Read again the first two paragraphs and the last two paragraphs of the selection. How do these paragraphs *frame*, or provide an organizational structure for, Britt's essay? What is the significance of the quotation in the first paragraph, and what personal meaning does Britt find in it?

3. Discuss how this selection illustrates the Part 2 theme, *Rumblings in the Culture*. For example, public sharing of faith (school prayer, the pledge of allegiance, posting of the Ten Commandments in public buildings, and prayers before public events) was once a central part of American culture. But as

Donna Britt says, we are becoming increasingly secular and suffering from "spiritual drift." Do you agree? Explain your reasons.

4. The author says she had a moment of clarity in church when she
    realized why she was there. Write about your own moment of
    clarity: a time when you clearly knew or understood something
    important for the first time.

FIRST THOUGHTS

To prepare yourself for the reading selection, answer the following questions, either on your own or in a group discussion.

1. Did you have a friend or family member who fought in Afghanistan or Iraq after September 11, 2001? Explain your answer.
2. What firsthand experience do you have of life in the military?
3. Preview the title, headnote, and first one or two paragraphs. What do you think will follow?

WORD ALERT

deployed (2) distributed, put into use or action
prepped (3) prepared, made ready
tenterhooks (4) a state of suspense or anxiety
substandard (5) below standard, unacceptable
charismatic (8) arousing popular devotion and enthusiasm
valiant (8) courageous, brave
fathom (10) comprehend, understand

❧ I'm Afraid to Look, Afraid to Turn Away

DENISE GONSALES

Gonsales is a military wife living in Rincon, Georgia. While her husband was stationed overseas, waiting for the war in Iraq to begin, she found out firsthand what a mixed blessing twenty-four-hour news coverage can be. She reminds us of the anxiety military families face while separated from their loved ones.

IT'S A STRESSFUL time for my family. I'm eight months pregnant and 1 my husband, Martin, a Black Hawk pilot based in Savannah, Ga., has been in Kuwait for more than two months. Not surprisingly, I have been glued to the television, watching events unfold in this latest conflict, praying for my husband's safe return. As hard as it is to wait, it's not the first time I've done it and I suspect it won't be the last.

My first husband, who died three and a half years ago, was part of 2 the 160th Special Operations unit **deployed** in 1993 to Somalia, where two Black Hawk helicopters were downed. Five of our dearest friends were killed during that mission. To my everlasting horror, I watched on CNN as the bodies of two of them were dragged through the streets of Mogadishu by a riotous crowd. My then 8-year-old daughter went to school the next day and saw a picture of one of the soldiers on the front page of our local paper. She told me that she would have been worried except that the soldier had blond hair and her daddy's was black. Once the military officially declared the soldiers' deaths, I had to deliver the terrible news to two of their wives.

While Army families are **prepped** to expect stresses and strains of 3 military service on their family life, I never thought the realities of war would affect me firsthand. Maybe I was in denial, maybe I just believed no nation in its right mind would take on America.

Martin was supposed to retire last February but he was caught in 4 the stop-loss that the military put on select jobs in the wake of September 11. He is now expected to retire in November of 2004. Even during peacetime, our family is on **tenterhooks,** wondering if he might be deployed to another far-flung region of the world. While I am certain we can endure his absence, I have seen many families fall apart from the constant separations.

It pains me that the American public doesn't fully comprehend 5 the sacrifices being made by soldiers during war, deployments and rotations. Incredibly, enlisted soldiers earn so little money that they qualify for food stamps. Many of them live in **substandard** military housing. Even so, they're willing to stick it out in the desert, where just having toilet paper is a luxury.

Their families sacrifice, too. Soldiers miss out on birthdays, an- 6 niversaries, children's sports events and summer vacations. There's a good chance Martin may miss the birth of our son next month. But I've learned over the years to have a backup plan so my family can have a sense of normalcy. Two of my best friends, Dan and Jennifer, will take Martin's place in the delivery room.

My access to Martin has been limited, but I keep thinking about 7 the wives of soldiers who fought in World War II. Their husbands were away for years on end with little communication, so I try and keep a stiff upper lip and remain grateful for the contact I do have. Other wives have not been so fortunate—their husbands don't write home. This creates more stress for their families.

I've received about 10 letters from my husband since he's been 8 gone. It takes them about 20 days to get to me. He's a **charismatic** kind of guy, very funny. Even in his letters he makes a **valiant** attempt to keep me uplifted. Between us we renamed this conflict "Operation Enduring Loneliness." I've gotten probably four or five phone calls. We had a three-minute conversation last Tuesday. He said, "D, I've been trying for 45 minutes to get through to you. There's a meeting and I have to go. Please don't worry, I love you and I'm really sorry I can't talk longer." I said "Martin, I don't care if it's 20 seconds, I'm just glad to hear your voice."

Being able to watch events unfold in real time has been a mixed 9 blessing. I'm terrified of what I might see and yet I find it impossible to turn the television off while my husband is fighting this war. I can't help but worry that the Somalia experience will play out in living rooms across the country. My children, in their teens now, are equally interested in watching the coverage. They know that Martin's unit, the Third Infantry Division, is leading the push to Baghdad. They constantly ask questions about his location and whether he is in harm's way. No doubt they sense my fear.

As nerve-racking as it was when President Bush announced that 10 the war had begun, it was in some ways a relief. My biggest fear was that our troops would sit over there all summer and morale would suffer. My heart just pours out to Iraqi families; as a mother, I can't imagine living with my two kids in a neighborhood that's being bombed. I can't even **fathom** that. And as terrified as I am for Martin, I can't imagine being an Iraqi wife whose husband is leaving to go fight the Americans. At least I know my husband has a fighting chance.

COMPREHENSION CHECK

Purpose and Main Idea

1. What is the author's topic?
    a. TV coverage of the war
    b. a soldier's responsibilities
    c. the war in Iraq
    d. a military family's sacrifices
2. What is the author's central idea?
    a. Americans do not fully comprehend the sacrifices that soldiers and their families make in times of war.

  b. Most people never think that the realities of war will affect them firsthand.
  c. Watching coverage of the war on TV has both advantages and disadvantages.
  d. Military families are prepared for the stress of seeing their loved ones go off to war.

3. Which one of the following is the author's primary purpose?
  a. to persuade readers that TV coverage of a war in progress is distressing
  b. to inform readers about the sacrifices that military families must make
  c. to explain to readers what she and her family are going through as they await her husband's return
  d. to entertain readers with her husband's adventures as a soldier

Details

4. Where is the author's husband, Martin, based?
  a. Mogadishu
  b. Savannah, Georgia
  c. Iraq
  d. Somalia

5. The author's first husband was part of which unit?
  a. Operation Enduring Loneliness
  b. the Third Infantry Division
  c. the Black Hawk pilots
  d. the 160th Special Operations unit

6. The author says that when the war began, it was a relief in some ways because
  a. she had worried that the soldiers' morale would suffer.
  b. fighting would be harder in winter than in summer.
  c. she did not know how long the war would last.
  d. she had no idea where her husband was stationed.

7. The author cites all but which one of the following as sacrifices that our soldiers have to make?
  a. deployments and rotations
  b. communication with families
  c. substandard housing
  d. little pay

8. The author calls watching events unfold in real time on TV a "mixed blessing" because

a. she gets information that is both immediate and accurate.
b. her family can keep up with the troops' location and events.
c. she is both afraid of and interested in watching the news.
d. news coverage can be stressful and nerve-racking.

Inferences

9. You can infer that during the Iraq war, the author might have been least likely to support which one of the following?
    a. food stamps for soldiers
    b. news interviews with Iraqi families
    c. the use of conventional weapons
    d. antiwar demonstrations by celebrities

10. Based on the author's details, which word best describes her view toward Iraqi families?
    a. fearful
    b. angry
    c. sympathetic
    d. charitable

WORKING WITH WORDS

Complete the sentences below with these words from Word Alert:

substandard   charismatic   prepped   fathom
tenterhooks   deloyed   valiant

1. Some of our most _____ celebrities, such as Elvis and Madonna, have been known by their first names only.
2. No one would want to live in _____ housing.
3. During the horror movie, the audience waited on _____ for something to happen.
4. Students may fear being called on when they know that they cannot _____ the answer to a question.
5. Because of their _____ efforts, the troops saw a swift end to the war.
6. Unbelievably, the soldier made a safe landing even though the parachute had not _____ .
7. The students who had _____ for the test made higher scores than those who had not studied.

THINKING DEEPER

Ideas for discussion and writing

1. Based on your experiences or on what you have read or heard, what are the advantages and disadvantages of military life?

2. Read again paragraphs 5 and 6. Do you agree or disagree with the author's view that the American public does not fully understand the sacrifices that soldiers and their families make during wartime? Explain your reasoning.

3. Discuss how this selection illustrates the Part 2 theme, *Rumblings in the Culture.* For example, did you watch the coverage of the Iraq war on one of the twenty-four-hour news stations? What were your emotional reactions while watching the coverage? In what ways do you think that continuous coverage of a war is either helpful or harmful? How has the idea of "all the news, all the time" shaped today's culture?

4. Write about one event or action that you either did or did not support during the Iraq war, and explain your reasons.

FIRST THOUGHTS

To prepare yourself for the reading selection, answer the following questions, either on your own or in a group discussion.

1. Do you own a cell phone? If so, where and when do you use it?
2. If you could write a list of good manners for cell phone users, what would they be?
3. Preview the title, headnote, and first one or two paragraphs. What do you think will follow?

WORD ALERT

surreal (3) odd, dreamlike
prodded (5) stimulated or prompted to act
etiquette (5) rules of behavior and manners prescribed by society or authority
disconcerting (6) disturbing, upsetting
gorges (9) narrow passages having steep sides
gullies (9) deep ditches cut by running water
eyesores (9) things that are unpleasant or offensive to view
hail (10) to signal or call out
gulch (18) a small ravine, a narrow valley

❧ Cell Phones Destroy Solitude of Wilderness

THE ASSOCIATED PRESS

Are cell phones a blessing or a curse? In this article, the authors examine a disturbing phenomenon: a day in the woods disrupted by the ringing of cell phones.

H IGH ABOVE THE TREES and surrounded by sky, the Adirondack 1 peaks can seem far removed from the everyday world.

Unless, of course, the guy next to you is jabbering on his cell ₂ phone.

Such a **surreal** scene played out on Mount Marcy's summit in ₃ front of state forester Jim Papero. He remembers it well: "It was cold and windy. Beautiful. You could hear the wind whistling and everything, then this . . . he was talking to his stockbroker."

Cell-phone chatter, already common at restaurants and shopping ₄ malls, is heard more and more often in the wilderness. Hikers and campers are tapping into personal directories to ask directions and apologize for dinner delays, to bum rides and call in sick.

This is not amusing to many campers, hunters or others who ap- ₅ preciate nature's quiet. The problem has **prodded** New York environmental officials, who also worry about hikers using cell phones as lifelines, to promote phone **etiquette** in the wilderness.

"To be walking down a trail or expend the effort it takes to climb ₆ one of the high peaks, and to see someone on the telephone . . . it's **disconcerting**," says Stu Buchanan, regional director of the state Department of Environmental Conservation.

There's no backwoods cell-phone epidemic just yet. But calls from ₇ the wild have become noticeable recently, now that wireless phones reach an estimated 74 million users nationwide.

What can be a mere irritant in civilization can be a lifesaver in the ₈ wild. Rescues have been launched after timely calls for help from remote areas. Even many "Ridge Runners," whose job is to help hikers on the Appalachian Trail, now carry cell phones.

Problem is, cell phones aren't reliable in the wild because cell tow- ₉ ers tend to be far apart. Then there's the problem of getting a phone to work in **gorges, gullies** and other pockets amid peaks. It's a Catch-22 because efforts to build cell towers in remote areas are often opposed by locals and conservationists concerned about rural **eyesores.**

Even when phones can **hail** a signal in the backwoods, rescuers ₁₀ complain about trivial "emergencies." Rangers in New York report picking up the phone to hear hikers asking directions or complaining about sprained wrists.

Rick Donovan, owner of an outdoor gear store in the Berkshire hills ₁₁ at Great Barrington, Mass., has received cell-phone queries about how to light the camp stove. Or worse: "They're calling my store and asking me for a ride. What happened to the days of walking down the mountain?"

Baxter State Park in Maine has banned the use of cell phones on ₁₂ park grounds, as it had earlier excluded radios and cassette players.

Park naturalist Jean Hoekwater says the ban in part targets nui- 13
sance calls the likes of, "Honey? Guess what I'm in front of right now. A
big moose!"

New York has no bans yet, but the state-sponsored effort to dis- 14
courage frequent and nonemergency use of cell phones is to begin
this summer with brochures, videos and trailhead postings.

Can education work? Michele Morris, senior editor of *Backpacker* 15
magazine, calls it the key. She's hoping for new attitudes of self-
reliance and consideration.

Stephen Jacobs, an associate professor of information technology 16
at the Rochester Institute of Technology, predicts the problem will
"auto correct" over time as more people consider it rude to ring.

Don't expect cell phones to disappear from the woods any time 17
soon, though. A survey by *Backpacker* last year found cell phones a
popular item on readers' "to buy" lists.

Meanwhile, some high-end cell phones can pull in signals from 18
satellites, eliminating the need for towers. With the right equipment, even the deepest, most remote **gulch** can be just a phone call
away.

COMPREHENSION CHECK

Purpose and Main Idea

1. What is the author's topic?
   a. the wilderness
   b. cell phones
   c. solitude
   d. etiquette

2. Which of the following sentences from the selection states the
   author's central idea?
   a. Paragraph 4, first sentence "Cell-phone chatter. . . ."
   b. Paragraph 7, first sentence "There's no. . . ."
   c. Paragraph 11, last sentence "What happened. . . ."
   d. Paragraph 17, first sentence "Don't expect. . . ."

3. The author's primary purpose is to
   a. persuade readers to give up cell phones.
   b. express a feeling about nature.
   c. inform readers that a problem exists.
   d. entertain us with a wilderness tale.

Details

4. State forester Jim Papero heard a man talking on his cell phone to
    a. his wife.
    b. a friend.
    c. a park ranger.
    d. a stockbroker.

5. Efforts to build cell towers in remote areas are opposed by people who are concerned about
    a. excess noise.
    b. gorges and gullies.
    c. rural eyesores.
    d. traffic.

6. Cell phones are not reliable in the wild because
    a. batteries may run down.
    b. cell towers tend to be far apart.
    c. they are an eyesore.
    d. calls cannot be received from remote areas.

7. Which one of the following predicts that irritating cell-phone use will "auto correct" over time?
    a. Rick Donovan
    b. Jean Hoekwater
    c. Michele Morris
    d. Stephen Jacobs

8. What is the organizational pattern in paragraph 8?
    a. definition
    b. process
    c. generalization then example
    d. comparison and contrast

Inferences

9. Rescuers would consider all of the following as trivial emergencies except which one?
    a. a sprained wrist
    b. a need for directions
    c. a request for a ride
    d. a snakebite

10. In the wilderness, where do cell phones probably work best?
    a. in gorges
    b. along gullies

c. in a valley

d. on high ground

WORKING WITH WORDS

Complete the sentences below with these words from Word Alert:

disconcerting	gullies	gorges
etiquette	prodded	gulch
eyesores	surreal	hail

1. This section of the city is littered with burned-out buildings, overflowing garbage dumpsters, and other _____ .

2. Will's girlfriend reminded him that she had a birthday coming up, and that _____ him to buy her a gift.

3. Although it is easy enough to _____ a taxi, getting one to stop is harder.

4. The heavy rains caused flooding and dug _____ in the ground along roadways and through fields.

5. We visited a small western town that was just a _____ cut through the foothills.

6. When you are trying to concentrate on your driving, the sound of a horn honking can be _____ .

7. If you are invited to dinner at the White House, it would be a good idea to brush up on the rules of _____ for formal dinners.

8. Although I like exploring caves, I've never felt comfortable squeezing through _____ in the rock.

9. If you've ever been to Mardi Gras, you know how _____ an experience it is to see the streets lined with huge floats and people dressed in strange costumes.

THINKING DEEPER

Ideas for discussion and writing

1. Do you agree with the authors that cell phones disturb the peace of the wilderness and other places? What are your views regarding cell phone use and misuse?

2. Discuss the concept of "etiquette." What are good manners to-day? What rules have changed? What rules are still important?

3. Discuss how this selection illustrates the Part 2 theme, *Rumblings in the Culture*. For example, the introduction of any-thing new into American culture brings with it new ideas and behaviors that may cause controversy. How has the use of cell phones and other pieces of new technology affected our public behavior?

4. Write about an annoying behavior by completing this sentence: *I wish people wouldn't. . . .* Explain your reasons.

FIRST THOUGHTS

To prepare yourself for the reading selection, answer the following questions, either on your own or in a group discussion.

1. What do you know about the history of oral contraceptives?

2. What impact do you think the pill has had on American women's lives?

3. Preview the title, headnote, and first one or two paragraphs. What do you think will follow?

WORD ALERT

aspirations (5) desires for achievement or advancement
depleted (8) used up, emptied out
incarnation (9) embodiment or form
circumvented (12) avoided, overcame
constraining (12) confining, restraining
cohorts (16) people within a group
resurgence (19) renewal or revival
complementary (19) supplying mutual needs, completing

৯ The Power of the Pill

CLAUDIA GOLDIN AND LAWRENCE F. KATZ

Claudia Goldin is the Henry Lee Professor of Economics at Harvard University, and Lawrence F. Katz is a professor of economics at Harvard University. Both are research associates at the National Bureau of Economic Research in Cambridge, Massachusetts.

THE PILL—THE female oral contraceptive—turned 40 this past year 1 and, in its lifetime, has changed not only the sexual lives of American women, but their economic ones, as well.

It is a middle-age medical miracle. Slimmed down in its progestin 2
and estrogen content from the original Enovid pill, it remains the contraceptive of choice of American women.

Almost 80 percent of women now between 45 and 55 took the pill 3
at some time.

The pill was an overnight success The fraction of married women 4
(under 35 years) who were "on the pill" came close to its historic maximum just five years after its release in 1960. But the pill did not immediately become as common among young unmarried women, and
that is a large part of our story concerning the social impact of the pill.

We have sought to understand how the pill affected the **aspira-** 5
tions and career choices of young women in the late 1960s and how it
enabled women to be accepted as equals in the most prestigious, highly
paid and demanding occupations.

Up until 1970, less than 10 percent of medical students were 6
women, while the comparable figures for law (4 percent), dentistry
(1 percent) and business (3 percent) were even lower. But just a
decade later the share was about one-third in medicine and business,
more than one-third in law, one-fifth in dentistry. By the early 1990s,
women were more than 40 percent of all first-year medical and law
students, and more than 35 percent of all first year MBA and dentistry
students.

Did the pill play a role in these changes? We think the answer is 7
"yes." A safe, reliable, easy-to-use, female-controlled contraceptive
enabled young women to enter careers that involved extensive and
up-front time commitments in education. But how?

A young woman beginning a degree program had to evaluate—in 8
addition to the financial costs of her education—the social consequences of a career track. If she did not marry before her professional
education began and lacked an almost foolproof contraceptive such
as the pill, she would have to pay the penalty of abstinence or cope
with considerable uncertainty regarding pregnancy. If she delayed
marriage (as many did), she would have to consider the social consequences of a **depleted** marriage market.

In its early high-dose **incarnation** the pill was monumentally 9
more reliable than other contraceptive methods. (Its other pluses are
that it is female-controlled, non-messy and can be taken well in advance of sex.)

The pill allowed a woman to "have it all." She could have sex and 10
plan for a future career. In addition, the pill encouraged an increase in

the age at first marriage. A career woman who decided to delay marriage would encounter a depleted marriage market if the typical age at first marriage were low. But if the marriage age for college graduates rose, as it did throughout the 1970s, the delay would involve far less of a penalty.

But what accounts for the lag of almost 10 years from the pill's 11 introduction in 1960 to the start of the career response for young women?

The explanation is simple. Single women in the 1960s were 12 thwarted from obtaining the pill by archaic state laws. As late as 1960, 30 states prohibited advertisements regarding birth control, and 22 had some prohibition on the sale of contraceptives. Married persons easily **circumvented** these laws, but the laws had **constraining** effects on young, single women. As the laws were relaxed, they were able to obtain the pill and, subsequently, the marriage age rose and career aspirations changed.

By the late 1960s and early 1970s almost all states had lowered the 13 age of legal majority to 18 and granted to youth the rights of adults through "mature minor" decisions. These legal changes, by the way, were not driven by a desire to extend family-planning services nor by feminist action.

Rather, they were motivated by the same factors that led to the 14 26th Amendment (1971) lowering the voting age to 18. The Vietnam War had awakened Americans to the inconsistency between the rights and responsibilities of young people.

With sufficient ingenuity, a determined unmarried woman could 15 have obtained the pill without benefit of the law. But our cross-state statistical analysis for 1971 shows that pill use among young women was considerably higher in states having more lenient laws regarding the rights of minors. The laws mattered. Until 1969 few, if any, college health clinics made family planning services available to students without regard to age or marital status. By the mid-1970s, most on large campuses did.

To measure trends in pill usage for young, unmarried women we 16 have used two retrospective surveys from the 1980s. Taken together, our data show that the widespread use of the pill among young unmarried women began more than five years after it did for married women. More important, the data also show that pill use among single, college-graduate women began to greatly increase with **cohorts** born at about 1948. These were precisely the cohorts that first began to enter professional schools around the 1970s.

The timing of the changes in the fraction of females among first- 17
year professional students and the use of the pill could, of course,
have been a coincidence. But we have additional, and more convincing, evidence that the relationship was causal.

Young unmarried women in states that lowered the age of major- 18
ity or had passed legislation extending the mature minor decision (or
had judicial rulings that did so), were considerably more likely to use
the pill. Also, the age at first marriage increased for college-graduate
women who turned 18 years old at about the time that the state laws
changed. That is, the availability of the pill to young college women
appears to have led to an increase in the age of first marriage. The increased age at first marriage among college graduate women is striking. Among women born from the early 1930s to the end of the 1940s,
about 50 percent married before age 23. But among women born in
1957, only 30 percent married before age 23.

The case for the pill as the primary factor driving women's career 19
decisions is strong. But it was not the only factor. The **resurgence** of
feminism, anti-discrimination legislation and legalized abortion (nationwide in 1973 by Roe vs. Wade and earlier in several states) are
some others. We have found that abortion legalization was not as po-
tent as the pill in encouraging later marriage for college women, although its impact on careers was **complementary.**

Young American women in the late 1960s had hoped to follow in 20
their mothers' footsteps, but in just a few years their aspirations had
changed radically. Our work shows that the pill had a large effect on
career and marriage. Without the pill these changes would, presum-
ably, have come later. How much later, though, we do not know.

COMPREHENSION CHECK

Purpose and Main Idea

1. What is the authors' topic?
   a. motherhood versus career
   b. birth control methods
   c. effects of the pill
   d. contraceptive devices
2. The central idea of the entire selection is best stated in which one
   of the following sentences?
   a. Invented decades ago, the pill was an overnight success.
   b. The pill is a safe, reliable, easy-to-use form of birth control.

    c. The oral contraceptive, best known as "the pill," is a powerful form of birth control.

    d. The pill has changed the lives of American women both sexually and economically.

3. In this selection, the authors' purpose is to

    a. persuade readers that the pill is still the most effective form of birth control.

    b. explain how the pill affected young women's career choices in the late 1960s.

    c. entertain readers with anecdotes about women's reproductive choices in earlier times.

    d. inform readers about the wide variety of contraceptive devices on the market today.

Details

4. Until 1970, less than what percent of women were medical students?

    a. 10 percent

    b. 4 percent

    c. 3 percent

    d. 1 percent

5. For young women in the 1960s, all but which one of the following were possible social consequences of a career track?

    a. a depleted marriage market

    b. abstinence in the absence of marriage or reliable birth control

    c. the financial costs of an education

    d. uncertainty regarding pregnancy

6. According to the authors, when did the widespread use of the pill among young, unmarried women begin?

    a. before it did for married women

    b. about the same time as it did for married women

    c. soon after it did for married women

    d. more that five years after it did for married women

7. According to the authors, lowering the age of legal majority to eighteen resulted from which one of the following?

    a. a desire to extend family-planning services

    b. feminist action

    c. the Vietnam War

    d. women's desire to "have it all"

8. According to the authors, which one of the following, along with the pill, had a complementary effect on careers?

    a. the resurgence of feminism
    b. abortion legalization
    c. antidiscrimination laws
    d. lowering the voting age

Inferences

9. In paragraph 12, second sentence, which one of the following is the most likely meaning of *thwarted?*
    a. pressured
    b. alienated
    c. required
    d. blocked

10. Based on the authors' details in this selection, they would most likely agree with which one of the following statements?
    a. Young women today are about as likely as men to pursue professional careers.
    b. In addition to its effects on marriage, the pill also affected the divorce rate.
    c. Without the introduction of the pill into American life, women would not have the opportunities they have today.
    d. Legislators should fight to keep abortion legal.

WORKING WITH WORDS

Complete the sentences below with these words from Word Alert:

> complementary   constraining   aspirations   depleted
> circumvented   resurgence   incarnation   cohorts

1. From time to time, fashions of the past have seen a _____ in popularity.
2. Jan's parents wanted her to follow in their footsteps and become an attorney, but her _____ were to pursue a career in architecture.
3. Age and skill are two _____ factors that may keep a young person from getting a driver's license.
4. Environmentalists fear that our high energy consumption will leave us with _____ oil reserves.
5. When the family resemblance is great, a child may seem to be the _____ of a parent.
6. Police can point to many instances where people have _____ laws, to their own regret.

7. Baby Boomers and the Silent Generation are two _____ that researchers have studied.

8. The blue tablecloth was _____ to the china's blue and white pattern.

THINKING DEEPER

Ideas for discussion and writing

1. What do you know or have you read or heard about women's rights in the 1960s? How were women's choices then different from the opportunities available to them today?

2. What are your views concerning marriage, family, and career? What do you think is the ideal age to marry or have children? Do you think both parents should work? Can women (or men) successfully combine family and career? How do your views differ from or reflect those of your parents?

3. Discuss how this selection illustrates the Part 2 theme, *Rumblings in the Culture*. For example, the authors attribute several changes in marriage and career patterns to the widespread use of the pill during the late 1960s. How have these changes affected women's and men's lives for better or worse?

4. What are your life and career goals? Do you feel any constraints that would prevent you from achieving your goals? Write about your aspirations and how you plan to achieve them.

FIRST THOUGHTS

To prepare yourself for the reading selection, answer the following questions, either on your own or in a group discussion.

1. Do you believe that the tobacco industry is responsible for smoking-related illnesses?

2. What do you know about the lawsuits several states and the federal government have brought against the tobacco industry?

3. Preview the title, headnote, and first one or two paragraphs. What do you think will follow?

WORD ALERT

blatant (2) unpleasantly obvious, offensive
deception (3) trick, the act of misleading
contends (3) asserts, maintains
poses (3) presents, puts forward
persistence (4) continuing effort despite setbacks
heartening (8) encouraging, strengthening
looming (9) coming into view in a threatening way

❧ The War on Tobacco: Where There's Smoke, There's Money

DAVE BARRY

Dave Barry is a noted humorist and columnist for the Miami Herald. *His columns are widely syndicated, and he has published several books. In this selection, he suggests that something other than a concern for public health is behind the U.S. Justice Department's lawsuit against the tobacco industry.*

THERE IS BIG NEWS in the War on Smoking. The U.S. Justice Department has filed a lawsuit against the cigarette industry, boldly   1 charging that the industry was lying—and KNEW it was lying—when it claimed that it never had sexual relations with Monica Lewinsky.

Whoops! Wrong lie! The Justice Department is charging that for 2 many years, the tobacco industry, on purpose, did not tell people that cigarettes were bad for them. To cite just one **blatant** example, on numerous documented occasions during the 1950s and 1960s, R.J. Reynolds deliberately failed to run an advertising campaign using the slogan: "Winston Tastes Good, AND Gives You Lung Cancer!"

As a result of this type of clever **deception,** the Justice Department 3 **contends,** smokers did not realize that cigarettes were hazardous. This is undoubtedly true of a certain type of smoker; namely, the type of smoker whose brain has been removed with a melon scoop. Everybody else has known for decades that cigarettes are unhealthy. I have known many smokers, and I have never heard one say: "You know why I stick these unnatural wads of chemically processed tobacco into my mouth, set them on fire and suck hot gases deep into my lungs? Because I sincerely believe it **poses** no health risk!"

When I first experimented with cigarettes, as a young teenager in 4 the early '60s, I knew they were unhealthy, because my dad, a heavy smoker, warned me of the dangers. "Son," he told me many times, "Hack hack hack haarrwwwGGGHHHHKK (spit)." But I tried cigarettes, anyway, because like all teenagers, I expected to live a minimum of 50,000 years, and I figured it was no big deal if I knocked a few centuries off the end. I thought that smoking would make me look older and more attractive to women—that I'd fire up an unfiltered Camel and, boom, I'd sprout muscles and vast quantities of body hair. Unfortunately, this did not happen, although I did manage, through **persistence** and hard work, to develop a cigarette habit that enabled me to spend the next 15 years smelling like a low-grade dump fire.

Eventually, I realized I had to kick my habit. This was before the 5 development of nicotine patches, so I had to devise some other way to get my nicotine "fix" while I was quitting. The method I came up with was: cheating. So I continued to smoke cigarettes for several years after I quit. Then I finally got desperate and really did quit, using the "cold turkey" method, which gets its name from the fact that it is no more difficult than inserting a frozen 20-pound Butterball completely into your left nostril.

My point is that, when I smoked, I knew it was unhealthy, and so 6 did every smoker I ever knew. Nevertheless, the Justice Department believes that we smokers were victimized by the tobacco industry, and so, on behalf of the federal government, it has filed a huge lawsuit against the federal government for spending gazillions of taxpayer dollars to support the tobacco industry.

Whoops! Wrong again! In fact, the Justice Department is suing the 7 tobacco industry for many billions of dollars. Needless to say, the to-bacco industry would obtain this money by selling more cigarettes. In fact, the sale of cigarettes is the financial heart and soul of the War On Smoking. Cigarette companies are already selling cigarettes like crazy to pay for the $206 billion anti-tobacco settlement won by the states, which are distributing the money as follows: (1) legal fees; (2) money for attorneys; (3) a whole bunch of new programs that have absolutely nothing to do with helping smokers stop smoking; and (4) payments to law firms.

Of course not all the anti-tobacco settlement is being spent this 8 way. A lot of it also goes to lawyers. And some money is actually being spent on educational campaigns that nag teenagers about smoking. As you would imagine if you have ever nagged a teenager, these cam-paigns are highly effective, provided that we define "effective" as "not effective." In fact, according to a University of Michigan study that I am not making up, the percentage of high-school seniors who smoke cigarettes has actually INCREASED in the past five years. This is **heart-ening** news, because it means that as older smokers die off, there will be fresh blood to support the War On Smoking.

The only danger I see **looming** ahead is that the tobacco industry 9 will get tired of serving as the bag person for the anti-smoking effort and actually quit selling cigarettes. In that case, the only way to keep the anti-tobacco money flowing in would be for the various govern-ments to join forces with the legal community and sell cigarettes di-rectly to the public out of post offices. This would be similar to the way we've tackled the gambling problem in this country, which is to have the states run massive lottery operations. It makes perfect sense to me! Of course, I have a turkey up my nose.

COMPREHENSION CHECK

Purpose and Main Idea

1. What is the author's topic?
    a. smoking
    b. the tobacco industry
    c. the war on tobacco
    d. quitting smoking

2. Which of the following sentences best expresses the author's cen-
    tral idea?
    a. The U.S. Justice Department is engaged in a war with the to-
        bacco industry and its officials.
    b. The war on tobacco is more about money than about any
        wrongdoing on the part of the tobacco industry.
    c. Like the war on drugs, the U.S. government's war on tobacco
        is doomed to failure.
    d. Despite the tobacco settlement, people are going to keep on
        smoking.

3. The author's primary purpose is to
    a. express his views about the dangers of smoking.
    b. persuade readers that money, not concern for our health, is
        behind the war on tobacco.
    c. inform readers that the U.S. Justice Department has won a
        settlement against the tobacco industry.
    d. entertain us by making fun of the U.S. Justice Department's
        war on tobacco.

Details

4. The Justice Department's lawsuit charged that the tobacco in-
    dustry
    a. forced young people to buy cigarettes.
    b. lied about the dangers of smoking.
    c. used illegal advertising tactics.
    d. made cigarettes available to minors.

5. As a teenager, the author tried smoking for all but which one of
    the following reasons?
    a. He was influenced by cigarette advertising.
    b. He was not afraid of cutting his life short.
    c. He believed that smoking would make him look older.
    d. He thought smoking would make him attractive to women.

6. The author eventually kicked the habit by
    a. using nicotine patches.
    b. cheating.
    c. quitting cold turkey.
    d. taking cold showers.

7. According to the author, the government's war on smoking is
    financed by
    a. taxpayers.

b. cigarette advertising.

c. the U.S. Justice Department.

d. the sale of cigarettes.

8. The sentences in paragraph 9 are related by

   a. process.

   b. sequence.

   c. comparison.

   d. definition.

Inferences

9. Based on the details in paragraphs 7 and 8, you can infer that the author's attitude toward lawyers is

   a. favorable.

   b. unfavorable.

   c. undecided.

   d. objective.

10. By calling the tobacco industry "the bag person for the anti-smoking effort," the author is making a comparison between the U.S. Justice Department and

   a. big business.

   b. a drug cartel.

   c. a state lottery.

   d. organized crime.

WORKING WITH WORDS

Complete the sentences below with these words from Word Alert:

persistence   deception   looming   poses
heartening   contends   blatant

1. In the long run, _____ pays off when it comes to studying and scoring well on tests.

2. Looking out across the ocean, we saw storm clouds _____ in the distance.

3. For a long time after the car had passed, we could still hear the _____ sounds of the boom box.

4. *Catch Me if You Can* is a movie about a young man's _____ in assuming the identity of someone else.

5. Honesty is your best defense when someone _____ that you are
    cheating.
6. It was _____ to see all the cards and letters that my grand-
    father's friends had sent him when he was in the hospital.
7. When your instructor _____ a question, you must be prepared
    to answer.

THINKING DEEPER

Ideas for discussion and writing

1. Discuss your views on smoking and the tobacco industry's re-
    sponsibility to consumers. Do you agree or disagree that the to-
    bacco industry should have been more straightforward about the
    hazards of smoking? Do you think that lawsuits against the to-
    bacco industry serve the public or not?
2. Discuss the author's use of humor in this selection and its effect
    on the reader. What was your response to the selection? Do you
    think that a serious treatment of the subject would have been
    more or less effective? Explain your answer.
3. Discuss how this selection illustrates the Part 2 theme,
    Rumblings in the Culture. For example, until about the 1960s,
    smoking was considered acceptable behavior in the United
    States. Smoking was permitted in offices and restaurants. Not
    only did airlines permit smoking in flight, but at one time flight
    attendants passed out complimentary packs of cigarettes to pas-
    sengers. Even the military included cigarettes with soldiers' C-
    rations. How have our cultural attitudes and values and even our
    laws regarding smoking changed? What reasons can you give to
    account for the change?
4. Think about your own youth and the efforts of parents, teachers,
    and others to discourage you from smoking. Which of their tac-
    tics worked? Which ones did not, and why? Explain your answer
    in writing.

FIRST THOUGHTS

To prepare yourself for the reading selection, answer the following questions, either on your own or in a group discussion.

1. What do you know about the cultural influences that affect the way people function in groups?
2. In a group setting, do you prefer the role of participant or leader?
3. Preview the title, headnote, and first one or two paragraphs. What do you think will follow?

WORD ALERT

In a textbook chapter, the words to watch may appear in boldface, italics, or a special color.

participants (1) group members who interact within the group
leaders (1) those who guide the group and facilitate its actions
leadership (1) those who influence or inspire the group to succeed at its task
Confucian principle of i (5) a philosophy that requires long-term group affiliation and identity
intuitive-affective decision-making approach (13) an approach that values emotions and impressions over reasoning
centralized decision-making process (14) an approach that places decision-making authority on those whose force of personality, rather than their position within the group, makes them leaders
proposal-counterproposal negotiating (15) reaching decisions through offers and counteroffers until one side gives in

✺ Participating in Groups

ROY M. BERKO, ANDREW D. WOLVIN, AND DARLYN R. WOLVIN

📖 *This textbook reading is excerpted from Chapter 10 of* Communicating, *8th edition. The entire chapter is about*

From *Communicating*, 8th ed, Roy M. Berko, Andrew D. Wolvin, and Darlyn R. Wolvin, (Boston: Houghton Mifflin, 2001).

roles and procedures for working in groups. The excerpt
focuses on cultural influences on group participation.
When reading from textbooks, remember that headings
may signal topics, main ideas, or important details.

GROUPS ARE MADE up of people. Those who comprise a group play 1
the roles of leaders, leadership, and participants. **Participants** are
those members of a group who interact to bring about the actions of
the group. **Leaders** are those who guide the group. **Leadership** refers
to those who influence the group to accomplish its goal.

Members of groups, whether they are assuming the participant or 2
leader role, come to that group with cultural influences. These influences affect the way in which group members function.

CULTURAL DIFFERENCES IN GROUPS

Each of us is a product of the culture in which we were brought up. We 3
learn the customs and patterns of our culture, and these carry over into
all phases of our lives. Research shows that people from different cultures possess varying attitudes about making independent decisions
and being a group participant, procedures for working in groups, making decisions, procedural structure, and using information.

Cultures and Groups

"The United States has the highest individualism index. We [European 4
Americans] are, without doubt, the most individualistic culture on
earth."[1] This individualism—putting oneself before group loyalty—
has a strong historical base; the United States was founded by adven-
turers and dissidents. In this culture, membership in groups (except
those that are mandatory because of a person's work or academic environment) tends to be voluntary. While recognizing that there may be
traditions, such as membership in a particular religion, European
Americans tend to decide on their own whether they want to belong to
a group. You, for example, choose whether to participate in a social
group or a fraternal organization. Once a part of the group, if you don't
like being a member, you can resign.

Because of this ability to join and leave a group, allegiance tends 5
not to be a lifelong commitment. This, however, is not the case in
other parts of the world. For example, in many East Asian countries,

Confucianism is the basic philosophy of much of the population. The **Confucian principle of i** requires that a person be affiliated and identify with a small and tightly knit group of people over long periods of time. These long-term relationships work because group members aid and assist each other when there is a need; sooner or later those who assisted others will have to depend on those they aided. This mutually implied assistance pact makes for group interdependence.[2]

Native Americans use group discussion "as a means to maintain or restore harmony."[3] It is important for group members to work toward consensus. "In the absence of consensus, talk goes on interminably, with great respect for the conventions of oratory."[4] Discussion continues "until those in opposition feel it is useless or impolite to express further disagreement."[5] 6

Not only does the attitude toward being in groups vary by culture, but there is a difference in the training needed in certain cultures for group participation. Because they participate in groups to a limited degree, many European Americans need to learn about group operational methods when they enter into organizations. The same is true of people from other countries having a high degree of individualism, such as Australia, Great Britain, Canada, New Zealand, and Denmark.[6] In contrast, people from societies where group adherence is stressed have a clearer sensitivity about how groups operate since they are encased in groups all their lives. Those areas and countries that are the least individualistic are found in Asia (Japan, China, Vietnam) and South America.[7] 7

Cultural differences also are reflected in the way a person works in a group. In many East Asian countries, for example, the Confucian principle of i leads to a strong distaste for purely business transactions. This is carried over into meetings, where the tendency is to mix personal with public relationships. Business meetings, for example, may take place over a long period of time in order for people to establish personal relationships; include activities like sports and drinking; foster an understanding of the personalities of the participants; and develop a certain level of trust and a favorable attitude.[8] 8

A good example of where the business is mixed with the personal is in Japan, which is known as a nation stressing group culture, where individualism is submerged, and expression occurs in hidden ways. This, of course, is almost the opposite of how European Americans operate. In the United States, individuals work in groups to get *tasks* accomplished. In Japan, the individual's sense of identity *is* the group. This is based on a long history of ruling families who created a social structure 9 that bound families, villagers, and strong leaders together. In the United States, the stress has been on rugged individualism, with the group coming second to the individual. In Japan, the word for describing a group is *we*. In the United States, groups often are divided between "us" and "them." For example, administrators and faculty members are part of the same group—the university—but too often find themselves on opposite sides in decisions.

Contrasts in Cultural Group Decision Making

If the assumption is made that one of the important tasks of a group is decision making, another cultural variation comes into play. It is important to realize, when working in decision-making groups, that there are vast cultural differences in how people think, apply forms of reasoning, and make decisions. 10

In the Western view, it is generally believed that people can discover truth if they apply the scientific method of decision-making process. The familiar problem-solving sequence has four segments: identify the problem, search for solutions, test those solutions, and put a solution into practice. The final decision is often based on a majority vote of the membership, with those who will have to implement or live with the decision often not part of the decision-making team. For example, few students are included in university discussions on curriculum requirements. In Japan, on the other hand, everyone affected by the decision is included in the process.[9] 11

Other societies use different decision-making approaches. For example, for the Chinese, "decision-making is more authoritative than consensual; decisions are made by higher authorities without the inclusion of subordinates."[10] 12

"Middle-Easterners can be described as using an **intuitive-affective decision-making approach.** Broad issues that do not appear to be directly related to the issue at hand are brought up; issues are linked together on the basis of whether or not the speaker likes the issues."[11] Although subordinates are consulted informally, the leader always makes the final decision.[12] 13

Work groups in Mexico tend to use a **centralized decision-making process.** Mexicans often view authority as being inherent within the individual, not his or her position. Making trade-offs is common for Mexican negotiators, including adding issues that are not part of the original business at hand.[13] 14

Cultural Contrast of the Role of Information for Groups

Even the information or ideas that are used for making decisions may [15] differ among cultures. European American negotiators tend to compartmentalize issues, focusing on one issue at a time instead of negotiating many issues together. "They tend to rely on rational thinking and concrete data in their negotiations."[14] In the United States, negotiating toward the final decision usually takes on a form of **proposal-counterproposal negotiating,** in which a plan or solution is presented and then a counteroffer is made. For example, in a group meeting concerning salary negotiations, the employees propose a particular salary and explain why they think this is the appropriate amount. Management then typically makes an offer of a lesser amount and offers counterarguments. This process continues until an amount is agreed on. The negotiations may be accompanied by a threat of the workers' going out on strike, an action unheard of in some other cultures.

The French, on the other hand, seem to "have no problem with [16] open disagreement. They debate more than they bargain and are less apt than Euro-Americans to be flexible for the sake of agreement.... They start with a long-range view of their purpose, as opposed to Euro-Americans, who work with more short-range objectives."[15]

"Japanese negotiators make decisions on the basis of detailed in- [17] formation rather than persuasive arguments."[16]

Because this book is directed primarily at individuals who will find [18] themselves most often participating in groups in the U.S. culture, the material in this chapter deals mainly with participant and leader conventions and patterns typical in the United States. However, because of the multiculturalism of this country, you likely will be working with people and in social situations with individuals from a variety of cultural backgrounds. Also, with the internationalization of business, it is becoming more and more common for the businesspeople from the United States to be working in international settings, so knowledge of other cultures' group procedures can be helpful.

Male and Female Roles in Groups

Besides cultural differences based on nationality, the cultural roles of [19] males and females play an important role in leader and participant operational modes.

Is gender a factor in group tasks or maintenance? Generally studies [20] on leadership and group process indicate that differences do occur in the way men and women operate in a group. For example, "women tend to be more process-oriented than men. Men are more goal-oriented. For women, the process is as important, or more important, than the product."[17] Other studies indicate that "individuals prefer managers who possess masculine characteristics."[18] This carries over into courtrooms, where men are more likely than women to be selected as foreperson of a jury.[19] Research in educational groups indicates that students believe classes led by women are more discussion oriented, and classes taught by men are more structured and emphasize content mastery.[20] In addition, male college professors are perceived to be less supportive and less innovative than are female instructors.[21]

"Being the only member of one's sex in a mixed-gender group 21 affects the perceptions of other group members and often skews the opportunities to communicate and the feedback one receives."[22] In addition, men are perceived to be more dominant and women more submissive during group communication involving both men and women, whether the communication is verbal or nonverbal.[23] And research on juries shows that male jurors typically offer 40 percent more comments during deliberation than do female jurors.[24] It also has been shown that "male students initiate more interactions with teachers than female students initiate" and that males tend to dominate classroom talk.[25]

Thus, it appears that there are differences, or at least perceived 22 differences, between the genders as they participate in groups in the European American culture.

COMPREHENSION CHECK

Purpose and Main Idea
1. What is the authors' topic?
   a. intercultural communication
   b. gender roles and culture
   c. cultural attitudes and behaviors
   d. cultural differences among groups
2. Which one of the following sentences best states the authors' central idea?
   a. Paragraph 2, sentence 1, "Members of groups. . . ."
   b. Paragraph 2, sentence 2, "These influences. . . ."
   c. Paragraph 3, sentence 3, "Research shows. . . ."
   d. Paragraph 22, last sentence, "Thus, it appears. . . ."

3. The authors' purpose is to
    a. inform readers about the ways in which cultural differences influence group participation.
    b. express concern that people from different cultures do not follow the U.S. conventions of group participation.
    c. persuade readers that cultural differences are of little importance in group participation.
    d. entertain readers with examples of common mistakes that people make when interacting in groups.

Details

4. All but which one of the following are characteristic of group participation in the United States?
    a. Participation tends to be voluntary.
    b. Allegiance to the group is a lifelong commitment.
    c. Individuals choose whether to belong to a group.
    d. The group comes second to the individual.

5. According to the authors, which one of the following leads to a strong distaste for purely business transactions?
    a. the centralized decision-making process
    b. the intuitive-affective decision-making approach
    c. the Confucian principle of i
    d. proposal-counterproposal negotiating

6. Which nation is known for stressing group culture and mixing business with the personal?
    a. New Zealand
    b. Japan
    c. United States
    d. Mexico

7. The authors offer all but which one of the following as examples of the ways in which U.S. females are perceived in group settings?
    a. A woman is more likely than a man to be selected as foreperson of a jury.
    b. Women are perceived as more submissive than men during group communication that involves both men and women.
    c. Female students appear to initiate fewer interactions with teachers than do male students.
    d. Female instructors are perceived to be more supportive and more innovative than male instructors.

8. Which one of the following paragraphs is organized by generalization, then example?

a. paragraph 6
b. paragraph 8
c. paragraph 9
d. paragraph 15

Inferences

9. Based on the context in which it is used, what does the word
   consensus in paragraph 6 mean?
   a. loyalty
   b. affiliation
   c. agreement
   d. solution

10. Based on the authors' information, an employee who seems un-
    willing to take credit for an accomplishment most likely finds his
    or her identity in
    a. individualism.
    b. national or ethnic pride.
    c. religious teachings.
    d. group loyalty.

WORKING WITH WORDS

Complete the sentences below with these words from Word Alert:

proposal-counterproposal negotiating   leaders
centralized decision-making process   leadership
intuitive-affective decision-making approach   participants
Confucian principle of i

1. In Middle Eastern cultures, the final decisions of groups are
   made by their _____ rather than by subordinates.
2. In the United States, _____ is the decision-making process
   used in contract negotiations between union leaders and employers.
3. A group's _____ are the ones responsible for carrying out its
   tasks.
4. Those who follow the _____ are known for their long-term
   group loyalty.
5. The research and development team members owed their success in coming up with a new product to the _____ that had inspired them.

6. The committee seemed upset that some members brought up unrelated issues because they were unfamiliar with that culture's _____ .

7. Because of their _____ the group followed the lead of a trusted member rather than that of the appointed leader.

THINKING DEEPER

Ideas for discussion and writing

1. According to the authors, the attitude toward being in groups varies by culture. For example, Americans tend to put their own interests before group interests, but Japanese are more prone to place group interests first. Where do you place your primary loyalty: to self, family, work, country, or something else, and why?

2. In paragraphs 19–22, the authors discuss gender differences in group participation. Discuss what these differences are and provide examples of any differences you have noticed in the way in which men and women perform in class or in groups. Also discuss any problems that have arisen in groups as a result of gender differences.

3. Discuss how the cultural differences in groups explained in this excerpt illustrate the Part 2 theme, *Rumblings in the Culture.* For example, in college courses and in the workplace, you will interact with people from different cultures in group activities or on work teams. What have you learned from the authors that will help you communicate effectively and overcome any problems you may encounter while working with a diverse group of people?

4. Using the following informal outline of paragraphs 9–14 as a guide, fill in the missing details. The outline is partially completed for you.

HOW PEOPLE IN DIFFERENT CULTURES MAKE DECISIONS

1. Western cultures
    a. Process used: scientific method
    b. Final say: majority vote of members, with those affected often not part of the team

2. Some Asian cultures
   a. Process used: authoritative rather than consensual
   b. Final say for Japanese: _____
   c. Final say for Chinese: _____
3. Middle-Easterners
   a. Process used: _____
   b. Issues discussed: broad issues, those that the speaker likes
   c. Final say: _____
4. Mexico
   a. Process used: _____
   b. Authority placed: _____
   c. Negotiators' roles: making trade-offs, adding unrelated issues

PART THREE

Against All Odds

❧

We humans are resilient creatures. We are able to bounce back from hardship and disaster with grace and dignity. We surmount obstacles, conquer our fears, reach milestones, and move on to accept new challenges. We are survivors.

We are inventors and trailblazers, too. Tell us it can't be done, and we will do it. Tell us we can't win, and we will set records. We may not live in a perfect world, but we believe that a better life is within our grasp.

We are the ordinary people who cope with disabilities, break bad habits, learn new skills, and strive to open doors that others have closed. These actions define, in part, who we are.

The Part 3 selections are about the will to persevere against all odds to meet a challenge or reach a goal. As you read and think about the selections, ask yourself these questions: What is the achievement, and how is it won? What is the obstacle, and how is it overcome? What is the lesson for me?

FIRST THOUGHTS

To prepare yourself for the reading selection, answer the following questions, either on your own or in a group discussion.

1. What stories have your grandparents or other family members told you about their past?

2. What do you know or have you read about the Jews who were sent to concentration camps during World War II?

3. Preview the title, headnote, and first one or two paragraphs. What do you think will follow?

WORD ALERT

reflection (1) careful consideration, mental concentration
transit (2) passage, passing through or across
extermination (2) getting rid of by complete destruction
coincidence (3) events that are accidental but seem planned
typhus (5) an infectious disease caused by fleas, lice, or mites
gruel (6) a thin, watery food made by boiling oats or another meal in water or milk
reassured (7) restored confidence

❧ I Saw Anne Frank Die

IRMA SONNENBERG MENKEL

In this selection, which the author wrote at the age of 100, she recalls her experiences in the Bergen-Belsen concentration camp, where she was imprisoned by the Germans during World War II. The article appeared in Newsweek *in 1997.*

I TURNED 100 YEARS OLD in April and had a beautiful birthday party 1
surrounded by my grandchildren, great-grandchildren and other
family members. I even danced a little. Willard Scott mentioned my

name on television. But such a time is also for **reflection.** I decided to overcome my long reluctance to revisit terrible times. Older people must tell their stories. With the help of Jonathan Alter of *Newsweek,* here's a bit of mine:

I was born in Germany in 1897, got married and had two children 2 in the 1920s. Then Hitler came to power, and like many other Jews, we fled to Holland. As the Nazis closed in, we sent one daughter abroad with relatives and the other into hiding with my sister and her children in The Hague. My husband and I could not hide so easily, and in 1941 we were sent first to Westerbork, a **transit** camp where we stayed about a year, and later to Bergen-Belsen, a work and transit camp, from where thousands of innocent people were sent to **extermination** camps. There were no ovens at Bergen-Belsen; instead the Nazis killed us with starvation and disease. My husband and brother both died there. I stayed for about three years before it was liberated in the spring of 1945. When I went in, I weighed more than 125 pounds. When I left, I weighed 78.

After I arrived at the Bergen-Belsen barracks, I was told I was to be 3 the barracks leader. I said, "I'm not strong enough to be barracks leader." They said that would be disobeying a command. I was terri- fied of this order, but had no choice. It turned out that the Nazi com- mandant of the camp was from my home town in Germany and had studied with my uncle in Strasbourg. This **coincidence** probably helped save my life. He asked to talk to me privately and wanted to know what I had heard of my uncle. I said I wanted to leave Bergen- Belsen, maybe go to Palestine. The commandant said, "If I could help you, I would, but I would lose my head." About once every three weeks, he would ask to see me. I was always afraid. It was very danger- ous. Jews were often shot over nothing. After the war, I heard he had committed suicide.

There were about 500 women and girls in my barracks. Conditions 4 were extremely crowded and unsanitary. No heat at all. Every morn- ing, I had to get up at 5 and wake the rest. At 6 a.m., we went to roll call. Often we had to wait there for hours, no matter the weather. Most of the day, we worked as slave labor in the factory, making bullets for German soldiers. When we left Holland, I had taken only two changes of clothes, one toothbrush, no books or other possessions. Later I had a few more clothes, including a warm jacket, which came from some- one who died. Men and women lined up for hours to wash their clothes in the few sinks. There were no showers in our barracks. And no bedding. The day was spent working and waiting. At 10 p.m., lights out. At midnight, the inspection came—three or four soldiers. I had to say everything was in good condition when, in fact, the conditions were beyond miserable. Then up again at 5 a.m.

One of the children in my barracks toward the end of the war was Anne Frank, whose diary became famous after her death. I didn't know her family beforehand, and I don't recall much about her, but I do remember her as a quiet child. When I heard later that she was 15 when she was in the camps, I was surprised. She seemed younger to me. Pen and paper were hard to find, but I have a memory of her writing a bit. **Typhus** was a terrible problem, especially for the children. Of 500 in my barracks, maybe 100 got it, and most of them died. Many others starved to death. When Anne Frank got sick with typhus, I remember telling her she could stay in the barracks—she didn't have to go to roll call.

There was so little to eat. In my early days there, we were each given one roll of bread for eight days, and we tore it up, piece by piece. One cup of black coffee a day and one cup of soup. And water. That was all. Later there was even less. When I asked the commandant for a little bit of **gruel** for the children's diet, he would sometimes give me some extra cereal. Anne Frank was among those who asked for cereal, but how could I find cereal for her? It was only for the little children, and only a little bit. The children died anyway. A couple of trained nurses were among the inmates, and they reported to me. In the evening, we tried to help the sickest. In the morning, it was part of my job to tell the soldiers how many had died the night before. Then they would throw the bodies on the fire.

I have a dim memory of Anne Frank speaking of her father. She was a nice, fine person. She would say to me, "Irma, I am very sick." I said, "No, you are not so sick." She wanted to be **reassured** that she wasn't. When she slipped into a coma, I took her in my arms. She didn't know that she was dying. She didn't know that she was so sick. You never know. At Bergen-Belsen, you did not have feelings anymore. You became paralyzed. In all the years since, I almost never talked about Bergen-Belsen. I couldn't. It was too much.

When the war was over, we went in a cattle truck to a place where we stole everything out of a house. I stole a pig, and we had a butcher who slaughtered it. Eating this—was bad for us. It made many even sicker. But you can't imagine how hungry we were. At the end, we had absolutely nothing to eat. I asked an American soldier holding a piece of bread if I could have a bite. He gave me the whole bread. That was really something for me.

When I got back to Holland, no one knew anything. I finally found 9
a priest who had the address where my sister and daughter were. I
didn't know if they were living or not. They were. They had been hidden by a man who worked for my brother. That was luck. I found them
and began crying. I was so thin that at first they didn't recognize me.

There are many stories like mine, locked inside people for decades. 10
Even my family heard only a little of this one until recently. Whatever
stories you have in your family, tell them. It helps.

COMPREHENSION CHECK

Purpose and Main Idea

1. What is the author's topic?
    a. World War II
    b. Anne Frank
    c. the Jewish religion and traditions
    d. memories of the concentration camps

2. What is the central idea of this selection?
    a. The horrors of life in a concentration camp should not be
        forgotten.
    b. Many Jews were sent to be exterminated in concentration
        camps.
    c. Anne Frank died of typhus in a concentration camp.
    d. Being a barracks leader helped save the author's life.

3. The author's primary purpose is to
    a. express her viewpoint about war.
    b. persuade older people to tell their stories.
    c. inform us about life in a concentration camp.
    d. explain what it is like to starve.

Details

4. A transit camp to which the author was sent first was
    a. Bergen-Belsen.
    b. Westerbork.
    c. The Hague.
    d. Auschwitz.

5. The author was married around
    a. 1897.
    b. 1920.

  c. 1941.

  d. 1945.

6. The author worked for the Nazis

  a. as a nurse.

  b. cooking food.

  c. sewing clothes.

  d. making bullets.

7. At different times in the concentration camps, the author had all but which one of the following to eat?

  a. bread

  b. coffee

  c. meat

  d. soup

8. The organizational pattern in paragraph 2 is

  a. sequence.

  b. comparison and contrast.

  c. cause and effect.

  d. definition.

Inferences

9. One reason that the author may not have wanted to talk about her story is that

  a. her children were not interested.

  b. she could not remember what happened.

  c. it would bring back terrible memories.

  d. she had no one to encourage her.

10. Which of the following is the most likely reason that the author was ordered to be barracks leader?

  a. The Nazis thought she had leadership capabilities.

  b. The other prisoners wanted her for their leader.

  c. She was stronger than most of the others.

  d. The commandant knew her family and wanted to help her.

WORKING WITH WORDS

Complete the sentences below with these words from Word Alert:

  extermination reflection transit gruel

  coincidence   reassured typhus

1. At first, Barbara's grandmother, Amanda Burton, did not want to tell her story, but on _____ , she decided that she would.

2. At the orphanage where she grew up, the children were fed _____ and little else.

3. Some of the children in the orphanage died of _____ as a result of the unsanitary conditions.

4. When Amanda was a young woman, she took a job with a company whose business was the _____ of mice and insects.

5. She spent several hours each day in _____ from home to work.

6. By an amazing _____ , Amanda met a woman who turned out to be her long-lost sister.

7. The meeting _____ both women that they had a family after all and were not alone in the world.

THINKING DEEPER

Ideas for discussion and writing

1. Discuss what the Holocaust means to you. What do you know about this historical event?

2. Do you think people who have endured great suffering should be encouraged to tell their stories? Do you believe that it is important to remember terrible events? Why or why not? What other stories and memories should older people be encouraged to tell their children and others?

3. Discuss how this selection illustrates the Part 3 theme, *Against All Odds*. For example, 6 million Jews were killed in concentration camps. That anyone survived was against all odds. But there were survivors, some of whom are still living today. Discuss any Holocaust survivors' stories that you have heard or read about. What else do you know of people who have survived the horrors of war? How have they overcome or learned to live with these experiences?

4. Write about a story from your past that you would like to pass on to your children.

FIRST THOUGHTS

To prepare yourself for the reading selection, answer the following questions, either on your own or in a group discussion.

1. What do you remember about your first day at school?
2. Was your first-day experience good or bad, and why?
3. Preview the title, headnote, and first one or two paragraphs. What do you think will follow?

WORD ALERT

defiance (2) resistance to force or authority, open hostility
counsel (2) advice, guidance
defective (3) faulty, abnormal
explicitly (4) fully and clearly expressed
illiterate (5) unable to read or write, having no formal education
naught (6) nothingness, nonexistence, insignificance
vaguely (9) not clearly expressed, indistinctly
precariously (9) dangerously
cascaded (9) fell, tumbled
resolve (13) determination, firmness of purpose

⅔ Back to School

TOM BODETT

The first day of school is a traumatic experience for some children. For others it is a time of great expectations. In this selection the author remembers his first day at school. Tom Bodett has been a commentator on National Public Radio's All Things Considered *and the host of* The End of the Road Review, *a radio variety show. He is the author of several*

From pp. 137–140 of SMALL COMFORTS by Tom Bodett. Copyright © 1987 by Tom Bodett. Reprinted by permission of Perseus Books Publishers, a member of Perseus Books, L.L.C. Permission conveyed through Copyright Clearance Center, Inc.

books, including Small Comforts, *from which this selection is taken.*

HE COULDN'T HAVE WEIGHED much more than his new raincoat. It 1 was so new, in fact, that it wouldn't let his arms hang the way they should. They stuck out from his sides at an odd angle, and he could no more scratch his nose than he could turn his head strapped into the hood. He stood stiffly beside the road and watched me coming from a long way. As I passed him he looked at me with his lip curled under his front teeth in fear.

When I found him again in my rear-view mirror, I saw it wasn't me 2 he'd been looking at at all, but the big yellow school bus behind me. "Oh, that's right," I thought. "First day of school." I wanted to turn around and go comfort him, but was called off by something remembered in his expression. Yes, the kid was scared, but his eyes were fixed on the bus with such **defiance** that I knew he didn't need any **counsel.** He was going through with it. Brave as any soldier, he was going to get on that bus for the very first time. I drove on while a similar bus in a similar rain charged out of my memory in fourth gear.

I hadn't been to kindergarten. That's what had me worried. I knew 3 my colors and I could count past a hundred, but I couldn't spell at all. My mother assured me I didn't need to spell to go to first grade. That's what they wanted to teach me. But I wasn't so sure. My older brother was way up in the third grade, and he could spell like crazy. He had me convinced I was a mental **defective** and the nuns at our small parochial school would serve me for hot lunch the first day if I didn't get my act together.

Determined to measure up, I asked my brother what it took to 4 spell. "Lots of paper and some pencils," he said. The pencils were covered. I'd already sharpened the life out of all three fat number ones in my Roy Rogers pencil box, and their big pink erasers were good and broken in. It was the paper that had me worried. Mom had told me the school would give me what I needed, but I couldn't trust her. She wasn't going to school, and my brother, who was, had **explicitly** mentioned paper. So I stole the whole stack of typing paper from the kitchen drawer and slipped it under my brand-new yellow raincoat.

Standing by the mailboxes with my brother, I was probably as 5 scared as I ever have been since. Six years old and functionally **illiterate.** Buckled into an impossible raincoat I wasn't sure I could find my way out of without maternal assistance. The only thing I had going for

me was a Roy Rogers pencil box, a Davy Crockett lunch pail, and over
four hundred sheets of stolen typing paper. The hardest thing I ever
did in my life was step onto that bus.

I'd like to be able to say that all my worrying was for **naught,** but it 6
wasn't. Actually, as I reached this mythical place called Saint Sebast-
ian's Elementary, my worst fears were realized.

Upon approaching the first-grade classroom I was greeted by Sis- 7
ter Antonio. I'd never been so close to a nun before and wasn't sure just
how to act. When she smiled and said "Good morning," it was as if a
burning bush had spoken. Until that moment I had never heard a nun
speak. My only experience of them had been watching them in church
in their mysterious black-and-white robes. I had some twisted notion
that they were all related to Saint Peter—a good friend of Jesus'—and
none of these people were to be taken lightly. I nearly swallowed my
tongue as I stumbled past her into the room. That's where the real
trouble started.

All the desks were in neat rows, and each one had a little folded 8
card on top. "Find the desk with your name on it and take your seat,
Tommy," I heard her say from the door. Other kids I'd never seen before were gracefully finding their places and admiring their name
cards. I didn't even know what my name looked like. I stalled around
the aisles until there were only two empty seats. Taking my best shot, I
marched up, plopped down my Davy Crockett lunch pail, and col-
lapsed with relief into Tammy Beech's chair.

The details are fuzzy from there, but I think I was found out during 9
roll call. I **vaguely** remember Sister Antonio looming over my desk and
saying something like, "You don't even know your own name?" This
was the last thing I needed pointed out in the presence of my very first
peer group. Still in my raincoat, I clumsily got out of my chair and dis-
lodged the four hundred–odd sheets of paper that were **precariously**
stashed underneath. They **cascaded** across the floor in an impressive
display and proceeded to soak up the mud and water left by thirty
first-graders. First-graders being how they are about wiping their feet,
it's a good thing I brought as much paper as I did.

To say I could've died would be an understatement. I blushed so 10
hard my ears rang. The thing I remember most about picking up that
paper was the presence of the burning bush right behind me in eter-
nal silence, the cruel giggles of my classmates, and the pounding of
my broken little heart.

Of course, I lived through all this and went on to finish my first 11
year of school. I got used to Sister Antonio and, believe it or not, she

even taught me how to spell. I was never served up for hot lunch, and I played Joseph in the Christmas play.

All these memories came back to me when I passed that little guy 12 on the road. All the fear and uncertainty that come with a strange new land. All the pain and humiliation that go with screwing it up. And everything we learn in the process. It never stops, and it never seems to get any easier.

I must say, though, how encouraged I was by that small face along 13 the road. Biting his lip in terror, but with pure **resolve** in his eye, he reminded me all over again of the best lesson I ever learned. If you want to go somewhere, you gotta get on the bus.

COMPREHENSION CHECK

Purpose and Main Idea

1. What is the author's topic?
   a. education
   b. teaching
   c. problems in school
   d. first day of school

2. What is the central idea of this selection?
   a. Education is the most important life experience a child can have.
   b. Parochial schools differ from public schools in a number of important ways.
   c. Looking back on our first day of school reminds us of the fear we felt and the lessons learned.
   d. Children today use many of the same school supplies as did children of the past.

3. The author's primary purpose is to
   a. express what it was like to be a first grader.
   b. persuade us to make the first day of school easier for kids.
   c. inform us about what first grade is like in a parochial school.
   d. entertain and amuse us with his memories of his first day of school.

Details

4. Before the author went to first grade, he did not know
   a. colors.

    b. numbers.

    c. how to write.

    d. how to spell.

5. The author had everything he needed for the first day of school except

    a. pencils.

    b. paper.

    c. pencil box.

    d. lunch pail.

6. By the end of first grade, the author says he had done all of the following except which one?

    a. He learned how to spell.

    b. He played Joseph in the Christmas play.

    c. He joined the school choir.

    d. He got used to Sister Antonio.

7. Looking back on his first day of school, the author says that he remembers all of the following except which one?

    a. his classmates' names

    b. the fear and uncertainty

    c. his classmates' giggles

    d. the pounding of his heart

8. The organizational pattern in paragraph 3 is

    a. definition.

    b. cause and effect.

    c. comparison and contrast.

    d. sequence.

Inferences

9. The author could not find the right seat because

    a. there were not enough desks.

    b. the nun frightened him.

    c. he did not know his own name.

    d. he could not read.

10. Which of the following sayings means about the same thing as "If you want to go somewhere, you gotta get on the bus."

    a. Nothing ventured, nothing gained.

    b. You have to start somewhere.

    c. Time and tide for no man wait.

    d. Opportunity strikes only once.

WORKING WITH WORDS

Complete the sentences below with these words from Word Alert:

precariously	defective	vaguely	naught
illiterate	defiance	resolve	
explicitly	cascaded	counsel	

1. The high diver balanced _____ on his toes before plunging into the pool.
2. Despite the fact that education is available for everyone in the United States, many people are still _____ .
3. This electric pencil sharpener must be _____ because I cannot make it work.
4. The angry driver shook his hand in _____ at the flagger who was directing traffic during road construction.
5. Marta had been having trouble outlining her research paper, but with new _____ she tried again.
6. After the spring thaw, waterfalls _____ down the mountainside.
7. When you are struggling with a problem, it may help to seek the _____ of those who have had experience with similar problems.
8. Before trying to assemble the toy, read the directions, which are _____ stated on the box.
9. Although the time you spend studying may seem for _____ , when you score high on a test, you know it was worth it.
10. If you only _____ understand what a lecturer is saying, you will have a hard time deciding what notes to take.

THINKING DEEPER

Ideas for discussion and writing

1. Discuss what the author means by "If you want to get somewhere, you gotta get on the bus." Do you think this is good advice? Why or why not?
2. Compare your first day at school with the author's first day. What similarities and differences do you see? Discuss first-day or first-time experiences in general, for example, your first day at college

or your first day at work. What do they all have in common? What kinds of lessons do we learn from first-day or first-time experiences?

3. Discuss how this selection illustrates the Part 3 theme, *Against All Odds*. For example, put yourself in the place of a child going to school for the first time. Getting on the bus, as the author sug-gests, is a big step. In taking it, the child beats the odds in the sense that he or she overcomes fear and finds self-confidence. Throughout school, what are some other big steps we take— either academically or socially—that help us beat the odds, or not?

4. In the last paragraph, the author says that seeing the little boy waiting for the bus made him remember all over again the best lesson he ever learned. Write about the best lesson you ever learned in school.

FIRST THOUGHTS

To prepare yourself for the reading selection, answer the following questions, either on your own or in a group discussion.

1. Are you a smoker or a nonsmoker?

2. Have you ever tried to quit smoking? Describe your experience.

3. Preview the title, headnote, and first one or two paragraphs. What do you think will follow?

WORD ALERT

raging (2) moving or speaking with great violence or anger
grope (9) to search blindly or uncertainly
intervals (10) amounts of time between events
oxygenate (12) treat, combine, or infuse with oxygen
combatting (12) fighting, opposing
vivid (13) bright, lifelike, realistic
abstinence (13) self-denial, the act of refraining from indulging an appetite

❧ How I Quit Smoking, If I Really Did

HELEN PARRAMORE

Helen Parramore retired from Valencia Community College as a humanities professor. In this selection, she explains her struggles with a smoking habit. The selection ran in The Orlando Sentinel's *"My Word" column in April 1998.*

O N Aug. 27, 1967, at 3:30 in the afternoon, with my five kids in the 1
station wagon on the way to the pound to pick out a puppy in Gainesville, I quit smoking.

The only other date I remember with certainty is 1066, when the 2
Battle of Hastings occurred. That's because my high-school history teacher had a **raging** fit in class one day, quite as memorable as the

battle itself, when everyone missed the question on a test. In my mind, quitting smoking is associated with the Battle of Hastings.

In 1967, everybody smoked. Nobody talked about quitting. I don't 3 know why I thought I should. Nobody encouraged me. I had quit six or seven times before this memorable date, but that was the *last* time I quit.

To do it, I had to figure out how to live in a world of smokers.   4

How could I take a coffee break without a cigarette?   5

How could I keep others from blowing smoke in my face?   6

Would I never be able to have a drink or socialize with friends?   7

After dinner in the evening or when chatting on the phone, what 8 could I do instead of smoking?

I chose Life Savers. I had to **grope** to find the roll in my purse, then 9 unravel the wrapper, offer one to a friend, pry one loose and pop it into my mouth. I had to suck, then wrap up the rest and put the roll away. The sugar gave me a little lift and reward—the same motions and effects of smoking.

I learned that my craving was as predictable as the clock. Every 20 10 minutes, when I wanted to smoke, I popped a Life Saver and promised myself to wait 10 minutes. Ten minutes later, I had forgotten about it and was content until the craving hit again. So, actually, I quit smoking forever in 10-minute **intervals.**

In the following weeks, the time between cravings gradually in- 11 creased. Every time I waited, I gained a few seconds. Within three months, cravings were down to about four times a day—a manageable problem.

I began bicycling and swimming because I found that physical ex- 12 ercise eased my cravings. Years later, I read that exercise gets rid of the sticky, brown gunk that coats the lungs of smokers and helps **oxygenate** our body and brains. Exercise is a natural "upper." Without knowing what I was doing, I was **combatting** the depression that accompanies withdrawal while helping my lungs to heal.

After the worst was over, I began having **vivid** dreams about smok- 13 ing. In these dreams, I would light a cigarette, telling myself I could have one occasionally. Then I would light another and another, and I would see that both of my hands held a full pack of cigarettes. I awoke from these dreams depressed and confused. Had I really quit? Or had I lied to myself all along? I still occasionally have that dream—a reminder to myself that, despite 31 years' **abstinence,** I am still a smoker.

If you've tried to quit and can't, try again. Remember, nobody does 14 it the first time. You're battling true addiction. It isn't easy, but you can do it 10 minutes at a time.

COMPREHENSION CHECK

Purpose and Main Idea

1. What is the author's topic?
   a. addiction
   b. bad habits
   c. smoking
   d. cigarettes

2. Which one of the following best expresses the author's central idea?
   a. I quit smoking at 3:30 p.m. on August 27, 1967.
   b. In the 1960s, smoking was accepted behavior.
   c. Smoking, like drinking, is a true addiction.
   d. Quitting smoking is a battle that I must keep fighting.

3. The author's primary purpose is to
   a. inform us about the effects of smoking.
   b. entertain us with the ways others have quit smoking.
   c. persuade smokers to keep trying to quit.
   d. express how difficult it is to quit smoking.

Details

4. Why did the author quit smoking in 1967?
   a. Everybody smoked in 1967.
   b. Her friends encouraged her to quit.
   c. She had quit in the past.
   d. She says she does not know why.

5. To live in a world of smokers, the author had to figure out how to do all of the following except which one?
   a. Continue smoking when under stress.
   b. Take a coffee break without a cigarette.
   c. Keep others from blowing smoke in her face.
   d. Have a drink or socialize without a cigarette.

6. To quit smoking, the author tried all of the following methods except which one?
   a. eating Life Savers
   b. bicycling
   c. swimming
   d. nicotine patches

7. The author says that the time between cravings for cigarettes
   a. gradually increased.
   b. gradually decreased.

    c. stayed the same.

    d. stopped suddenly.

8. The overall organizational pattern in this selection is
    a. definition: the author explains what addiction means.
    b. cause and effect: the author explains the dangers of smoking.
    c. comparison and contrast: the author compares smoking with alcohol addiction.
    d. process: the author explains how she quit smoking.

Inferences

9. When the author says that she is still a smoker after 31 years of abstinence, she means that she
    a. has not really quit.
    b. does not want to quit.
    c. still has cravings.
    d. does not know why she should quit.

10. When the author says you can stop smoking "10 minutes at a time," she probably means that
    a. you can never stop smoking.
    b. Addiction is an ongoing battle.
    c. it takes 10 minutes to stop smoking.
    d. eventually, the cravings will stop.

WORKING WITH WORDS

Complete the sentences below with these words from Word Alert:

abstinence   oxygenate   vivid   raging
combatting   intervals   grope

1. The tornado was _____ outside, rooting up trees and tearing houses off their foundations.

2. Smoking interferes with your lungs' capacity to _____ the blood.

3. Tourists visit New England in the fall to see the _____ leaves and enjoy the cool weather.

4. Because the rain fell off and on, we were able to walk to the library during one of the dry _____ .

5. In the dark, I had to _____ for the light switch.

6. A smoker's lungs will heal themselves after a long _____ from smoking.

7. If you do not get enough sleep, you will be spending most of your time in class _____ the urge to doze.

THINKING DEEPER

Ideas for discussion and writing

1. Discuss various forms of addictive behavior, including smoking. What are some of the reasons that people engage in addictive behavior?
2. Discuss the steps in the process the author went through to quit smoking. How does her experience compare either to your own or to that of someone you know who has tried to quit smoking?
3. Discuss how this selection illustrates the Part 3 theme, *Against All Odds*. For example, the author suggests that battling addiction may be a lifelong process, which means that those who succeed do so against all odds. What success stories do you know about people who battled their addictions and won?
4. Have you ever tried to break a habit or to battle an addiction? Were you successful? What strategies did you use? Write about your experience.

FIRST THOUGHTS

To prepare yourself for the reading selection, answer the following questions, either on your own or in a group discussion.

1. Do you know or can you imagine what it would be like to be blind?

2. What are some of the things you do as a sighted person that you would not be able to do if you were blind?

3. Preview the title, headnote, and first one or two paragraphs. What do you think will follow?

WORD ALERT

hemorrhaged (3) bled excessively
mannequins (4) models of the human body, dummies for displaying clothes
fainthearted (4) timid, lacking courage
eerie (5) causing fear or uneasiness, mysterious
hapless (7) luckless, unfortunate
misconstrued (8) misunderstood
patronizing (8) looking down on, being condescending
exotic (10) unusual, different, intriguing
interloper (11) one who interferes with the affairs of others
ricochet (14) to rebound at least once from a surface

ൠ Navigating My Eerie Landscape Alone

JIM BOBRYK

Jim Brobryk is a California writer and executive. In this selection from Newsweek, *March 8, 1999, he explains what it is like to have lost his sight.*

NOW, AS I STROLL down the street, my right forefinger extends five 1 feet in front of me, feeling the ground where my feet will walk.

Before, my right hand would have been on a steering wheel as I 2
went down the street. I drove to work, found shortcuts in strange
cities, picked up my two daughters after school. Those were the days
when I ran my finger down a phone-book page and never dialed Information. When I read novels and couldn't sleep until I had finished
the last page. Those were the nights when I could point out a shooting
star before it finished scraping across the dark sky. And when I could
go to the movies and it didn't matter if it was a foreign film or not.

But all this changed about seven years ago. I was driving home for 3
lunch on what seemed to be an increasingly foggy day, although the
perky radio deejay said it was clear and sunny. After I finished my
lunch, I realized that I couldn't see across the room to my front door. I
had battled glaucoma for 20 years. Suddenly, without warning, my
eyes had **hemorrhaged.**

I will never regain any of my lost sight. I see things through a port- 4
hole covered in wax paper. I now have no vision in my left eye and only
slight vision in my right. A minefield of blind spots make people and
cars suddenly appear and vanish. I have no depth perception. Objects
are not closer and farther; they're larger and smaller. Steps, curbs and
floors all flow on the same flat plane. My world has shapes but no features. Friends are **mannequins** in the fog until I recognize their voices.
Printed words look like ants writhing on the pages. Doorways are un-
lit mine shafts. This is not a place for the **fainthearted.**

My cane is my navigator in this **eerie** landscape. It is a hollow 5
fiber-glass stick with white reflector paint and a broad red band at the
tip. It folds up tightly into four 15-inch sections, which can then be
slipped into a black holster that attaches to my belt with Velcro.

Adults—unless they're preoccupied or in a hurry—will step aside 6
without comment when they see me coming. Small children will either be scooped up apologetically or steered away by their parents.
Only teenagers sometimes try to play chicken, threatening to collide
with me and then veering out of the way at the last moment.

While I'm wielding my stick, strangers are often afraid to commu- 7
nicate with me. I don't take this personally—anymore. Certainly they
can't be afraid that I'll lash at them with my rod. (Take *that,* you **hapless** sighted person! Whack!) No, they're probably more afraid *for* me.
Don't startle the sword swallower. Don't tickle the baton twirler.

The trick for the sighted person is to balance courtesy with con- 8
cern. Should he go out of his way or should he get out of the way? Will
his friendliness be **misconstrued** by the disabled as pity? Will an offer
of help sound **patronizing?** These anxieties are exaggerated by not
knowing the etiquette in dealing with the disabled. A sighted person

will do nothing rather than take the risk of offending the blind. Still, I refuse to take a dim view of all this.

When I peer over my cane and ask for help, no one ever cowers in 9 fear. In fact, I think people are waiting for me to give them the green light to help. It makes us feel good to help.

When I ask for a small favor, I often get more assistance than I ever 10 expect. Clerks will find my required forms and fill them out for me. A group of people will parade me across a dangerous intersection. A salesclerk will read the price tag for me and then hunt for the item on sale. I'm no Don Juan, but strange (and possibly **exotic**) women will take my hand and walk me through dark rooms, mysterious train stations and foreign airports. Cabbies wait and make sure I make it safely into lobbies.

It's not like it's inconvenient for friends to help me get around. 11 Hey, have disabled parking placard—will travel. Christmas shopping? Take me to the mall and I'll get us front-row parking. Late for the game? *No problema.* We'll be parking by the stadium entrance. And if some inconsiderate **interloper** does park in the blue zone without a permit, he'll either be running after a fleeing tow truck or paying a big fine.

Worried about those age lines showing? Not with me looking. Put 12 down that industrial-strength Oil of Olay. To me, your skin looks as clear and smooth as it was back in the days when you thought suntanning was a good idea.

So you see, I'm a good guy to know. I just carry a cane, that's all. 13

None of this is to make light of going blind. Being blind is dark and 14 depressing. When you see me walking with my cane, you may think I'm lost as I **ricochet** down the street. But you'll find more things in life if you don't travel in a straight line.

COMPREHENSION CHECK

Purpose and Main Idea

1. What is the author's topic?
   a. disabilities
   b. blindness
   c. traveling
   d. solitude
2. Which of the following best states the author's central idea?
   a. Various organizations exist to help the blind.
   b. Blindness has several causes.

    c. My life changed when I became blind.

    d. Strangers are afraid of helping the blind.

3.   The author's primary purpose is to
    a. persuade readers to help those who are blind.
    b. entertain us with stories of famous blind people.
    c. express what his life is like now that he is blind.
    d. inform us of the many things we can do to help the blind.

Details

4.   The author is completely blind in
    a. the left eye.
    b. the right eye.
    c. both eyes.
    d. neither eye.

5.   His navigator is
    a. his daughter.
    b. any stranger.
    c. his cane.
    d. a seeing-eye dog.

6.   Since his hemorrhage, his vision has changed in all but which one of the following ways?
    a. He has no depth perception.
    b. People's features are distinct.
    c. Steps, floors, and curbs are on the same flat plane.
    d. He has blind spots.

7.   According to the author, sighted people should learn to
    a. ignore blind people.
    b. go out of their way to help.
    c. get out of the blind person's way.
    d. balance courtesy with concern.

8.   In paragraphs 4 and 5, the author's details are mainly
    a. reasons.
    b. descriptions.
    c. steps in a process.
    d. time markers.

Inferences

9.   As he says, the author is "a good guy to know" for all of the following reasons except
    a. he has a disabled person's permit.
    b. he can get you front-row parking.

    c. he does not inconvenience his friends.

    d. he knows exactly how old you are.

10. When the author says in paragraph 8 "I refuse to take a dim view of all this," he is

    a. showing that he has a sense of humor.

    b. suggesting that sighted people are inconsiderate.

    c. revealing his feelings of anger and frustration.

    d. asking for the reader's pity.

WORKING WITH WORDS

Complete the sentences below with these words from Word Alert:

fainthearted	hemorrhaged	mannequins	ricochet	exotic
misconstrued	patronizing	interloper	hapless	eerie

1. On our trip to Asia, we visited many _____ places.

2. Who is this _____ who keeps trying to break into the line?

3. Chris served the Ping-Pong ball and watched it _____ off the table.

4. I am sorry for the mistake; I must have _____ your meaning.

5. After her fall, Nancy's nose _____ and her friends took her to the emergency room.

6. The hurricane's _____ victims were overwhelmed by the help strangers offered.

7. Sports like mountain climbing and white-water rafting are not for the _____ .

8. As a sign that spring was coming, the store _____ were all dressed in pastel colors.

9. Don't take that _____ attitude with me; I can do this project as well as you can.

10. Being in the deep woods on a moonless night is _____ because you literally cannot see your hand in front of you.

THINKING DEEPER

Ideas for discussion and writing

1. Discuss the author's views about sighted people and their treatment of him. If necessary, read again paragraphs 7 through 10.

Using what the author says as an example, what lessons can we all learn about communicating with and getting along with those who have any disability?

2. Discuss the author's use of descriptive details and humor. Identify specific paragraphs or sentences where the details seem especially vivid or the author's sense of humor is displayed. Why do you think the author chose these details? What effect do they have on the reader, and how do they suit the author's purpose?

3. Discuss how this selection illustrates the Part 3 theme, *Against All Odds*. For example, what legislation and attitude changes have improved life and working conditions for the disabled? What more needs to be done to help them beat the odds?

4. Using this selection as an example, write about your own attempts to cope with a disability or to help someone who is disabled—either a friend or a family member. Or write about a disabled person you admire.

FIRST THOUGHTS

To prepare yourself for the reading selection, answer the following questions, either on your own or in a group discussion.

1. Who are some athletes you admire and why?

2. What female athlete can you name who has set a record or made a name for herself?

3. Preview the title, headnote, and first one or two paragraphs. What do you think will follow?

WORD ALERT

scrutinized (2) examined carefully
pioneers (5) those who venture into unknown or unclaimed territory
commonplace (14) ordinary
intense (21) extreme in degree
honed (27) sharpened
detrimental (42) harmful, damaging

❧ Drive

SHANNON SHELTON

The author, a staff writer for the Orlando Sentinel, *writes about female athletes who have competed successfully with their male counterparts. Following the publication of this article on May 18, 2003, Annika Sorenstam competed admirably for two days of qualifying rounds at the PGA Colonial Classic but did not make the cut, and Suzy Whaley competed in the Greater Hartford Open. The general agreement was that both golfers' performance in their respective tournaments scored a victory for female athletes.*

Orlando Sentinel, May 18, 2003, p. C11

EVERY golfer has a bad round. Every kicker has a kick blocked or the 1 ball hook wide left or right. Every athlete has experienced the feeling of losing a game, match or tournament.

But for the most part, your losses and mistakes aren't **scrutinized** 2 for decades. You aren't held up as poster child for arguments about participation in athletics.

Unless you're a woman.   3

From Billie Jean King in 1973 to Annika Sorenstam today, women 4 who have attempted to compete with men instantly become poster children for the debate over a woman's place in sports. On one end are groups that paint such women as pioneers for opening doors for female athletes. The other side expresses concern that if the women come up short, they will set back social acceptance of female athletes in general. In between, of course, are those who say women shouldn't compete with men.

Talk to the women athletes themselves, and most fall squarely in 5 the middle. They say they're just playing the sports they love and that they want to test themselves at the highest level. While understanding their roles as **pioneers,** their main goal isn't to make a political statement. And if there is failure, they find it the height of a double standard to be judged more harshly.

"It took a few days for me to realize that I was still a good player," 6 said Katie Hnida, a kicker at New Mexico who last season became the first woman to play in a Division I-A college football game.

In the Las Vegas Bowl on Christmas Day against UCLA, Hnida had 7 an extra-point attempt blocked; it was her first attempt of the season. Much of the media attention Hnida received was positive, but she was stung by the negative reaction she received in some media outlets.

"It was my first kick," she said. "I was tremendously disappointed 8 about it being blocked, but then I had people saying that I had just proven that women shouldn't be out there.

"You definitely get put under a microscope."   9

Hnida, like many other "first women," applauds Sorenstam's deci- 10 sion to play in the PGA Tour's Bank of America Colonial Classic [May 25] in Fort Worth, Texas. Mildred "Babe" Didrikson Zaharias is the last woman to play in a PGA event, in 1945. Sorenstam will do it in the age of 24-hour television, radio and Internet sports access, putting her under a microscope Didrikson couldn't have imagined.

Suzy Whaley will continue the trend in July when she plays in 11 the PGA Tour's Greater Hartford Open after qualifying for the event last fall.

No matter how Sorenstam does at The Colonial, the women who 12
have been pioneers before feel it's unfair to judge her skill only on that
weekend's results.

"Annika's got to march to her own drum," said Ann Meyers, the 13
first woman to participate in an NBA training camp. "Should she be
judged on the results of one tournament? No. Her performance over
10–15 would be a better way to see how well she can compete."

TIMES HAVE CHANGED

It has been nearly 30 years since Billie Jean King's 6–4, 6–3, 6–3 victory 14
over Bobby Riggs in tennis' "Battle of the Sexes," and public opinion
about women in sports has changed dramatically. Women's participation in sports from the recreational to professional levels is **commonplace,** and few question whether women should have the right to
compete. But with women's leagues available in most sports, a new
question is why some women choose to compete with men.

Hnida said that playing against men exposes her to the highest 15
level of competition. Meyers said she enjoyed the challenge as well.

"It's a part of the joy of sport," said Donna Lopiano, the executive 16
director of the Women's Sports Foundation. "Whenever you take risks,
you can say that you have reached the highest of highs and lowest
of lows."

It's that feeling that likely attracted women like Manon Rheaume 17
to become the first woman to play on an NHL team when she was a
goalie with the Tampa Bay Lightning in a preseason game against the
St. Louis Blues in 1992. Or Ila Borders to play pro baseball when she
pitched in the independent Northern League with the Saint Paul Saints
in 1997.

But there's also the extra pressure that comes when a woman 18
chooses to compete against men. King felt it perhaps more than any
woman, since she competed against Riggs at a time when women
weren't typically seen as competitive athletes.

"It was all about social change," King said. "Back in '73, everyone 19
thought women were total chokes and folded like a napkin.

"That's not true. Both genders choke." 20

Although the "Battle of the Sexes" was more of a publicity event 21
than a serious match and although Riggs was 55 and King was 27,
the pressure on King was **intense.** Despite the age difference, Riggs
and many others believed no woman would be good enough to beat
a man.

But even though the number of women breaking through the gen- 22
der barrier in sports grows larger each year, a lot of the same questions
remain. For instance, tennis commentator John McEnroe has been
quoted as saying any good male college tennis player could beat Se-
rena and Venus Williams, currently ranked first and second in the world.

"Annika is probably thinking this is the time to put her best foot 23
forward," King said. "Because of how Annika is as an athlete, I think
she will do very well. This is how you really find out if you have the
nerves to handle the pressure."

BASKETBALL BREAKTHROUGH

In the late '70s, Meyers was one of the top women's basketball players 24
in the nation. She led UCLA to a national championship in 1978 and
competed on the U.S. team that won an Olympic silver medal in 1976.

After her graduation in '78, she was the first draft pick in the newly 25
formed Women's Basketball League. But opportunity knocked when
the NBA's Indiana Pacers offered her a tryout in 1979. She signed as a
free agent and participated in a three-day rookie/free-agent camp. To
this day, she remains the only woman to sign with an NBA team.

"It was an opportunity," said Meyers, whose brother, David, played 26
at UCLA and with the NBA's Milwaukee Bucks. "How do you turn
down something when it's offered to you? You never want to look back
and say 'What if?'"

Meyers, the widow of Hall-of-Fame pitcher Don Drysdale, said her 27
intention was to simply make it in the NBA as a basketball player, not
as a female player. Playing against men wasn't an issue for her. She
makes the point that most top female athletes have **honed** their skills
against men.

"I'd grown up playing basketball against men," Meyers said. "In 28
my mind, it wasn't a big deal. Don't tell me that [Annika] hasn't played
against men before."

But Meyers remembers that her presence was a problem for some 29
of the men she faced. While not outwardly hostile, she said other players were hesitant about the idea of playing against a woman.

"They were scared of being as aggressive with their hand checks, 30
wondering if they reached out they might feel something they weren't
supposed to," Meyers said, laughing. "For sure, they played their hardest, but I'm sure they were on pins and needles."

Meyers faced the same with Coach Bob "Slick" Leonard, who she 31
said wasn't accustomed to the idea of women competing with men.

Her biggest supporter was assistant coach Jack McCloskey, who later became the general manager of several NBA teams. She said his inclusion in team talks peppered with colorful language let other players know Meyers was to be treated like everybody else.

Ultimately, Meyers was cut and did end up in the now-defunct 32 WBL. She later found success as a broadcaster. She met Drysdale through her broadcasting career.

Still, Meyers looks back and wishes she could have made the Pac- 33 ers and hopes Sorenstam will continue to pursue whatever opportunities she feels are best for her despite what detractors might say.

The talk about how a Sorenstam failure could set back women's 34 golf or the doubts that Sorenstam can compete with the men sound familiar to Meyers.

"As much as things change, these are the same things that hap- 35 pened to me 24 years ago," Meyers said.

PRESSURE CAN BE GREAT

Hnida just wanted to play football. A former soccer player, she took up 36 football at Littleton (Colo.) Chatfield High.

The rest of the story is typical: She fell in love with the sport and 37 ended up going 4-of-5 on field-goal attempts and 83-of-87 on extra-point attempts. She ended up walking on at Colorado but was released after a year.

When she left, Hnida felt she became "Exhibit A" when it came to 38 women playing football. She remembers seeing her picture on the front page of a local sports section, illustrating a negative article about her participation.

"I was just an 18-year-old kid," she said. "It was hard to take." 39

Not willing to give up her dream, she ended up walking on at New 40 Mexico. She didn't participate in a game during the regular season, but got the opportunity in a bowl game to try an extra point in a 27–13 loss to UCLA.

Hnida should get more opportunities to become the first woman 41 to score in a Division I-A game as a senior this fall. She appreciates that Coach Rocky Long and her teammates treat her as they would any other player on the team. Getting another chance is something that should be given to any athlete, she said.

Although Sorenstam's supporters outnumber her detractors, the 42 idea that a bad performance would be **detrimental** to women's golf has been heard frequently. Tiger Woods' comments are the most prominent:

He said her participation was great but could be detrimental to women's golf if she performed poorly.

That's a double standard the "first women" hate.   43

"The future of women in sports is not riding on this one tourna- 44 ment," Hnida said. "What matters is that she is able to do this. It's just one stinkin' tournament."

COMPREHENSION CHECK

Purpose and Main Idea

1. What is the author's topic?
   a. famous female athletes of the past
   b. women in professional sports today
   c. female athletes who compete with men
   d. sports in which women have excelled

2. Which one of the following sentences best states the author's central idea?
   a. Over the past 30 years, public opinion about women in sports has changed dramatically.
   b. It is not unusual to find successful female athletes in all major sports today.
   c. Arguments about women's participation in athletics persist despite their achievements.
   d. Why some women choose to compete with men is a question of interest to many sports observers.

3. The author's primary purpose is to
   a. explain why women compete with men in sports.
   b. entertain readers with examples of female athletes' successes.
   c. inform readers about the achievements of great female athletes.
   d. persuade readers that a debate about women in sports exists.

Details

4. According to most female athletes, why do they compete with men?
   a. They want to make a political statement.
   b. They love their sport and want to test themselves.
   c. They want to open doors for other female athletes.
   d. They believe there is a double standard for men and women.

5. Which woman became the first to play in a Division I-A college football game?
   a. Manon Rheaume
   b. Brandi Chastain
   c. Donna Lapiano
   d. Katie Hnida

6. Which game was more of a publicity event than a serious match?
   a. the 1992 preseason game between the Tampa Bay Lightning and the St. Louis Blues
   b. the Colonial Classic in which Annika Sorenstam competed
   c. the "Battle of the Sexes" between Bobby Riggs and Billie Jean King
   d. the 1997 Northern League game in which Ila Borders pitched for the St. Louis Saints

7. Ann Meyers is best known as which one of the following?
   a. the first woman to play on an NHL team
   b. the only woman to sign with an NBA team
   c. the winner of an Olympic silver medal
   d. one of three women to play in a PGA tournament

8. The author's details consist mainly of
   a. facts about female athletes' accomplishments.
   b. opinions about women's role in professional sports.
   c. reasons that explain why some female athletes excel.
   d. examples of women who are tops in their sports.

Inferences

9. In paragraph 42, "detractors" means which one of the following?
   a. fans
   b. players
   c. promoters
   d. opponents

10. In paragraph 9, when Katie Hnida says, "You definitely get put under a microscope," she probably means which one of the following?
    a. You must meet certain requirements.
    b. Doctors monitor your physical condition.
    c. The media analyze your performance.
    d. Your teammates keep an eye on you.

WORKING WITH WORDS

Complete the sentences below with these words from Word Alert:

> detrimental   commonplace   intense
> scrutinized   pioneers   honed

1. As a young boy, Tiger Woods _____ his golf skill by practicing for many hours daily.
2. Though once only rarely seen, cell phones have now become _____ .
3. Burglars like to work in the dark, where their actions will not be _____ by nosy neighbors.
4. Some female athletes are regarded as _____ for competing in sports formerly reserved for men.
5. Athletes who want to stay at the top of their game refrain from activities that are _____ to their health and performance.
6. When the heat is _____ , you should stay indoors to avoid sunstroke.

THINKING DEEPER

Ideas for discussion and writing

1. Discuss as many high-profile women athletes as you can think of who are changing our ideas about women's role in sports.
2. Consider a sport, such as soccer, that both men and women play professionally. Compare men's and women's teams in terms of their styles of play, attitudes toward the game, and treatment of fans. What can male and female athletes learn from each other that will improve their game?
3. Discuss how this selection illustrates the Part 3 theme, *Against All Odds*. For example, until recently women's sports have not received the interest either from fans or from potential sponsors that men's sports have. Women athletes have always struggled against these odds. Discuss how this may be changing.
4. Write about a female athlete you admire, or write about a sport in which you would like to see more women participate.

FIRST THOUGHTS

To prepare yourself for the reading selection, answer the following questions, either on your own or in a group discussion.

1. What is your attitude toward elderly people?

2. How do people show respect or disrespect toward the elderly?

3. Preview the title, headnote, and first one or two paragraphs. What do you think will follow?

WORD ALERT

consign (1) entrust, deliver, turn over to the care of another
maligned (2) spoke evil of, showed ill will toward
tribulations (2) great suffering or distress, hard times
forbearance (2) restraint and tolerance
inconspicuous (5) not obvious, not noticeable
posthumously (7) after death
template (8) pattern
begrudge (12) to envy the possession of, to give reluctantly

⅔ Longevity and Livability

ARGUS J. TRESIDDER

*Argus J. Tresidder is from northern Virginia. He was 91 in
1998 when this selection ran in* Newsweek. *He asks readers
to be more tolerant of the elderly.*

I AM A MEMBER of the generation that has outlived the conventional 1
life span. We are often accused these days of threatening the financial stability of Medicare and Social Security by being too numerous and too demanding. Our critics say we hide behind the powerful American Association of Retired Persons for protection from the efforts of younger people, especially those called baby boomers, to **consign** us to ice floes or canoes launched out to sea without paddles. They are evidently afraid that our rapidly increasing percentage of the

population is using up too much air, food, water and health care and there won't be enough left over for them as they approach the entry age of our generation.

I hear such comments as "You know, these senior citizens keep 2 telling us that they barely have enough to live on, but you can be sure that they have a neat pile of stocks and bonds stashed away." Or "Did you ever notice how quick they are to claim their discounts as seniors?" And "Of course, they expect us to pay for the Medicare that will run out before we get to it." I should like to put in a word for my **maligned** generation. For the most part, we are law-abiding, tax-paying, even productive citizens. I think that we have earned the right to a little respect, and even perhaps admiration, for having reached old age and its **tribulations** and tragedies with courage and **forbearance.**

Let me present my credentials as a self-appointed spokesman for 3 the growing generation of septuagenarians, octogenarians and nonagenarians. The centenarians, bless them all, need no defense. There aren't enough of them yet to be much of a threat, and everybody marvels at their durability. I'm only in the nonagenarian stage, which I call the "no-no period"—no fatty food, no salt, no alcohol and no sex. Incidentally, I'm also legally blind.

I'm a second-generation American of sturdy German-English stock. 4 I've had a moderately successful, generally useful life in several careers as a university instructor, a naval officer during World War II, a corporate executive for a time, a Foreign Service officer and, finally, a professor of English at the Marine Corps Command and Staff College at Quantico, Va.

After my final retirement, from Quantico at the age of 75, my wife 5 and I lived in a pleasant home in a dormitory suburb of Washington. Our daughter and her two sons lived near us. At last I had leisure to be a full-time writer, though my success with editors had been less than distinguished. I had published six books and many articles in various periodicals, and I was listed in a couple of **inconspicuous** literary Who's Whos. It was a happy time. I was healthy and active and had lots of friends. I imposed on Medicare very little until I lost my vision after problems with glaucoma, cataracts and a detached retina.

During this period of adjustment, my wife, who had seen me 6 through seven operations, became very ill. I was able to help take care of her for three years until her death in 1995. Her loss left me to shape a plan for growing old alone.

I taught myself to touch-type, and I've written novels, several children's stories, plays and a book about my Foreign Service experience 7 in South Africa in the 1960s. After years of disappointments over manuscripts that publishers have rejected, I continue to churn out more and more pages, hoping that, even **posthumously,** someone will discover me as a writer. My daily hours on the typewriter have given me the illusion of being productive. I keep thinking about the artists and authors and composers who have done their best work in old age. I should know by now that I don't really have the necessary talent or inspiration to be so late a bloomer, but it's fun to keep trying. Quite a high pile of books, edited by my faithful volunteers, is waiting for someone else to read.

No part of my day is idle. I rise at 7 and have the light breakfast 8 that one of my home caretakers has left in the refrigerator the previous evening. I can manage the buttons on a microwave. Then I wait for my walker of the day. We go out for more than an hour every day, walking in a nearby rugged park. If the weather is really bad—we don't mind a little rain or snow—we go to my basement, where I have an electric treadmill and a stationary bicycle. Best of all, we talk. Companionship is the spice of life for the elderly. A shower and several hours of concentrated typing follow until my caretaker arrives at noon. In the afternoon, I listen to Library of Congress Talking Books and keep up with events on radio and in recorded magazines. Another helper, my bookkeeper, comes in to write checks that I sign in a **template.** Three evenings a week, my friendly readers come by.

Sometimes I'm invited to parties. Twice I've taken plane trips 9 alone to visit friends in other cities—once to speak at a reunion of my naval students—now all over 70. I may even attend my 70th college reunion this coming June. My 11-year-old car, which has less than 10,000 miles on its odometer, is available, driven by others, to take me on errands or to see a doctor.

The most wonderful part of this orderly, busy life is that it has 10 brought me friends, including the best neighbors I have ever had. They provide me with cookies and vegetables from their gardens and make up most of my pool of walkers.

I still find the world interesting, though badly run, and look for- 11 ward with intense curiosity to the possibility of observing the simultaneous change of century and millennium. I'd really like to be around to experience Armageddon, if the doomsayers are right. I am especially curious to learn if computers not programmed beyond the 20th century will blow up in frustration.

There are many more oldsters like me, still full of creaking vitality, 12 who do not find life boring or the sky always dark. Don't **begrudge** us our perks or resent our drain on natural and financial resources. You might make better use of our experience and possible wisdom to help in reducing the nation's growing cultural illiteracy and even perhaps as models for the young. At any rate, please be more tolerant of us!

COMPREHENSION CHECK

Purpose and Main Idea

1. What is the author's topic?
   a. respect for the elderly
   b. baby boomers' attitudes
   c. perks for seniors
   d. medical care for the aged

2. Which of the following sentences from the selection states the author's central idea?
   a. paragraph 1, first sentence "I am a member. . . ."
   b. paragraph 2, last sentence "I think that. . . ."
   c. paragraph 3, first sentence "Let me present. . . ."
   d. paragraph 12, second sentence "Don't begrudge. . . ."

3. The author's primary purpose is to
   a. entertain readers with funny stories about growing old.
   b. inform us about the perks for senior citizens.
   c. persuade readers to treat the elderly with more respect.
   d. express what he thinks about baby boomers' problems.

Details

4. The author says his generation is often accused of all but which one of the following?
   a. being too numerous and demanding
   b. threatening the financial stability of social security
   c. using too much air, food, water, and health care
   d. taking jobs that should go to younger people

5. The author has pursued all but which one of the following careers?
   a. insurance salesman
   b. university instructor
   c. naval officer during World War II
   d. corporate executive

6. Now that he is retired, the author says that he has the leisure to be a full-time
   a. lecturer.
   b. teacher.

c. writer.
d. traveler.

7. The author says that he finds the world
   a. confusing.
   b. disappointing.
   c. intensely boring.
   d. interesting but badly run.

8. In paragraph 8, the author's dominant organizational pattern is
   a. sequence: He relates a series of events in his typical day.
   b. generalization then example: He says that no part of his day is idle and lists examples to explain what he does.
   c. comparison and contrast: He compares his activities to those of other elderly people.
   d. process: He offers readers a plan for living a full and interesting life.

Inferences

9. If a *septuagenarian* is seventy or so years old and an *octogenarian* is eighty or so, then a *nonagenarian* (paragraph 3) is
   a. sixty or so.
   b. ninety or so.
   c. one hundred or so.
   d. of indeterminate age.

10. What the author enjoys most in his old age is
    a. writing.
    b. teaching.
    c. being with friends.
    d. walking in the park.

WORKING WITH WORDS

Complete the sentences below with these words from Word Alert:

inconspicuous	tribulations	maligned	begrudge
forbearance	posthumously	template	consign

1. Diandra showed great _____ in not eating the cookies when she wanted them so much.

2. Bats are one of the world's most _____ creatures only because so many people are offended by the way they look.

3. To make a calendar of your own, you can use my _____ as a guide.

4. Please do not _____ me the last piece of your cake; I will bake you another one.

5. When the author died, he left several manuscripts that his family agreed to have published _____ .

6. When a dog misbehaves, the most effective thing you can do is _____ him to the garage or somewhere else away from your company.

7. When Alden traveled to Ecuador and witnessed the _____ of poverty-stricken natives, he decided to stay and help.

8. If you do not want to be noticed, wear _____ clothing in neutral colors and conventional styles.

THINKING DEEPER

Ideas for discussion and writing

1. Discuss the author's careers and interests and the way he is spending his retirement. In what way is he similar to or different from elderly people that you know?

2. Discuss elderly people who have made a significant contribution to society. Who are these people, what have they done, and what makes them worthy of our respect and admiration?

3. Discuss how this selection illustrates the Part 3 theme, *Against All Odds*. For example, what can young people do now to lessen the odds that they will have poor health or inadequate income as they near old age? What are some of the tribulations of old age that the senior citizens you know are facing, and how are they dealing with them?

4. Write about an elderly person who taught you something of value.

FIRST THOUGHTS

To prepare yourself for the reading selection, answer the following questions, either on your own or in a group discussion.

1. What do you know about underdog racing or drag racing in general?

2. What kinds of cars do you think of when someone brings up the subject of drag racing?

3. Preview the title, headnote, and first one or two paragraphs. What do you think will follow?

WORD ALERT

emblem (4) symbol, badge, design
throwback (5) a reversion to a former type
staple (7) a basic element or feature
disparate (10) fundamentally different or distinct
unscathed (15) unharmed, uninjured
salvaged (16) rescued, saved from destruction or put to further use
tweaks (21) adjusts or fine-tunes, pinches or twists

❧ A Drag Racer

DAN MORSE

Dan Morse is a staff reporter for the Wall Street Journal, *in which this selection ran on May 25, 1999. He writes about a man who turns his Yugo's handicap to his advantage.*

D AVE BENTON REVS UP his engine as the announcer at Atco Race- 1 way calls the action over a scratchy public-address system. "Eighty cubic inches," announcer Max Scherwin tells the crowd of about 2,000. "I know motorcycles that got bigger motors than that."

And Mr. Benton is off. It's his third drag race of the morning, all in 2 a 1986 Yugo.

Let people laugh. 3

The arthritic 62-year-old challenges 17-foot dragsters, souped-up 4 Chevys, roaring Mustangs—taking full advantage of a handicapping system that gives his baby-blue hatchback up to an eight-second head start in quarter-mile dashes. Under the **emblem** "Underdog Racing," Mr. Benton has become something of a legend around New Jersey's weekend drag-racing circuit.

Mr. Benton is a **throwback** to a time when drag racing wasn't 5 about who could spend the most money muscling up a car. What drivers couldn't afford, they simply made themselves. A clutch release? Mr. Benton slapped an old air-conditioner magnet on the floorboard that he activates with a switch on the stick shift. To lighten the Yugo, he uses a battery from a garden tractor; gas is held in a 1-gallon oil tank taken from a Honda motorcycle.

In seven years of racing, he has cut his time to 14.785 seconds 6 from 21.9, hitting speeds of around 90 miles an hour.

But . . . a Yugo? The $3,990 car that Consumer Reports once called 7 "a grab bag of barely assembled nuts and bolts"? The vehicle that after it was launched with a slogan of "Everybody you know needs a Yugo" scored worst in its category on U.S. government crash tests? The car that for years became a **staple** on the joke circuit (Why do Yugos have rear-window defrosters? To keep your hands warm while you push it)?

Actually, in many ways, Mr. Benton is as unique as the Yugo.   8

A lifelong New Jersey resident, Mr. Benton was born with a club- 9 foot and wore a leg brace through grade school. At the age of nine, he took apart his first engine. "A '37 Chevy," Mr. Benton recalls. He remembers, he says, because "I never got it back together."

He studied forestry for a year in college but dropped out to pursue 10 a string of **disparate** careers: Porsche mechanic, cowboy, bulldozer operator, motivational speaker, instructor of automotive technology.

By 1986, Mr. Benton and his wife, Linda, a high-school math 11 teacher, decided to downsize from their '73 Cadillac and old Chrysler station wagon. The first compact they test-drove: an '86 Yugo GV. A half-mile into the ride, Mr. Benton was so taken by the car's pep and handling, they turned the thing around, zipped back to the dealer and bought it. As it happened, Yugo America Inc. was headquartered just up the road in Upper Saddle River. And in 1987, Mr. Benton got a job there, in the technical-services department.

Inside Yugo America, though, things weren't going well. The com- 12 pany had recalled its first 9,000 cars because some of the seat belts weren't bolted on according to specifications. And though Fortune magazine had singled the Yugo out as one of the products of the year in

1985, the car's sales fell consistently short of annual goals of 200,000; they never reached one-quarter of that.

In 1992, Yugo America filed for Chapter 17 bankruptcy liquida- 13 tion, stopped importing the vehicles and left American dealers to take dramatic measure to sell off inventory. One pitch: "Buy a Buick, Get a Free Yugo."

Mr. Benton was once again out of a job. But when his desire for an 14 inexpensive hobby drove him to New Jersey's amateur drag-racing circuit in 1992, Mr. Benton opted for the Yugo. His first quarter-mile time, 21.9 seconds, was only slightly faster than a greyhound could have run it.

One day, returning home from the Atco Raceway, Mr. Benton was 15 clipped by a passing Camaro. He was forced into the center guardrail, flipped four times—and walked away, **unscathed.** "Tough little cars," Mr. Benton says.

GETTING SERIOUS

After the wreck, Mr. Benton **salvaged** the 80 cubic-inch engine, Yugo's 16 largest ever, stuck it in a replacement Yugo he bought at a junkyard for $100 and really got serious about making a fast car.

Over the next five years, he ran about 400 races, generally compet- 17 ing in "bracket" divisions. Under that format, drivers submit the time they expect to run. Typically, Mr. Benton might submit a 14.91, while his competitor would post something like a 10.04. Then Mr. Benton would get his 4.87-second head start. The winner: whoever is closest to his predicted time—without going under it.

Still, he feels the need for speed. This winter, Mr. Benton rebuilt 18 the engine's short block, looking to shave more ticks off his time. And on May 15, he and two Yugo Underdog buddies—Pete Mulhern, 57, and Dave Greason, 63—have gathered in Mr. Benton's driveway to finish up the engine so Mr. Benton can unleash it the following day at the Atco Raceway.

Mr. Benton still limps. Mr. Mulhern also moves slowly: He has had 19 two heart attacks and suffers from emphysema. Mr. Greason, a diabetic, has had open-heart surgery and has a condition called essential tremor, which makes his head shake. He figures he doesn't have all that long to live. "It's winding down for me now," he says. "It's time to have some fun."

YUGO CENTRAL

Behind the three, a dark garage has been turned into a Yugo parts cen- 20
ter. Six engines lie on the floor. Exhaust systems rest against the wall.
Nuts and bolts are stored in old Planters Cheese Balls cans, or are scat-
tered on the concrete floor. The mess spills into the driveway, where
six parked Yugos extend into a weed-caked front yard.

Mr. Benton climbs behind the wheel, and flips the ignition 21
switch—piercing the quiet neighborhood with what sounds like a
lawn mower on steroids. Mr. Mulhern, wearing a white fishing cap and
reading glasses, **tweaks** the carburetor with a long, thin screwdriver.

Eventually, Mr. Benton declares the new engine ready for battle. 22

Early the next morning, Mr. Benton packs for the day: lunch, soft 23
drinks, a plastic sandwich-bag filled with vitamins and various medi-
cines. Mr. Mulhern arrives, and the two hitch the drag-Yugo to the
back of Mr. Benton's everyday-Yugo. They drive to the track, arriving
before most of the other racers, and start replacing the standard front
tires of the dragster with racing ones.

Within minutes, a younger man, Kevin Thomas, bounds up to 24
check out the car.

"I heard about you!" he says. "I heard about the Yugo!" Mr. 25
Thomas, who drags a Subaru station wagon, tells Mr. Benton he has a
turbo kit on order. "I want to become an Underdog too. I want to scare
some people."

DROPPING WEIGHT

Other racers and spectators wander by, some shaking their heads, 26
some laughing. But the jokes don't last long in this crowd. Mostly, it's
Mr. Benton's mechanical skills that impress his fellow racers—and
have helped him cut down the weight of the car to its current 1,340
pounds from about 2,000.

The morning goes well for Underdog Racing. On this day, Mr. Ben- 27
ton is racing only against cars his own size and speed, in the "Sports-
man Import" division. In his second practice run, Mr. Benton sets a
new personal record: 14.785 seconds.

He eventually loses in the semifinals to a Mazda RX-7, but he has 28
done well enough for a swing by the awards stand after the race.
He picks up a trophy, $85 in prize money (he has won money just
three times before) and climbs back into the dragster. En route to his
space in the pits, Mr. Benton drives by hundreds of fans and racers—

cracking open his driver's side door and thrusting the 18-inch gold trophy into the air. The crowd cheers.

Mr. Mulhern has been waiting patiently in his lawn chair, by now 29 exhausted from an afternoon in the warm sun.

"We did it again," Mr. Benton says, showing him the cash.   30

COMPREHENSION CHECK

Purpose and Main Idea

1. What is the author's topic?
    a. the Yugo automobile
    b. drag racing
    c. drag racer Dave Benton
    d. repairing cars

2. Which of the following sentences from the selection states the author's central idea?
    a. paragraph 1, first sentence "Dave Benton revs. . . ."
    b. paragraph 4, last sentence "Under the emblem. . . ."
    c. paragraph 5, first sentence "Mr. Benton is. . . ."
    d. paragraph 8, " Actually, . . . Mr. Benton. . . ."

3. The author's primary purpose is to
    a. persuade readers to take up drag racing.
    b. express his admiration for Dave Benton.
    c. inform us of the history of drag racing.
    d. entertain us with an account of Benton and his Yugo.

Details

4. Mr. Benson's drag racing record is
    a. 14.785 seconds.
    b. 21.9 seconds.
    c. 2.000 seconds.
    d. 17 seconds.

5. Benton has had all the following health or physical problems except which one?
    a. arthritis
    b. clubfoot
    c. diabetes
    d. a limp

6. Who or what influenced Benton to take up drag racing?
    a. his family

    b. the desire for an inexpensive hobby

    c. Mr. Mulhern and Mr. Greason

    d. Yugo America, for which he worked

7. Benton's fellow racers are impressed most by his
    a. personality.
    b. physical condition.
    c. racing ability.
    d. mechanical skills.

8. In paragraphs 12 and 13, the author's organizational pattern is
    a. sequence.
    b. cause and effect.
    c. comparison and contrast.
    d. classification.

Inferences

9. In paragraph 25, why do you suppose Mr. Thomas thinks his Subaru is a candidate for underdog racing?
    a. The Subaru is a car that people laugh at.
    b. Like the Yugo, it is an unlikely racing car.
    c. He does the mechanical work on the car himself.
    d. It is an inexpensive car.

10. Why do people laugh at the Yugo as a racing car?
    a. The Yugo is an inexpensive car.
    b. In 1985 Fortune named it one of the products of the year.
    c. It scored poorly on government crash tests.
    d. The Yugo has a reputation for being poorly made.

WORKING WITH WORDS

Complete the sentences below with these words from Word Alert:

    unscathed   disparate   emblem   tweaks
    throwback   salvaged   staple

1. Caroline emerged from the accident _____ except for a tiny scratch on her forehead.

2. After the fire, some of the family's possessions could be _____, but others were destroyed.

3. Bread is a _____ of the diet in most parts of the world.

4. Sometimes when Steve's computer locks up, he _____ one of the wires to get it working again.

5. Since our research needs are _____ , the methods that work for me may not work for you.

6. Our uniform consists of navy pants or skirt and a red blazer with the company's _____ on the pocket.

7. Deadly Nightshade's latest album is a _____ to their early years as a musical group.

THINKING DEEPER

Ideas for discussion and writing

1. Discuss how Dave Benton became a drag racer and why he chose the Yugo.

2. Discuss other people you have known who have pursued an interest in unconventional ways and have achieved success.

3. Discuss how this selection illustrates the Part 3 theme, *Against All Odds*. For example, how are the Yugo's reputation and Benton's age and physical condition working against him as a drag racer? How has he overcome these odds?

4. Write about a hobby or personal interest that has enhanced the quality of your life.

FIRST THOUGHTS

To prepare yourself for the reading selection, answer the following questions, either on your own or in a group discussion.

1. What do you know about the Spanish Inquisition?

2. What happened to Spanish Jews during the Inquisition?

3. Preview the title, headnote, and first one or two paragraphs. What do you think will follow?

WORD ALERT

expulsion (1) the act of being driven out or forced to leave

refuge (1) protection, shelter, safety

unleavened (2) lacking an agent such as yeast that causes rising, as with bread

nominally (3) existing in name only, insignificant

linger (9) to remain, to be slow in leaving

cognizance (10) knowledge, recognition, awareness

saga (11) a long, detailed report

compelling (12) urgently requiring attention, forcing

obscurity (14) the state of being unknown or difficult to understand

genealogy (22) a record of a person's or family's descent, lineage

intermediary (24) one who acts as a mediator or a go-between

exhilarated (27) refreshed, energized, invigorated

confiscated (32) seized by authority or as if by authority

vengeance (35) punishment in return for a wrong, extreme violence or force

❧ Scholars and Descendants

KATHLEEN TELTSCH

In this selection we learn what scholars have uncovered about Spanish Jews who settled in the American West and their descendants.

"Scholars and Descendants," Kathleen Teltsch, NEW YORK TIMES, November 11, 1990. Copyright © 2000 by the New York Times Co. Reprinted with permission.

A FTER SEVERAL CENTURIES, scholars are uncovering the history of 1
Spanish Jews who converted to Catholicism under threat of **expulsion** by Spain's monarchs in 1492 and then found **refuge** and obscurity in the mountains of New Mexico.

Although most of these early colonizers lived as practicing Cathol- 2
ics, a significant number, often called "conversos," continued to cling
secretly to Jewish traditions, lighting candles on Fridays, reciting Hebrew prayers, circumcising baby boys, baking **unleavened** bread,
keeping the Sabbath.

Researchers are now finding evidence that some **nominally** Chris- 3
tian families have handed down Jewish traditions, and have done it
amid a fear-inspired secrecy that seems hardly to have lessened over
five centuries.

In the past two or three years, in remote areas of the Southwest, 4
hundreds of gravestones have been found in old Christian cemeteries
with Hebrew inscriptions or Jewish symbols often combined with the
cross.

Stimulated by the scholarly inquiries, or on their own, young de- 5
scendants of converso families are searching to find their roots, Jewish
and Christian, and comparing their findings.

A few of these descendants have returned to Judaism. Others are 6
slowly establishing fragile ties to mainstream Jewish congregations.

"I've been here 20 years, and only in the last two or three, after ob- 7
serving me carefully, a handful of these people have made contact
with me," said Rabbi Isaac Celnik of Congregation B'nai Israel in Albuquerque.

Some come to services, always sitting by themselves, he said. He 8
has been invited five or six times to their homes to lead prayers, often
because an elderly relative wants to renew ties to the ancient faith.

Still, distrust toward outsiders **lingers.** "These people lived in fear 9
of persecution for so long, they still look over their shoulders," Rabbi
Celnik said. "They are historically conditioned over centuries to be
suspicious and alert."

HERITAGE OF SECRECY IS HANDED DOWN

There are perhaps 1,500 families in New Mexico who have some **cog-** 10
nizance of their Jewish heritage, said Frances Hernandez, a professor
of comparative literature at the University of Texas at El Paso. "They
range from those with only blurred memories of Jewish customs or
family legends to others who really are aware of their Judaic background

and know what it means," she said. "We're talking of people who survived 200 generations of stress and secrecy, and it's a wonder anything
survives."

In pursuing the conversos' **saga,** historians are interviewing fami- 11
lies and using data in church records in Mexico City and New Mexico
on baptisms, weddings and burials. They have also examined Spanish
shipping manifests dating from the 1490's.

A few months before Columbus's voyage in 1492, Spain enacted 12
the Edict of Expulsion, **compelling** Jews to leave or convert to Catholicism under threat of death. Perhaps half of the estimated 200,000 Jews
in Spain began an exodus to Portugal, other European countries and
North Africa. Others became "New Christians."

But even New Christians who prospered found themselves still 13
persecuted, possibly out of envy. And some only pretended to convert.
Under continuing pressure from the Inquisition, which began to be
felt in Portugal as well, some of the persecuted seized opportunities to
come to the New World.

When the Inquisition stretched its reach to Mexico, they fled 14
again, crossing deserts and hostile Indian country to the frontier of
what is now New Mexico. There they found a measure of safety and
obscurity.

"We only have started to scrape the surface," said Dr. Stanley 15
Hordes, co-director of a research project on the secret Jews, or "Crypto-
Jews," at the University of New Mexico's Latin American Institute.

Dr. Hordes, who spoke at the recent third annual meeting of the 16
New Mexico Jewish Historical Society, believes that converso families
who fled to remote areas like New Mexico's Mora, Charma and Rio
Grande valleys could have settled the first Jewish community in what
is now the United States.

But other historians and Jewish scholars dispute Dr. Hordes's con- 17
clusion, saying Christian families carrying on some Jewish practices
or dietary laws do not constitute a Jewish community. Shearith Israel,
the Spanish and Portuguese Synagogue established in New Amster-
dam in 1654, is considered the first Jewish congregation in North
America.

Rabbi Marc D. Angel of Shearith Israel said the remnants of 18
Crypto-Jews in New Mexico was a tribute to the human spirit, but he
questioned the claim to an early community.

"What concerns me is that because of their dramatic story with a 19
movie-like quality, there will be an eagerness to receive them into Judaism and forget there is a formal procedure for re-entry after separa-

tion that requires instruction, patience and sincerity," he said. "There are no short-cuts."

GETTING TO KNOW DISTANT RELATIVES

Dr. Hordes's own inquiry began in 1981 soon after he became New 20 Mexico state historian. His doctoral dissertation at Tulane University was about Crypto-Judaism in Mexico in the 17th century.

"People began dropping into my office, leaning across my desk 21 and whispering, 'You know, so-and-so lights candles and does not eat pork.'" Repeated such visits led him to undertake the research project, together with Dr. Thomas C. Atencio, a sociologist at the University of New Mexico.

Since 1988, they have interviewed almost 50 converso families, in- 22 cluding many who practiced Jewish customs without understanding them, because their families had done so. In the process, the researchers introduced descendants who did not know they were related and who now are comparing their own **genealogy** searches.

Daniel Yocum, a 23-year-old engineering student, suspected 23 he had Jewish roots on his mother's side. He discovered a wedding photograph of his late grandfather wearing a fringed prayer shawl. He has boyhood memories of him baking round, unleavened bread at certain seasons and butchering livestock in the traditional Jewish way.

Nora Garcia Herrera, his mother, elaborates on her son's recollec- 24 tions, recalling that her father and mother disagreed about the family's religious practices. "He said it was all right not to kneel to the saints because you don't need an **intermediary** to talk to God," she recalled. She objected and called him "Judio," Spanish for "Jew," which her children guessed was a bad word. Her father and grandfather were circumcised by an old man in their community. When he died, her father carved a gravemarker with a Star of David.

Ramon Salas, 26, a manufacturing analyst at Digital Equipment in 25 Albuquerque, discovered that he was related to Daniel Yocum after tracing his own lineage 17 generations. He computerized his findings and says he has found evidence that Crypto-Jewish families, who often intermarried, used code names so they would recognize each other.

Mr. Salas said that, when he asked another cousin if they shared 26 Jewish roots, she shot back, "Use your good Jewish head and you'll come to the realization you have Jewish blood."

"I remember I was **exhilarated;** it knocked my head off," Mr. Salas 27
said. But as one who was raised as a Catholic, and in the eyes of his
church will always be a Catholic, he is torn about making a choice. Judaism has an appeal—he lights Sabbath candles—but he does not
want to lose his attachment to the Catholic community.

MEMORY AND MYTH ARE INTERTWINED

Dennis Duran, a corporate official who lives in Santa Fe, came to the 28
historical society meeting with a copy of his family tree going back 14
generations and showing his kinship to the Salas family. He has col-
lected data suggesting their ancestors were among the Jews who came
with Don Juan de Oñate in 1598 to colonize New Mexico. Mr. Duran,
who is 36, formally converted to Judaism even before beginning his
search for his Jewish heritage.

He has recollections of his grandfather secretly praying daily at 29
sundown in a cellar where the family kept fruit and wine, and of playing games as a child with tops, similar to the dreidel of Jewish origin.

Paul Marez, a 24-year-old graduate student, is the only one in his 30
family who attends temple services. Family members are practicing
Catholics, but he recalls his grandmother preparing for the Sabbath
and, after a relative's death, observing a period of mourning and turning mirrors to the wall, as in the Jewish custom.

A number of the young adults are counseled about Judaism by 31
Loggie Carrasco, a teacher with a magnetic style. Rabbi Celnik calls
her Mama Loggie. "Young people look to her for validation because
she is so knowledgeable," he said. "She is their rabbi."

Ms. Carrasco said she has traced her family to Seville and Madrid 32
in the early 1600's. She said one ancestor, Manuel Carrasco, was tried
in Mexico City by the Inquisition in 1648 for carrying matzo under his
hat, which he tried to explain was a remedy for headache. His sugar
plantations were **confiscated** and he disappeared.

While protectively withholding the names of conversos, Rabbi 33
Celnik said that for many months he gave religious instruction to an
artist from Taos who came weekly, arising at 4 a.m. to travel here. The
rabbi also prayed with a dying elderly woman who lived as a Catholic
but cherished her Jewish roots.

"I went to see her in the hospital," he said. "Her eyes brightened 34
when I came into the room, and she recognized me. It happened to
be Passover, and I placed a morsel of matzo on her lip. It meant a lot
to her."

STARTING TO RECONCILE TWO DISPARATE FAITHS

Rabbi Celnik said that, among the conversos who go to church, there 35
is a segment that very much wants to return to Judaism. An equally
small segment want to be Catholic and Jewish; they are comfortable in
both traditions. "But there also is a very small group committed to
vengeance against those who return to Judaism, and this is regarded
as a genuine threat," the rabbi said. "They are afraid of their own
cousins."

Rabbi Celnik said this may be the opportune moment for Crypto- 36
Jews to embrace their heritage openly because 1992 marks the 500th
anniversary of both Columbus's voyage and the Expulsion Edict.

The International Jewish Committee, Sepharad '92, formed to 37
commemorate the the anniversary of the expulsion, would welcome
the support of the New Mexicans, said Andre Sassoon, the committee
vice president.

Would they be regarded as genuinely Jewish? "We're a tolerant 38
people," Mr. Sassoon said.

"Personally, whether someone is truly a Jew or not, only God can 39
judge, and not mortals."

COMPREHENSION CHECK

Purpose and Main Idea

1. What is the author's topic?
    a. the Old West
    b. New Mexico's secret Jews
    c. Judaism
    d. Catholicism

2. The author's central idea is stated in
    a. paragraph 1, "After several. . . ."
    b. paragraph 2, "Although most. . . ."
    c. paragraph 3, "Researchers are. . . ."
    d. paragraph 5, "Stimulated by. . . ."

3. The author's purpose is to
    a. express her own religious beliefs.
    b. persuade readers to search out their religious roots.
    c. inform readers about New Mexico's secret Jews.
    d. entertain readers with reports of strange religious rituals.

Details

4. According to the author, scholars have uncovered
    a. practicing Catholics living in New Mexico.
    b. ancient recipes for making unleavened bread.
    c. the history of Spanish Jews who converted to Catholicism.
    d. the reason the Jews left Spain.

5. Historians are using all but which one of the following sources to uncover the *conversos'* saga?
    a. interviews with families
    b. court records
    c. data from church records
    d. Spanish shipping manifestos

6. Spanish Jews came to New Mexico because they
    a. sought economic freedom.
    b. were fleeing the Spanish Inquisition.
    c. preferred New Mexico to other places.
    d. had relatives in the west.

7. Evidence of the secret Jews' existence consists of all of the following except which one?
    a. gravestones engraved with Hebrew symbols found in Christian cemeteries
    b. Christians who have handed down Jewish traditions
    c. family members who disagree about their family's religious practices
    d. Jews who have no question about their heritage

8. The author's organizational pattern in paragraph 2 is
    a. process.
    b. definition.
    c. sequence.
    d. classification.

Inferences

9. Based on the details in paragraph 29, a *dreidel* is
    a. a child's toy.
    b. an adult game.
    c. a book.
    d. a puzzle.

10. Some historians and scholars do not believe that New Mexico's secret Jews were the first Jewish community, probably because
    a. Christian families practiced Jewish customs.
    b. Christians observed Jewish dietary laws.

c. they practiced Judaism secretly rather than communally.
d. they were Christians, not Jews.

WORKING WITH WORDS

Complete the sentences below with these words from Word Alert:

intermediary	unleavened	obscurity	refuge
confiscated	cognizance	expulsion	saga
exhilarated	vengeance	nominally	
compelling	genealogy	linger	

1. When two people are quarreling, a neutral party may serve as the _____ to help them resolve their differences.

2. When a storm broke at the theme park, visitors ran into the stores seeking _____ from the lightning and heavy rain.

3. It was only after their _____ from school that the students realized the seriousness of what they had done.

4. If you spill a bottle of perfume on the floor, the fragrance may still _____ even after mopping.

5. The thought of sleep was so _____ that Angela decided to put off studying and take a nap.

6. People in search of their family's roots may decide to have their _____ traced.

7. In the Old West, an outlaw would seek _____ on someone who had wronged him.

8. _____ bread is a traditional Jewish food served at Passover and other meals.

9. After a brief period of fame, some celebrities spend the rest of their lives in _____ .

10. On a tip from the landlord, the police broke into the apartment and _____ thousands of dollars worth of stolen property.

11. Tony always feels _____ after an exciting game of racquetball.

12. The detective asked the accused bank robbers if they had any _____ of their partner's whereabouts.

13. Although _____ a member of the organization, Terry did not participate in its activities.

14. Let me know when you have several hours to kill, and I will
    tell you the _____ of my first attempt to get my driver's
    license.

THINKING DEEPER

Ideas for discussion and writing

1. Discuss the meaning of the title "Scholars and Descendants" as it
   relates to the author's central idea and details.
2. Discuss how this selection is about a past that was lost and then
   recovered.
3. Discuss how this selection illustrates the Part 3 theme, *Against All
   Odds*. For example, throughout history people have been willing
   to do almost anything to protect their religious freedom. In this
   selection, how did the Spanish Jews avoid persecution?
4. Write about something important that you lost and then recovered, or write about something you lost that you wish you could
   recover.

29

FIRST THOUGHTS

To prepare yourself for the reading selection, answer the following questions, either on your own or in a group discussion.

1. What do you know about parables, fables, or folktales?
2. What is the purpose of such a story?
3. Preview the title, headnote, and first one or two paragraphs. What do you think will follow?

WORD ALERT

fetlocks (1) tufts of hair above and behind a horse's hooves
anlage (1) foundation for a future development, potential
threshed (2) beat, stomped, tossed about
embankment (2) mound of earth or stone built to hold back water or support a roadway
parapet (2) a low protective wall or railing
peered (2) looked intently or searchingly
fraction (4) fragment, small amount or part

❧ From *The Grapes of Wrath*

JOHN STEINBECK

John Steinbeck is one of our great American authors. His novel The Grapes of Wrath, *from which this selection is taken, is about the plight of migrant workers who fled the dust bowl during the Depression to find work picking fruit and vegetables in California. This selection is Chapter Three of the book, and many have called it a parable, or instructive tale.*

THE CONCRETE HIGHWAY was edged with a mat of tangled, broken, 1
dry grass, and the grass heads were heavy with oat beards to catch

"Chapter 3", from *The Grapes of Wrath* by John Steinbeck, copyright 1939, renewed © 1967 by John Steinbeck. Used by permission of Viking Penguin, a division of Penguin Putnam Group (USA), Inc.

on a dog's coat, and foxtails to tangle in a horse's **fetlocks,** and clover
burrs to fasten in sheep's wool; sleeping life waiting to be spread and
dispersed, every seed armed with an appliance of dispersal, twisting
darts and parachutes for the wind, little spears and balls of tiny thorns,
and all waiting for animals and for the wind, for a man's trouser cuff or
the hem of a woman's skirt, all passive but armed with appliances of
activity, still, but each possessed of the **anlage** of movement.

The sun lay on the grass and warmed it, and in the shade under 2
the grass the insects moved, ants and ant lions to set traps for them,
grasshoppers to jump into the air and flick their yellow wings for a second, sow bugs like little armadillos, plodding restlessly on many tender feet. And over the grass at the roadside a land turtle crawled,
turning aside for nothing, dragging his high-domed shell over the
grass. His hard legs and yellow-nailed feet **threshed** slowly through
the grass, not really walking, but boosting and dragging his shell
along. The barley beards slid off his shell, and the clover burrs fell on
him and rolled to the ground. His horny beak was partly open, and his
fierce, humorous eyes, under brows like fingernails, stared straight
ahead. He came over the grass leaving a beaten trail behind him, and
the hill, which was the highway **embankment,** reared up ahead of
him. For a moment he stopped, his head held high. He blinked and
looked up and down. At last he started to climb the embankment.
Front clawed feet reached forward but did not touch. The hind feet
kicked his shell along, and it scraped on the grass, and on the gravel.
As the embankment grew steeper and steeper, the more frantic were
the efforts of the land turtle. Pushing hind legs strained and slipped,
boosting the shell along, and the horny head protruded as far as the
neck could stretch. Little by little the shell slid up the embankment
until at last a **parapet** cut straight across its line of march, the shoulder
of the road, a concrete wall four inches high. As though they worked
independently the hind legs pushed the shell against the wall. The
head upraised and **peered** over the wall to the broad smooth plain of
cement. Now the hands, braced on top of the wall, strained and lifted,
and the shell came slowly up and rested its front end on the wall. For a
moment the turtle rested. A red ant ran into the shell, into the soft skin
inside the shell, and suddenly head and legs snapped in, and the ar-
mored tail clamped in sideways. The red ant was crushed between
body and legs. And one head of wild oats was clamped into the shell by
a front leg. For a long moment the turtle lay still, and then the neck
crept out and the old humorous frowning eyes looked about and the
legs and tail came out. The back legs went to work, straining like ele-

phant legs, and the shell tipped to an angle so that the front legs could not reach the level cement plain. But higher and higher the hind legs boosted it, until at last the center of balance was reached, the front tipped down, the front legs scratched at the pavement, and it was up. But the head of wild oats was held by its stem around the front legs.

Now the going was easy, and all the legs worked, and the shell 3 boosted along, waggling from side to side. A sedan driven by a forty-year-old woman approached. She saw the turtle and swung to the right, off the highway, the wheels screamed and a cloud of dust boiled up. Two wheels lifted for a moment and then settled. The car skidded back onto the road, and went on, but more slowly. The turtle jerked into its shell, but now it hurried on, for the highway was burning hot.

And now a light truck approached, and as it came near, the driver 4 saw the turtle and swerved to hit it. His front wheel struck the edge of the shell, flipped the turtle like a tiddly-wink, spun it like a coin, and rolled it off the highway. The truck went back to its course along the right side. Lying on its back, the turtle was tight in its shell for a long time. But at last its legs waved in the air, reaching for something to pull it over. Its front foot caught a piece of quartz and little by little the shell pulled over and flopped upright. The wild oat head fell out and three of the spearhead seeds stuck in the ground. And as the turtle crawled on down the embankment, its shell dragged dirt over the seeds. The turtle entered a dust road and jerked itself along, drawing a wavy shallow trench in the dust with its shell. The old humorous eyes looked ahead, and the horny beak opened a little. His yellow toe nails slipped a **fraction** in the dust.

COMPREHENSION CHECK

Purpose and Main Idea

1. What is the author's topic?
   a. the desert landscape
   b. desert weather conditions
   c. a busy highway
   d. a land turtle's journey

2. Which of the following best states the central idea of the selection?
   a. A desert highway is a dangerous place for both animals and people.
   b. A turtle crosses a highway, carrying on nature's processes.

    c. The desert landscape is filled with life.

    d. Dust and heat are characteristic of desert weather.

3. The author's *primary* purpose is to

    a. express his feelings about nature.

    b. teach readers facts about turtles.

    c. describe desert life.

    d. relate an instructive story.

Details

4. The turtle in this story is

    a. very young.

    b. old.

    c. in the middle of its life.

    d. of indeterminate age.

5. In the first paragraph the author describes the process of

    a. plant growth.

    b. fertilization.

    c. seed dispersal.

    d. soil erosion.

6. What did the turtle do when he came to the embankment?

    a. He stopped and remained at the foot of it.

    b. He walked in the opposite direction.

    c. He crawled parallel to it.

    d. He climbed to the top of it.

7. What became lodged under the turtle's shell?

    a. a clover burr

    b. a head of wild oats

    c. an ant lion

    d. a sow bug

8. The author's details are mainly

    a. facts.

    b. examples.

    c. descriptions.

    d. reasons.

Inferences

9. Based on the details in paragraph 4, what has happened to the oat seeds?

    a. Insects ate them.

b. The turtle destroyed them.

c. They have died.

d. They have been planted.

10. The best statement of this tale's underlying message is that

a. if you want to get somewhere, you have to cross the road.

b. some mountains are too high to climb.

c. the potential for survival is part of our nature.

d. nature can be an unfriendly place.

WORKING WITH WORDS

Complete the sentences below with these words from Word Alert:

embankment	fraction	anlage	parapet
fetlocks	threshed	peered	

1. The little boy _____ from between the blinds, watching his dad leave for work.

2. We live in a beautiful city where even the _____ below the interstate highway is planted with flowers.

3. Don't tempt me with even a _____ of a slice of that pie because I am trying to watch my weight.

4. The telephone line workers _____ through my yard in their heavy boots, smashing my flowers.

5. Holding the small egg that had fallen out of the nest, Tina knew that it possessed the _____ of life.

6. We climbed to the top of the tower and stood along a _____ looking out across a wide valley.

7. After the race, the horse's _____ were wet with sweat.

THINKING DEEPER

Ideas for discussion and writing

1. Trace the turtle's journey. Where is he going, and what happens along the way?

2. Discuss Steinbeck's use of descriptive details. Identify passages in the story that create especially vivid images in your mind.

3. Discuss how this selection illustrates the Part 3 theme, *Against All Odds*. For example, life is a struggle for all living things—including humans. If tales are meant to be instructive, then what does this one teach us by the example of the turtle's journey and the oat seed's progress?

4. Write about a process of nature or a natural wonder that has always fascinated you.

FIRST THOUGHTS

To prepare yourself for the reading selection, answer the following questions, either on your own or in a group discussion.

1. What does the term *baby boom* mean to you?
2. What do you know about post–World War II prosperity in America?
3. Preview the title, headnote, and first one or two paragraphs. What do you think will follow?

WORD ALERT

In a textbook chapter, the words to watch may appear in boldface, italics, or a special color.

prosperity (1) wealth, affluence
recessions (1) extended declines in business activity
per capita (3) per person
suburbs (6) residential areas near a city
homogenized (8) made similar, became uniform
mergers (14) acts of blending two companies together or of one company absorbing another
inflation (16) persistent increase in prices or decline in purchasing power
consolidation (17) combining or uniting into one system
indicted (19) accused of wrongdoing

❧ The Postwar Booms: Babies, Business, and Bigness

MARY BETH NORTON, DAVID M. KATZMAN, DAVID W. BLIGHT, HOWARD P. CHUDACOFF, THOMAS G. PETERSON, WILLIAM M. TUTTLE, JR., PAUL D. ESCOTT, AND WILLIAM J. BROPHY

This textbook reading is excerpted from Chapter 28 of A People and a Nation, *Brief Sixth Edition. The entire chapter is*

about postwar America from 1945 to 1961. The excerpt
focuses on widespread growth in America's population and
economy. When reading from textbooks, remember that
headings may signal topics, main ideas, or important details.

THE POSTWAR ECONOMIC boom proved to be one of the longest pe- 1
riods of growth and **prosperity** the United States ever experienced. Its keys were increasing output and increasing demand. Despite
occasional **recessions** the gross national product more than doubled
between 1945 and 1961.

THE AFFLUENT SOCIETY

The Harvard economist John Kenneth Galbraith gave a name to the 2
United States during the postwar economic boom: the "affluent society." As U.S. productivity increased in the postwar years, so did Americans' appetite for goods and services. In the flush postwar years,
Americans bought as never before. Some families purchased two cars
and equipped their new homes with the latest appliances and amuse-
ments, such as television. Easy credit was the economic basis of the
consumer culture; when people lacked cash to buy what they wanted,
they borrowed money.

INCREASED PURCHASING POWER

When the economy produced more, Americans generally brought 3
home bigger paychecks and had more money to spend. Between the
end of the war and 1950, **per capita** real income (based on actual purchasing power) rose 6 percent. In the 1950s it jumped another 15 percent, and in the 1960s the increase was 32 percent. The result was a
noticeable increase in the standard of living. To the vast majority of
Americans, such prosperity was a vindication of the American system
of free enterprise.

BABY BOOM

The baby boom was both a cause and an effect of prosperity. After the 4
war the birth rate soared, and it continued to do so throughout the

From: Norton et al., *A People And A Nation*, Brief 6th Ed., (Boston: Houghton Mifflin, 2003),
501–503.

1950s. During the 1950s, the number of births exceeded 4 million per year, reversing the downward trend in birth rates that had prevailed for 150 years. Births began to decline after 1961 but continued to exceed 4 million per year through 1964. The baby-boom generation was the largest by far in the nation's history.

The baby boom meant business for builders, manufacturers, and 5 school systems. "Take the 3,548,000 babies born in 1950," wrote Sylvia F. Porter in her syndicated newspaper column. "Bundle them into a batch, bounce them all over the bountiful land that is America. What do you get?" Porter's answer: "Boom. The biggest, boomiest boom ever known in history."

Of the three cornerstones of the postwar economic boom— 6 construction, automobiles, and defense—two were directly related to the upsurge in births. Demand for housing and schools for all these children generated a building boom, furthered by construction of shopping centers, office buildings, and airports. Much of this construction took place in the **suburbs**. The postwar suburbanization of America in turn would have been impossible without automobile manufacturing, for the car provided access to the sprawling new communities.

HOUSING BOOM

Government funding helped new families to settle in the suburbs. 7 Low-interest GI mortgages and Federal Housing Administration (FHA) mortgage insurance made the difference for people who otherwise would have been unable to afford a home. This easy credit, combined with postwar prosperity, produced a construction boom. From 1945 to 1946, housing starts climbed from 326,000 to more than 1 million; they approached 2 million in 1950 and remained above 1.3 million in 1961. Never before had new starts exceeded 1 million.

HIGHWAY CONSTRUCTION

As suburbia spread, pastures became neighborhoods with astounding 8 rapidity. Highway construction was a central element in the transformation of rural land into suburbia. In 1947 Congress authorized construction of a 37,000-mile chain of highways, and in 1956 President Eisenhower signed the Highway Act, which approved funds for a 42,500-mile interstate highway system. Federal expenditures on highways swelled from $79 million in 1946 to $2.6 billion in 1961. State and local spending on highways also mushroomed. Highways both hastened suburbanization and **homogenized** the landscape. The high-speed trucking that highways made possible also accelerated the integration of the South into the national economy.

GROWTH OF THE SUBURBS

In the twenty-five years after the war, a mass movement was under 9 way from the cities to the suburbs. By 1970 more people lived in suburbs than in cities or in rural areas. A combination of motives drew people to the suburbs. Some wanted to leave behind the noise and smells of the city. Some white families moved out of urban neighborhoods because African American families were moving in. Many wanted houses that had yards, family rooms, extra closets, and utility rooms. People were also looking for a place where they could have a measure of political influence, particularly on the education their children received.

Highway construction in combination with the growth of subur- 10 bia produced a new phenomenon, the *megalopolis,* a term coined in the early 1960s to refer to the almost uninterrupted metropolitan complex stretching from Boston 600 miles south through New York, Philadelphia, and Baltimore all the way to Washington, D.C. "Boswash" encompassed parts of eleven states and a population of 49 million people, all linked by interstate highways. Other megalopolises also took shape.

GROWTH OF THE SUNBELT

Millions of Americans began their search for affluence by migrating to 11 the Sunbelt—roughly, the southern third of the United States. The mass migration to the Sunbelt had started during the war, when GIs and their families were ordered to new duty stations and war workers moved to defense plants in the West and South. The economic bases of the Sunbelt's spectacular growth were defense contractors, such as the aerospace industry, agribusiness, the oil industry, real-estate development, and recreation. Industry was drawn to the southern rim by right-to-work laws, which outlawed closed shops, and by low taxes. Government policies—generous tax breaks for oil companies, siting of military bases, and awarding of defense and aerospace contracts—were crucial to the Sunbelt's development.

MILITARY SPENDING

The third cornerstone of the postwar economic boom was military 12
spending. Between 1947 and 1961 the annual defense budget increased from $10 billion to $98 billion. Many defense contracts went
to industries and universities to develop weapons, and the government supported space research. Defense spending also helped stimu-
late rapid advances in the electronics industry. The ENIAC computer,
completed at the University of Pennsylvania in 1946, required 18,000
vacuum tubes. Then, in the 1950s, introduction of the transistor accelerated the computer revolution; the silicon microchip in the
1960s inaugurated even more stunning advances in electronics. The
microchip facilitated the shift from heavy manufacturing to high-
technology industries in fiber optics, lasers, video equipment, robot-
ics, and genetic engineering.

The evolution of electronics meant a large-scale tradeoff for the 13
American people. As industries automated, computerized processes
replaced slower mechanical ones, increasing productivity but pushing people out of jobs. Electronic technology also promoted concentration of ownership in industry. Sophisticated technology was
expensive, and small corporations were shut out of the market. Indeed, large corporations with capital and experience in high-tech
fields expanded into related industries.

CONGLOMERATE MERGERS

Corporate expansion was also marked by a third great wave of **merg-** 14
ers. The first two such movements, in the 1890s and 1920s, had tended
toward vertical and horizontal integration, respectively. The postwar
era was distinguished by conglomerate mergers. A *conglomerate* brings
together companies in unrelated industries as a hedge against insta-
bility in a particular market. International Telephone and Telegraph
(IT&T), for instance, bought up companies in several fields, including
suburban development, insurance, and hotels.

LABOR MERGER

The labor movement also experienced a postwar merger. In 1955 the 15
American Federation of Labor and the Congress of Industrial Organizations finally put aside their differences and formed the AFL-CIO.

Union membership grew slowly during the postwar years, increasing from 14.8 million in 1945 to 17.3 million in 1961. The main reason for the slow growth of union membership was a shift in employment patterns. Most new jobs were being created not in the heavy industries that hired blue-collar workers but in the union-resistant white-collar service trades.

The postwar economic boom was good for unionized blue-collar 16 workers, many of whom won real increases in wages sufficient to enjoy a middle-class lifestyle that previously had been the exclusive province of white-collar workers and professionals. And they were more protected against **inflation:** in 1948 General Motors and the United Auto Workers agreed on automatic cost-of-living adjustments (COLAs) in workers' wages, a practice that spread to other industries.

AGRIBUSINESS

The trend toward economic consolidation also changed agriculture. 17 By the 1960s it took money—sometimes big money—to become a farmer. In many regions only banks, insurance companies, and large businesses could afford the necessary land, machinery, and fertilizer. The movement toward **consolidation** threatened the survival of the family farm. From 1945 to 1961 the nation's farm population declined from 24.4 million to 14.8 million.

ENVIRONMENTAL COSTS

Rapid economic growth also exacted environmental costs, to which 18 most Americans were oblivious. Steel mills, coal-powered generators, and internal-combustion car engines polluted the air and imperiled people's health. America's water supplies suffered as well. Human and industrial waste befouled many rivers and lakes. And the extraction of natural resources—strip mining of coal, for example—scarred the landscape, and toxic waste from chemical plants seeped deep into the soil.

Defense contractors and farmers were among the country's worst 19 polluters. Refuse from nuclear weapons facilities polluted soil and water resources for years. Agriculture began employing massive amounts of pesticides and other chemicals. A chemical called DDT, for example, which had been used on Pacific islands during the war to kill mosquitoes and lice, was released for public use in 1945. During the next fifteen years, farmers eliminated chronic pests with DDT. In 1962, however, *Silent Spring* by Rachel Carson, a wildlife biologist, specifically **indicted** DDT for the deaths of mammals, birds, and fish. Because of Carson's book, many Americans finally realized that there were costs to human conquest of the environment. The federal government finally banned the sale of DDT in 1972.

But America had become a "throwaway" society. With its plastic 20 cups, paper plates, disposable diapers, and products—especially cars— that were intentionally made less durable than they might have been, Americans used a disproportionate amount of the world's resources. By the 1960s the United States, with only 5 percent of the world's population, produced and consumed more than one-third of the world's goods and services.

COMPREHENSION CHECK

Purpose and Main Idea

1. What is the authors' topic?
    a. aftereffects of World War II
    b. population growth in the suburbs
    c. ups and downs in American business
    d. the postwar economic boom
2. Which sentence best states the central idea of the entire passage?
    a. paragraph 1, first sentence "The postwar economic boom. . . ."
    b. paragraph 2, second sentence "As U.S. productivity. . . ."
    c. paragraph 3, last sentence "To the vast majority. . . ."
    d. paragraph 4, first sentence "The baby boom. . . ."
3. The authors' primary purpose is to
    a. express their opinions about the social changes in postwar America.
    b. entertain readers with vivid examples of postwar American life.
    c. explain the events that characterized the postwar boom.
    d. persuade readers that the boom had environmental costs.

Details

4. Which one of the following do the authors say was both a cause and an effect of prosperity?
    a. increased purchasing power
    b. the baby boom

    c. highway construction

    d. low-cost housing

5. Which one of the following is the name John Kenneth Galbraith gave to postwar America?

    a. "the beat generation"

    b. "the baby-boom era"

    c. "the counterculture movement"

    d. "the affluent society"

6. Rachel Carson's *Silent Spring* cited which one of the following as an environmental cost of rapid economic growth?

    a. strip mining

    b. toxic waste

    c. damage from use of DDT

    d. human and industrial waste

7. Which one of the following was not a cornerstone of the economic boom?

    a. conglomerate mergers

    b. defense spending

    c. construction

    d. automobiles

8. The dominant organizational pattern in paragraph 10 is which one of the following?

    a. process

    b. definition

    c. comparison and contrast

    d. cause and effect

Inferences

9. In paragraph 20, the authors' details imply that by the 1960s, Americans had become

    a. secure.

    b. affluent.

    c. wasteful.

    d. intolerant.

10. Based on the details in paragraphs 18–20, you can infer that the authors would be most likely to support which one of the following?

    a. disposable syringes

    b. offshore oil drilling

    c. electric automobiles

    d. revival of our steel industry

WORKING WITH WORDS

Complete the sentences below with these words from Word Alert:

consolidation   prosperity   inflation   indicted   suburbs
homogenized   recessions   per capita   mergers

1. Some criticize the press for trying and convicting those who are accused of crimes before they are formally _____ .
2. When the economy is experiencing a downturn, it is normal to wish for a return to _____ .
3. High prices and the decline in the value of the dollar are two common signs of _____ in our economy.
4. Tired of battling city traffic, we moved to the _____ for a less hectic life.
5. Do you know which state has the lowest _____ income in America?
6. In recent years, our economy has seen _____ among many companies that own hotels, insurance firms, and other businesses.
7. The spread of fast-food chains and other businesses has _____ our communities, making them all look alike.
8. One way to get out from under debt is through _____ of bills and loans.
9. After several _____ , business owners may be reluctant to expand.

THINKING DEEPER

Ideas for discussion and writing

1. What similarities and differences do you see between the postwar economy described in this excerpt and today's economy?
2. What kind of life do you want for yourself in the future? How confident are you that you will be able to earn enough money to buy the things you need and want for yourself and your family? What plans have you made to prepare for your economic future?
3. Discuss how the postwar boom explained in this excerpt relates to the Part 3 theme, *Against All Odds*. For example, few expected that there would be a baby boom following World War II or that America's economy would explode with growth. Citing details

from the excerpt and from any other sources you can find, explain the effects that the postwar boom had on American life.

4. Just as these authors cite various events as the keys to America's postwar prosperity, much of history deals with analyzing the events and trends that define a certain era. Right now, America is focused on combating terrorism. In fact, some historians have said that the twenty-first century actually began with the terrorist attacks on our nation on September 11, 2001, and that these events will shape our history for years to come. What are some important events that have occurred in your lifetime? Consider court decisions, national defense, education, scientific discoveries, and anything else that has had a significant impact on American life. Then write about one of these events. Explain what happened and why you think it is important.

Hard Questions

❧

When you woke up this morning, you probably wondered what the weather was going to be like, what you should wear, and what you should eat. Questions like these are easy, and we answer them almost without thinking. Life's hard questions require time and thought, and some of them may seem unanswerable.

What can we do to improve race relations and employment opportunities? How can we cure intractable diseases and stop epidemics? How can we prevent crime and protect our homeland? Scholars, scientists, and others are attempting to find solutions to the problems that these questions address.

The Part 4 selections are about confronting the hard questions and searching for answers. As you read and think about the selections, ask yourself these questions: What problem or challenge must I confront? What help is available to me? What actions will I take?

FIRST THOUGHTS

To prepare yourself for the reading selection, answer the following questions, either on your own or in a group discussion.

1. What are some of the effects on the children of divorced parents?

2. What problems arise when divorced parents who share custody of a child live far apart?

3. Preview the title, headnote, and first one or two paragraphs. What do you think will follow?

WORD ALERT

custody (3) care, supervision, or control

unresolved (3) undecided, unsettled

convert (6) to persuade or induce to adopt a particular religion, faith, or belief

turbulence (6) disturbance, agitation

cameo (9) brief appearance, as of an actor in a film

toll (10) the amount of loss or destruction caused by a disaster

❧ My Long-Distance Life

NICK SHEFF

In this selection, the author explains what it is like to divide his time between two parents living in different towns. Nick Sheff wrote this selection for Newsweek's *My Word column when he was a junior at Marin Academy High School in San Rafael, California.*

I WAS BORN IN Berkeley, where I lived in a small house in the hills sur- 1
rounded by firs and redwoods. My mom, my dad and me. As early as I can remember, there was arguing. When I was 4, my parents decided that they could no longer live together.

That same year, my mom moved to Los Angeles, and a therapist 2
was hired to decide where I would live. My dad called her my worry

doctor. Playing with a dollhouse in her office, I showed her the mother's room on one side and the father's room on the other. When she asked me about the little boy's room, I told her he didn't know where he would sleep.

Though I was very young, I accepted my parents' separation and 3 divorce and somehow knew it wasn't my fault. Yet I was intensely afraid. Not only was my mom more than 500 miles away, but she had a new husband. My dad had a new girlfriend, and my **custody** was **unresolved.** Everyone said I'd spend time with both parents, but I wanted to know where I would live.

The therapist finally decided I'd stay with my dad during the 4 school year and visit my mom on long holidays and for the summers. I began flying between two cities and two different lives. I've probably earned enough miles for a round-trip ticket to Mars. Some people love to fly, but I dreaded the trips.

For the first year, one of my parents would accompany me on the 5 flights. At 6, I started traveling on my own. I would pack my toys and clothes in a Hello Kitty backpack and say goodbye to my parent at the gate. The flight attendant would lead me onto the plane.

When I was 7, the woman sitting next to me on the plane tried to 6 **convert** me to Christianity. A few years later I was on a flight with such bad **turbulence** that the luggage compartments opened and the man behind me threw up. When I was 12 and on my way to L.A. for Christmas, a lady refused to check her bag and shoved a flight attendant. We couldn't take off for two hours; the police came and dragged her off, to the cheering of other passengers. But flying was just part of what made long-distance joint custody so difficult.

I remember the last day of school in the sixth grade. All my friends 7 made plans to go to the beach together—all my friends, but not me. I couldn't join them because I had to fly to L.A. It wasn't that I didn't want to see my mom and stepdad. I just didn't want to leave my friends. As the school year came to a close, I began to shut down. I hated saying goodbye for the summer. It was easier to put up a wall, to pretend I didn't care. My dad drove to school with my packed bags. My friends went off together and I headed to the airport.

Arriving in L.A., I was excited to see my mom and stepdad. It had 8 been almost three months since my last visit. But it took a while to adjust. Each set of parents had different rules, values and concerns.

I am 16 now and I still travel back and forth, but it's mostly up to 9 me to decide when. I've chosen to spend more time with my friends at the expense of visits with my mom. When I do go to L.A., it's like my stepdad put it: I have a **cameo** role in their lives. I say my lines and I'm off. It's painful.

What's the **toll** of this arrangement? I'm always missing somebody. 10 When I'm in northern California, I miss my mom and stepdad. But when I'm in L.A., I miss hanging out with my friends, my other set of parents and little brother and sister. After all those back-and-forth flights, I've learned not to get too emotionally attached. I have to protect myself.

Many of my friends' parents are divorced. The ones whose mom 11 and dad live near each other get to see both their parents more. These kids can go to school plays and dances on the weekends, and see their friends when they want. But others have custody arrangements like mine. One friend whose dad moved to New Hampshire sees him at Christmas and for one month during the summer. My girlfriend's dad lives in Alaska. They know what I know: it's not fair.

No child should be subjected to the hardship of long-distance 12 joint custody. To prevent it, maybe there should be an addition to the marriage vows: Do you promise to have and to hold, for richer and for poorer, in sickness and in health, as long as you both shall live? And if you ever have children and wind up divorced, do you promise to stay within the same geographical area as your kids? Actually, since people often break those vows, maybe it should be a law: if you have children, you must stay near them. Or how about some common sense? If you move away from your children, *you* have to do the traveling to see them.

In two years I'll go to college. I'll be living away from both homes, 13 which will present new problems, such as where I will spend holidays. Whatever happens, I'll continue to build my relationships with both my parents, my siblings and my friends.

Before I have children of my own, I'll use my experiences to help 14 make good decisions about whom I choose to marry. However, if I do get a divorce, I will put my children's needs first. I will stay near them no matter what happens.

COMPREHENSION CHECK

Purpose and Main Idea

1. What is the author's topic?
   a. family therapy following divorce
   b. long-distance joint custody

    c. divorce in the United States

    d. reasons for separation

2. The central idea of this selection is stated in

    a. paragraph 1, last sentence "When I was 4. . . ."

    b. paragraph 3, first sentence "Though I was. . . ."

    c. paragraph 11, last sentence "They know what. . . ."

    d. paragraph 12, first sentence "No child should. . . ."

3. The author's primary purpose is to

    a. inform us about the research on children of divorce.

    b. express his views on the reasons that marriages fail.

    c. entertain readers with amusing incidents in his long-distance life.

    d. persuade readers that divorced parents should live close to their children.

Details

4. Sheff's parents separated when he was how many years old?

    a. 4

    b. 6

    c. 7

    d. 12

5. Sheff's mother lives in

    a. Berkeley.

    b. Alaska.

    c. Los Angeles.

    d. San Francisco.

6. As a young child, what was Sheff's attitude toward his parents' divorce?

    a. He did not accept it.

    b. He knew it was not his fault.

    c. He did not believe in divorce.

    d. He lost respect for both parents.

7. At age 16, Sheff chose to

    a. live with his mother.

    b. live with his father.

    c. spend more time with his friends.

    d. live with someone other than his parents.

8. The author's overall organizational pattern is

    a. definition: He defines the term *joint custody.*

b. comparison and contrast: He compares children of divorce to children of intact families.
c. cause and effect: He explains why he thinks long-distance joint custody is unfair.
d. sequence: He traces his travels between his parents' homes.

Inferences

9. The author believes that divorced parents should
   a. move far away from each other.
   b. divorce only as a last resort.
   c. reconsider staying together.
   d. put their children's needs first.

10. As an alternative to long-distance joint custody, the author proposes that
   a. only one parent should have custody of the children.
   b. parents should maintain homes close to their children.
   c. children of divorce should be placed in foster homes.
   d. a law should be passed making divorce illegal.

WORKING WITH WORDS

Complete the sentences below with these words from Word Alert:

turbulence   unresolved   convert   custody   cameo   toll

1. If a financial dispute between individuals remains _____ , they may have to settle their differences in court.

2. During a presidential election, each candidate tries to _____ as many voters as possible to his or her point of view.

3. The most important decision to be made in a divorce case concerns who will have _____ of the children.

4. Moviegoers enjoy watching a film in which one of their favorite actors has a _____ , however brief.

5. Because of _____ in the air, several passengers on the flight suffered from motion sickness.

6. During the Middle Ages, the death _____ from plague was high.

THINKING DEEPER

Ideas for discussion and writing

1. According to the author, what has been the toll of his long-distance life? Using details from the selection, discuss how his parents' divorce has affected him.

2. Discuss the various custody arrangements available to divorced parents and the advantages and disadvantages of each.

3. Discuss how this selection illustrates the Part 4 theme, *Hard Questions*. For example, how do children cope with their divorced parents' custody arrangements? Also, criminal activity, drug use, and emotional distress are much higher for children of divorce. How can divorced parents protect their children from these consequences?

4. Write about what you think is the greatest problem associated with divorce.

FIRST THOUGHTS

To prepare yourself for the reading selection, answer the following questions, either on your own or in a group discussion.

1. In your opinion, what are the personal advantages and disadvantages of divorce?

2. What do you think the term *divorce culture* means?

3. Preview the title, headnote, and first one or two paragraphs. What do you think will follow?

WORD ALERT

disposition (3) mood or tendency
adherents (4) supporters of a cause or an individual
empirical (5) verified by observation or by experimental evidence
alluring (9) attractive, enticing, desirable
emancipating (9) freeing from bondage, oppression, or restraint
franchise (11) a right or privilege officially granted by government to an
   individual or group
attenuate (12) reduce, weaken, lessen
abrogates (13) abolishes, does away with
dismantle (21) to take apart, to end gradually and systematically
dissolution (27) termination or extinction, disintegration

❧ Creating a New Form of Inequality

BARBARA DAFOE WHITEHEAD

In this selection, reprinted from her book The Divorce Culture, *Barbara Dafoe Whitehead suggests that widespread acceptance of divorce has had damaging social consequences.*

From *The Divorce Culture* by Barbara Dafoe Whitehead. Copyright © 1997 by Barbara Dafoe Whitehead. Reprinted by permission of Alfred A. Knopf, a Division of Random House, Inc.

T HE SHIFT FROM a family world governed by the institution of mar- 1
riage to one ruled by divorce has brought a steady weakening of
primary human relationships and bonds.

Relationships are becoming more fleeting and unreliable. Chil- 2
dren are losing their ties to their fathers. Even a mother's love is not
forever, as the growing number of throwaway kids suggests.

Divorce is not the only force that has contributed to weaker family 3
ties and more fragile families. But it has been the most important force
in shaping a new cultural **disposition** about the meaning of family
breakup.

Divorce has been damaging not only because it has contributed to 4
family fragmentation and the paternal abandonment of children but
also because it has won influential **adherents** who defend family
breakup as necessary for individual psychological growth and freedom.

When the divorce revolution began 30 years ago, no one could 5
have predicted where it would lead, how it would change the shape
and content of family relationships, or whether it would deliver on its
promises of improving marriage and family life, especially for women.
Now we have a substantial body of experience and **empirical** evidence
on the impact of divorce. It tells us the cultural case for divorce has
been based on misleading claims, false promises and bankrupt ideas.

One claim made for divorce was that women would gain greater 6
equality and independence. Yet the evidence suggests that widespread divorce has generated new forms of inequality. It has contributed to greater economic insecurity and poverty among women
and children. It has been a principal generator of unequal opportunities and outcomes for children.

It is hard to think of any recent economic force that has been as 7
brutally efficient in transforming middle-class haves into have-nots.
In a high-divorce society—even if the wage gap continues to narrow,
jobs remain plentiful and child-support enforcement continues to be
more efficiently and aggressively pursued—women still are likely to
lose ground economically.

Nor can it be said that widespread divorce has moved us closer to 8
greater gender equality. In a society marked by high levels of divorce,
women not only bear double responsibilities for bread-winning and
child-rearing, but they bear them alone. Moreover, in a high-divorce
society the goal of involved, hands-on fatherhood becomes more difficult to attain.

Perhaps the most **alluring** claim for divorce has been its promise 9
of greater personal freedom. One popular book promises women "the

joy of handling your own money, learning to cope as a single mother, and the freedom to manage your time as you see fit." Another proclaims that "there is joy in **emancipating** oneself." Yet in ways not fully anticipated, divorced women's freedoms and opportunities often are quite limited. Single mothers in particular may find it difficult to achieve a satisfying blend of work and family.

Society's principal cheerleaders for expressive divorce have been 10 its most economically advantaged and well-educated women, but only their message, not their privilege, has been transmitted to their working-class "sisters."

Divorce frees many men from the daily tasks of home and family 11 life, and many men free themselves from the responsibilities of providing for their children. However, divorced fathers are not truly liberated. Their opportunities to share in the daily lives of their children are lost. As they lose their **franchise** as fathers, many men also lose a central reason for working hard and participating in the life of the community.

Divorced men also lose access to women's emotional and social 12 intelligence in building and sustaining relationships. Men's social, as well as family, ties **attenuate** after divorce. Although it is too soon to tell, fathers who abandon their children may be abandoned by their adult children when they become old, needy and dependent, leaving elderly men to the care and custody of strangers.

In a culture of divorce, children are the most "unfree." Divorce **ab-** 13 **rogates** children's right to be reasonably free from adult cares and woes, to enjoy the association of both parents daily, to remain innocent of social services and therapy, and to spend family time in ways not dictated by the courts.

More broadly, the divorce culture limits the family's freedom to 14 conduct its own relationships. The American family is founded on the principle of glorious voluntarism. However, the freedom to choose is not unfettered. Through marriage the individual becomes committed to a set of obligations, not only to the spouse but to children, relatives and the larger society. These obligations are voluntarily made and kept.

However, in a culture captive to divorce, the family becomes less 15 able or willing to govern itself. Parental commitments outside of marriage become increasingly involuntary and regulated. The obligation of fathers to provide for their children, an obligation freely accepted and (generally) faithfully honored by married fathers, becomes the focus of state enforcement. Parent-child relationships, once conducted without legal oversight, are governed by court-established visitation and custody arrangements.

Paternity, itself the voluntary recording of a father's name on a 16 birth certificate, an occasion once celebrated with cigars and champagne, becomes a matter of court-ordered and state-reimbursed blood tests. Adoption, the voluntary system of reassigning children to families, loses ground to a system of reshuffling children from biological parents to foster or residential care and back again. In brief, divorce and single parenthood invite, indeed often require, more active regulation of family relationships by the state.

Even though the state can require certain forms of parental sup- 17 port, mainly for the economic upkeep of children, it can do so at only minimal levels. The state cannot force divorced fathers to take higher-paying jobs or work extra shifts for their children's sake. It cannot require divorced parents to set aside their anger to assist each other in rearing their children.

Consequently, compared with a system in which parents share a 18 common household and voluntarily invest in their children, a legally supervised parenthood is almost by definition one in which the levels of parental investment are likely to be low and somewhat fitful, even if the regulatory controls are steadily improved and tightened. Thus, Americans are moving away from a high-investment child-rearing strategy when the requirements of a postindustrial economy require higher-level and longer-term parental and societal investments in children.

It does not require sophisticated statistical projections to make the 19 argument that Americans already have experienced too much divorce during the past 25 years and that the current trends cannot be sustained.

If we do not act to reduce divorces involving children, we will 20 surely become a nation with a diminished capacity to sponsor the next generation into successful lives as citizens, workers and family members. We will lose the capacity to foster strong and lasting bonds between fathers and children, between older and younger generations, and between children and the larger society.

Divorce is necessary in a society that believes in the ideal of affec- 21 tionate marriage, and in one that seeks to protect women from brutality and violence in marriage. But it is not necessary to abolish divorce to **dismantle** the divorce culture.

For parents, divorce is not a solo act but one that has enormous 22 consequences for children. It has spawned a generation of angry and bereaved children who have a harder time learning, staying in school and achieving at high levels. High and sustained levels of divorce also

have raided children's piggy banks, depriving them of the full resources that they might have had growing up in an intact family. The
cost of getting a divorce also has diverted family resources away from
children toward the professional service sector. An entire industry has
sprung up to harvest the fruits of family discord.

Finally, divorce is never merely an individual lifestyle choice with- 23
out larger consequences for the society. Divorce has contributed to
welfare dependency and given rise to an entire public bureaucracy de-
voted to managing and regulating the parental tasks and obligations
of raising children. It has imposed a new set of burdens on schools,
contributed to the tide of fatherless juveniles filling the courts, and increased the risks of unwed parenthood.

Once we acknowledge that divorce involves other stakeholders 24
and imposes costs on others, then we can begin to talk about high levels of divorces involving children as a social problem that must be
addressed rather than as an expression of individual freedom that
cannot be infringed.

A second and complementary step toward dismantling the di- 25
vorce culture is to treat divorce as a morally and socially consequen-
tial event. The ethic of expressive divorce recognizes the rights and
needs of the liberated self, but has nothing to say about the responsibilities of the obligated self. It has no language for talking about the
special obligations of parents to children or about the social trust invested in marriages with children. We still are reluctant to speak about
the moral obligations involved in divorces with children for fear of
"blaming" and thus psychologically burdening adults. Yet the truth is
that divorce involves a radical redistribution of hardship from adults
to children, and therefore cannot be viewed as a morally neutral act.

Changing the way we think about divorce will have several likely 26
consequences:

- If children are treated as key stakeholders and as those most at   27
  risk in the **dissolution** of the marriage, then parents, clergy, therapists, judges and policymakers will be more likely to attend to
  their interests.
- If divorce is regarded as a central source of disadvantage and fa-   28
  ther-loss for children, there may be a stronger effort at educating
  the public about the risks of divorce to children.
- If marriages with children are considered a kind of special trust,   29
  there will be greater societal effort aimed at preventing the dissolution of such marriages. Not all marriages can or should be

saved "for the sake of the children," but clearly of the six out of 10 divorces that involve children, some are salvageable.

- Members of the divorce establishment could take leadership in   30 divorce prevention. Therapists, lawyers and other professionals who profit from divorces involving children might, through their professional associations, support projects designed to reduce divorce among families with children.
- Scholars might put marriage back on their research agenda and   31 thereby add to our knowledge of what makes marriages succeed or fail.
- Clergy might renew their commitment and redouble their efforts   32 to provide pastoral care to married couples with children, especially at times when marriages likely are to be stressed. Within religious communities, older married couples might serve as mentors to younger couples.

COMPREHENSION CHECK

Purpose and Main Idea
1. What is the author's topic?
    a. a new form of inequality
    b. the divorce culture
    c. the case for divorce
    d. divorce and government regulation
2. Which of the following is the best statement of the author's central idea?
    a. In a world ruled by divorce rather than marriage, family ties are weakened.
    b. Defenders of divorce say that it is necessary for psychological growth and freedom.
    c. Widespread divorce has created new forms of inequality among women and children.
    d. Divorce makes families less self-sufficient and more dependent on government.
3. The author's *primary* purpose is to
    a. express her feelings about divorce.
    b. persuade us to change the way we think about divorce.
    c. inform readers that a divorce culture exists.
    d. describe different types of family relationships.

Details

4. According to the author, divorce has been damaging for all but which one of the following reasons?
   a. It has contributed to family breakup.
   b. Fathers have abandoned their children as a result of divorce.
   c. Divorce has won adherents who defend it as necessary for growth and freedom.
   d. It has caused couples to resolve their differences and get back together.

5. According to the author, which one of the following claims about divorce is false or misleading?
   a. Divorce has generated new forms of inequality.
   b. It has contributed to greater economic insecurity.
   c. Women have gained greater equality and independence as a result of divorce.
   d. Divorce has generated unequal opportunities and outcomes for children.

6. According to the author, who is the most unfree in a culture of divorce?
   a. men
   b. women
   c. society
   d. children

7. Which one of the following best expresses the author's opinion about divorce?
   a. Divorce is not necessary.
   b. Divorce has brought a steady weakening of primary human relationships and bonds.
   c. It is a lifestyle choice without social consequences.
   d. Divorce is a solo act for parents with few consequences for children.

8. The author's organizational pattern in paragraphs 26 through 32 can best be described as
   a. classification.
   b. cause and effect.
   c. comparison and contrast.
   d. generalization then example.

Inferences

9. The author's rejection of the divorce culture is based on
    a. experts' opinions.
    b. her upbringing.
    c. religious beliefs.
    d. moral values and social concerns.

10. The author rejects the "ethic of expressive divorce" because
    a. it ignores the fact that people have obligations and responsibilities to others.
    b. divorce is a morally neutral act.
    c. it blames adults for not being able or willing to work out their differences.
    d. the rights and needs of the liberated self supersede those of children and society.

WORKING WITH WORDS

Complete the sentences below with these words from Word Alert:

emancipating	dismantle	adherents	alluring
dissolution	franchise	abrogates	
disposition	attenuate	empirical	

1. It will take me months to _____ my office so that I can move into a larger one.

2. A big step toward the equality of women was the voting _____ established in the Nineteenth Amendment to the U.S. Constitution.

3. In any election, each candidate has _____ who are willing to contribute money or time to the campaign.

4. Vicki's little boy has such a good _____ that she hopes her second child will be as nice.

5. Scientific laws are based on research and the collection of _____ evidence.

6. A failure to abide by the terms of your rental agreement _____ your lease.

7. Many who watch the Academy Awards ceremony each year are more intrigued by the women's _____ gowns than by the awards.

8. Abraham Lincoln is credited with _____ the slaves.
9. Petty disagreements over a period of time can _____ the bonds of even the best friendships.
10. Trina watched the _____ of the chemical powder as she slowly stirred it into the beaker of water.

THINKING DEEPER

Ideas for discussion and writing

1. Throughout the selection, the author makes a distinction between divorce and *the divorce culture*. In paragraph 21 she says, "But it is not necessary to abolish divorce to dismantle the divorce culture." What does she mean? What *is* the divorce culture? How does the author suggest that we dismantle it?

2. Discuss the relationship between the ideas expressed in this selection and those expressed in Selection 31. For example, does Nick Sheff's experience as a child of divorce reinforce or contradict what Barbara Dafoe Whitehead says about the divorce culture? Explain your answer.

3. Discuss how this selection illustrates the Part 4 theme, *Hard Questions*. For example, some hard questions for society are: Whose needs does divorce serve? Who suffers? How does the author answer these questions? What are your answers?

4. The author of this selection discusses several consequences of divorce. Choose one of these consequences to write about and explain what you think can or should be done about it.

FIRST THOUGHTS

To prepare yourself for the reading selection, answer the following questions, either on your own or in a group discussion.

1. Do you believe that educators have correctly determined your needs as a student?

2. Do you think that male and female students have different needs?

3. Preview the title, headnote, and first one or two paragraphs. What do you think will follow?

WORD ALERT

unfathomable (1) not understandable, incomprehensible
cues (4) signals, hints, suggestions
procreation (7) sexual reproduction
agitation (12) emotional disturbance, restlessness
cognitive (14) involving or relating to thought processes
implicit (15) implied, suggested, not directly expressed
succinctly (17) expressing much in few words, concisely
tainted (22) morally corrupted
adulation (22) excessive flattery or admiration
exuberance (24) enthusiasm, joy

ૹ Have Today's Schools Failed Male Students?

PATRICIA DALTON

Patricia Dalton is a Washington, D.C., clinical psychologist. In this selection she suggests that in our attempt to overcome the disadvantages of female students, we may have shortchanged male students.

F OR ALL THE **unfathomable** horror of the shootings . . . at Col- 1
umbine High School, there was one thing that came as no surprise
to me.

It was boys who fired the guns in Littleton, Colo. Just as it was 2 boys who fired the guns in the school shootings in Pearl, Miss., in West Paducah, Ky., in Jonesboro, Ark., in Springfield, Ore., and . . . in Conyers, Ga.

It seems clear to me, both as a psychologist and as the mother of 3 two daughters and a son, that we should be concerned about how we are failing our boys.

I'm not suggesting that every boy is a potential killer. Far from it. 4 But from observing my patients and my son's friends, I think we are missing **cues.**

I can recall a teenage boy I saw some time ago in therapy. He had 5 changed schools after his parents divorced. His dad was concerned that he was not interested in sports and was not hanging around with the other guys. I knew that the boy was unhappy, but the underlying problem was that his behavior simply didn't fit his father's picture of being a man. His dad seemed surprised—even embarrassed—that his son was going through a hard time, as if real guys shouldn't have doubts and worries. What his son needed, I realized, was for his father to understand that real guys do have doubts and worries.

To really help boys, we need to think not only about issues such as 6 the violence they are exposed to and the availability of weapons; we also need to widen the lens and look at their daily lives, both in and out of school, and examine the expectations and messages they get from us.

Because of legitimate concerns about gender discrimination, for 7 years we tended to play down differences between boys and girls, even though research and common sense tell us they exist. Ask any parent who has raised children of both sexes. The differences show up at a young age, they persist, and they are probably there for good evolutionary reasons: They bring the sexes together and promote **procreation.**

More recently, as we've begun to acknowledge gender differences, 8 we've focused our attention on girls. Think of Mary Pipher's bestseller, *Reviving Ophelia,* which catalogued problems such as anorexia nervosa, bulimia and self-mutilation that girls are likely to exhibit. Think of Harvard professor of education Carol Gilligan and her research team as they described girls who are confident at 11 but confused by 16. And think of all the recent studies of single-sex education that have addressed almost exclusively the special needs of girls.

Where does all this leave boys?   9

The statistics that cross my desk are not encouraging. They sug- 10 gest that boys may be the more fragile sex. Approximately three out of every four children identified as learning disabled are boys. Boys are much more likely than girls to have drug and alcohol problems. Four of every five juvenile-court cases involve crimes committed by boys. Ninety-five percent of juvenile homicides are committed by boys. And while girls attempt suicide four times more often, boys are seven times as likely to succeed as girls—usually because they choose more lethal methods, such as guns.

While girls tend to internalize problems, taking their unhappiness 11 out on themselves, boys externalize them, taking their unhappiness out on others. Boys have more problems than girls in virtually every category you can think of with the exception of eating disorders.

The signs of depression my colleagues and I are likely to see in 12 girls are typically straightforward—sadness, tearfulness and self-doubt. In boys, depression is generally hidden behind symptoms such as irritability, **agitation** and explosiveness.

Since our kids spend the majority of their day in the structured 13 setting of school, that's where problems are most likely to come to light. Many boys think that their grade schools are boy-unfriendly. I well remember my son bursting into the kitchen one day after school, yelling "They want us to be girls, Mom, they want us to be girls!" A seventh-grader once told me he was planning that night to write a book report that was due the next day—"not like the perfect girls who did theirs three weeks ago."

We all know that boys mature more slowly than girls, and that they 14 reach the **cognitive** milestones essential for doing well at school later than girls do. Take reading, for example. Girls are usually ready to read earlier than boys. This means that average boys wind up feeling less successful, and learning-disabled boys can feel easily defeated.

What have schools done to accommodate these well-documented 15 differences in rates of maturity? Very little. Schools, like researchers, have been concentrating on girls. In recent years, some parents have been holding their boys back voluntarily, because they don't seem ready for first grade. Maturity differences persist through adolescence, although adults sometimes seem to ignore them. Teenagers seem to have an **implicit** understanding of them, though; boys are often a year or two older than the girls they date.

So here's a radical proposal: Have boys start school a year later 16 than girls so that the two sexes are more evenly matched.

Besides their different maturity rates, boys are more active than 17 girls and slower to develop control of their impulses. I'm not the first one to suggest this; even Plato observed that of all the animal young, the hardest to tame is the boy. A young boy put the matter to me **succinctly:** "I figured it out. I'm bad before recess."

But many schools have not accommodated boys' need to work off   18 excess energy. Instead, many have shortened lunch and recess periods in order to cram more class time into the day, as the pressure to become more competitive and test-oriented has increased.

A fifth-grade boy once told me, "School just sucks the fun out of   19 everything." And my high-school-age son, who enjoyed preschool and kindergarten so much that he left for first grade one day saying, "Ready to rock and roll," had changed his tune by middle school. "Mom," he said, "It's like going to prison."

While parents and schools have often failed to respond to these   20 signals, popular culture has picked up on them. Matt Groening once said that he created *The Simpsons* because of all the teachers who, when he was enjoying himself, would shoot him a look that said, "Take that stupid grin off your face right now."

Groening has it right. I hear a lot about *The Simpsons* from the kids   21 I see in therapy. Girls like *The Simpsons;* boys love the show.

One of the ways boys can blow off steam is sports. Yet even this   22 outlet is **tainted** by the student and adult **adulation** of athletes that pervades many of the big high schools. That's a problem for several reasons: It gives athletes an inflated idea of themselves and non-athletes feelings of inferiority and resentment. The boys I see in my office often tell me how sports provide an arena in which they can test themselves, and many feel like failures when they get cut from a team—something that is increasingly likely to happen in our highly competitive mega-schools. All kids need to exercise and play sports, and not just for the short time they have physical education. It would be good to see all schools offering intramural after-school sports to all students.

There's no question in my mind that, in our haste to make up for   23 the disadvantages that girls have historically suffered, we've tended to overlook the needs of ordinary boys.

Like everyone else, boys of all ages need adults to love them, ap-   24 preciate them and enjoy them, so that they can come to value and have faith in themselves. We need to help them find outlets for their natural **exuberance,** vitality and even devilishness. One of my favorite sights is the look on boys' faces on the baseball field as they steal bases—when it's good to be bad.

COMPREHENSION CHECK

Purpose and Main Idea

1. What is the author's topic?
    a. differences between boys and girls
    b. ways to help boys in school
    c. academic performance of boys and girls
    d. how we are failing boys

2. The central idea of this selection is stated in
    a. paragraph 1 "For all the unfathomable. . . ."
    b. paragraph 3 "It seems clear to me. . . ."
    c. paragraph 6 "To really help boys. . . ."
    d. paragraph 23 "There's no question. . . ."

3. The author's *primary* purpose is to
    a. entertain readers with a discussion of gender differences.
    b. inform readers of the ways in which schools are meeting the needs of female students.
    c. persuade readers that schools should address the needs of male students.
    d. express concern that girls are being overlooked in school.

Details

4. According to the author, we can really help boys by thinking about
    a. gender differences.
    b. girls' needs.
    c. violence and the availability of weapons.
    d. the expectations and messages that boys get from us.

5. According to the author, boys—not girls—may be the more fragile sex for all but which one of the following reasons?
    a. Boys attempt suicide four times more often than girls.
    b. Three out of every four learning-disabled children are boys.
    c. Boys are more likely than girls to have drug and alcohol problems.
    d. Boys commit 95 percent of juvenile homicides.

6. Which one of the following is a sign of depression in boys?
    a. self-doubt
    b. tearfulness
    c. irritability
    d. eating disorders

7. The author suggests that boys should start school a year later
    than girls because boys
    a. are not as smart as girls.
    b. mature more slowly than girls.
    c. are less active than girls.
    d. have more control over their impulses than girls.
8. The author's organizational pattern in paragraphs 14 through 17 is
    a. comparison and contrast.
    b. cause and effect.
    c. sequence.
    d. definition.

Inferences

9. Although schools have failed to address boys' needs, popular
    culture has picked up on them, as best expressed in which one of
    the following?
    a. Mary Pipher's *Reviving Ophelia*
    b. Matt Groening's *The Simpsons*
    c. the research of Carol Gilligan and her team
    d. Plato's *Republic*
10. Which of the following is an example of the way a boy might *ex-
    ternalize* his unhappiness?
    a. crying
    b. becoming anorexic
    c. attempting suicide
    d. swearing at a classmate

WORKING WITH WORDS

Complete the sentences below with these words from Word Alert:

unfathomable	exuberance	adulation	cues
procreation	cognitive	implicit	
succinctly	agitation	tainted	

1. Taking her _____ from her friends, who were dressed
    informally, Janet changed into jeans and a T-shirt.
2. Ron's red face and restlessness showed his _____ over not being
    able to find his keys.

3. The instructor said, "Your paper is too long and wordy; you need to express your ideas more _____."

4. In their _____, some fans go to extremes, such as attending every personal appearance of a favorite celebrity.

5. On Oscar night, winners cannot conceal their _____ at being selected.

6. Some crimes, such as those involving kids who kill their class-mates, seem _____ to otherwise knowledgeable people.

7. In a zoology class, you will study the _____ and behavior of var-ious animal species.

8. Reading, writing, and critical thinking are three _____ skills that students can develop and improve.

9. An attitude of disrespect is _____ in the behavior of drivers who swear at or make obscene gestures to others on the road.

10. While some people enjoy betting on the outcome of a game, others refrain, believing that gambling has _____ professional sports.

THINKING DEEPER

Ideas for discussion and writing

1. The author says that in focusing their attention on girls, the schools have failed male students. What evidence does she offer? What differences between boys' and girls' behaviors does the author believe that educators are not addressing?

2. Read paragraph 24 again. What relationship do you see between the ideas expressed in this paragraph and what the authors of Selections 31 and 32 say about the needs of children from divorced familes?

3. Discuss how this selection illustrates the Part 4 theme, *Hard Ques-tions*. For example, once we asked the question, "How have schools failed girls?" Having made the classroom more comfort-able for girls, now we seem to be shortchanging boys. What do you think schools can or should do to accommodate the needs of both sexes?

4. In paragraphs 11 and 12, the author compares the ways boys and girls handle problems. Does your own experience support the idea that girls internalize problems while boys externalize them? Write a paper in which you compare the way you and a friend or family member of the opposite sex handle problems.

FIRST THOUGHTS

To prepare yourself for the reading selection, answer the following questions, either on your own or in a group discussion.

1. What does the term *racial profiling* mean?
2. Under what conditions do you think that police officers should question or search individuals?
3. Preview the title, headnote, and first one or two paragraphs. What do you think will follow?

WORD ALERT

stammered (4) a way of speaking marked by uncontrollable pauses and repetitions
cheeky (8) bold, impertinent
seething (10) violent, excited, or agitated
concocted (10) devised, contrived, prepared by mixing ingredients
stark (12) harsh, grim, blunt
railed (14) expressed objection or criticism in bitter, harsh, or abusive language
chastens (16) restrains, subdues, punishes
nexus (19) means of connection, link, tie, connected series or group
disproportionate (19) out of proportion, as in size, shape, or amount
incessant (19) continuing without interruption

৯ Correspondence/Black & Middle Class: Both a Victim of Racial Profiling—and a Practitioner

STEVEN A. HOLMES

Steven A. Holmes writes for The New York Times. *In this selection, he suggests that the police are not the only ones who use the tactic of racial profiling.*

Correspondence/Black & Middle Class. Both a Victim of Racial Profiling—and a Practitioner by Steven A. Holmes, NEW YORK TIMES, April 25, 1999. Copyright © 1999 by the New York Times Co. Reprinted with permission.

T HE SPRING DAY was bright and sunny enough for sunglasses, yet 1
cool enough to require a sweatshirt and baggy sweat pants.

As I walked along a busy street in the predominantly white north- 2
west Washington neighborhood where I lived, I hardly thought that
my clothing or, more important, my dark skin would attract the attention of the police.

But sure enough, after a few blocks, a brown and white cruiser 3
from the Capital Police suddenly pulled alongside. A white police officer jumped out and demanded to know what I was doing there.

I live here, I **stammered,** somewhat stunned.   4

Incredulous, he asked to see some identification.   5

I produced a driver's license verifying that I lived a few blocks 6
away—that this was, indeed, my neighborhood. He seemed satisfied.

I was not. "Why are you stopping me?" I asked.   7

"There was a burglary in the area, and you fit the description of 8
the suspect," he answered, sounding surprised at what he clearly regarded as a **cheeky** question.

"Oh, yeah?" I replied. "Where?"   9

He quickly gave me the name of a street where the crime allegedly 10
had occurred and departed, leaving me standing on the sidewalk,
seething. I later called the local police precinct to check out this supposed burglary and was not surprised to find out that there was no report of any break-in on that street. The officer's explanation, I assumed,
had been **concocted** to cover up what really had happened—a random
stop of a black man who to the officer's eye did not fit the area.

The issue of whether the police target minorities for questioning 11
and searches has been thrust onto center stage. Figures compiled by
the New York City police show that in the 20 precincts where the Street
Crimes Unit has been most active, 63 percent of the people stopped
and frisked were minorities. Recently, investigators in New Jersey announced that a two-year study of random stops on the New Jersey
Turnpike showed that roughly three-fourths of the people whose cars
were halted and searched by state troopers were black or Hispanic.

The numbers are **stark,** and to civil-rights leaders and liberal 12
politicians the numbers are proof of the use of racial profiling by police. But the figures give little sense of the depth of anger of people like
me singled out evidently because of race or ethnicity.

The incident left me frustrated and irate. I thought: I'm a middle- 13
class black man who works hard, pays his taxes, keeps out of trouble
and tries to treat people with dignity and respect. Why should I be an
object of suspicion?

I **railed** at the injustice of it all. Yet, as my anger cooled, I asked my- 14
self a harder question: Hadn't I done the same thing myself?

I thought back to the time back in the early 1970s when, as a col- 15
lege student in New York City, I supported myself by driving a taxi at
night. In many ways, it was a great job for a student—flexible hours,
good pay, a way to meet interesting people, especially women. It could
also be dangerous. In three years, I was held up twice. Both times the
perpetrators were young black men.

Fear **chastens** you. I did not quit driving a taxi. But I became more 16
choosy about who I let in my cab. I still picked up black women, older
men, couples, families and men dressed in suits. But my sense of tolerance and racial solidarity was tested every time a casually dressed
young black man tried to hail my cab. Most times, I drove right by.

Like it or not, I was engaging in my own form of racial profiling. 17
What I was doing was playing the odds, playing it safe, taking no
chances. Looking back, I realized that those I declined to pick up
looked remarkably like I did when the cop stopped me as I walked
down a Washington street.

As I contemplated this, my anger spread to many targets: the police 18
officer who had confronted me, and the young black hoodlums whose
criminal behavior had made the officer suspicious of all African-
American men in the first place. And I resented the country's history
of racism, which helped to ensure that the presence of a black person
in a leafy, affluent neighborhood of Washington was still a rare sight.

The **nexus** of race, crime and stereotyping raises difficult ques- 19
tions that are often ignored. Even as crime rates tumble, young black
men still commit a **disproportionate** share of serious offenses, a fact
that is driven home in metropolitan areas by television's seemingly **incessant** airing of crime news. And whether the fear stems from real experience or media-driven perceptions, people—police and civilian,
white and black—play the odds all the time when it comes to how they
view and respond to young black men.

Too often the country fails to acknowledge how widespread the prac- 20
tice is. Some years ago, at a town hall meeting on race in Akron, Ohio,
then-President Clinton asked a group of whites who had joined him
onstage whether they felt fear when they saw a young black man on the
street who was not well dressed. A number sheepishly raised their hands.
Clinton thanked them for their honesty. I sat there wondering, "Mr. President, why don't you ask the black participants the same question?"

Even the seemingly clear-cut statistics on racial profiling don't tell 21
the whole story. New York's Street Crimes Unit did indeed stop and

frisk a disproportionately large number of black men. Yet in those same precincts, 71 percent of the suspects, as described by their victims, were black men.

On the flip side, New Jersey state troopers arrested or seized con- 22 traband from 13.5 percent of the minorities whose cars were searched on the turnpike, compared with 10.5 percent of the whites. At first blush that seems like a sizable difference. But then consider that the troopers stopped three times as many non-whites or Hispanics as others: Racial profiling hardly seems to be producing enough arrests to justify the effort—or the heartache.

That may be the biggest argument against targeting some people 23 as suspects based on their race, beyond the constitutional argument of equal treatment before the law. With crime rates tumbling in virtually every big city in the land, racial profiling may have outlived its usefulness. Perhaps if I were a young New York City cab driver today I would not be as wary of young black men as I once was. With the streets safer, it could be time for the public and the police to shed the kind of attitude I held nearly three decades ago—the attitude that followed me into middle-aged respectability on a Washington street.

COMPREHENSION CHECK

Purpose and Main Idea

1. What is the author's topic?
   a. racial profiling
   b. race relations
   c. race and ethnicity
   d. racial discrimination

2. Which of the following is the best statement of the author's central idea?
   a. Racial profiling is only one crime-fighting method.
   b. Racial profiling is not as prevalent as people think.
   c. The reality of racial profiling is that we all do it.
   d. Racial profiling is unfair to those who are singled out.

3. The author's *primary* purpose is to
   a. inform readers that racial profiling exists.
   b. express concern about the number of crimes committed by African Americans.
   c. persuade readers to shed stereotypical attitudes.
   d. entertain readers with his experiences as a taxi driver.

Details

4. According to the author, racial profiling is all but which one of the following?
   a. a legitimate crime-fighting technique
   b. the targeting of minorities as suspects
   c. a form of stereotyping
   d. unequal treatment under the law

5. In the author's opinion, he was stopped and questioned because he
   a. was dressed casually.
   b. fit the suspect's description.
   c. was a black man in a white neighborhood.
   d. might have information for the officer.

6. The author says that he should not be an object of suspicion for all of these reasons except which one?
   a. He works hard.
   b. He pays his taxes.
   c. He treats people with dignity and respect.
   d. He has been in trouble with the law.

7. According to the author, what may be the biggest argument against racial profiling?
   a. Crime rates are decreasing.
   b. It is an unfair tactic.
   c. Racial profiling may be unconstitutional.
   d. The country has a history of racism.

8. In paragraph 14 the word *yet* signals that the relationship between the first sentence and the second sentence is
   a. contrast.
   b. process.
   c. definition.
   d. example.

Inferences

9. Clinton's question at the town meeting in Ohio (paragraph 20) and the author's response to it illustrate his point that
   a. racial profiling is stereotyping.
   b. Clinton was not sensitive to his audience's needs.
   c. both blacks and whites engage in racial profiling.
   d. Ohioans are not willing to express their views.

10. The author suggests that people's fears of black men—whether real or imagined—stem from the fact that

a. cities have a higher crime rate than small towns.
b. the crime rate is highest among young black men.
c. crimes committed by minorities are widely publicized.
d. most police officers are racists.

WORKING WITH WORDS

Complete the sentences below with these words from Word Alert:

disproportionate	concocted	cheeky	nexus
stammered	seething	railed	
incessant	chastens	stark	

1. A good parent ————— a child for playing too near the street.
2. Some of the actors who won Oscars were so surprised that they ————— into the microphone, unable to speak.
3. ————— with anger, Lyn shook her fist at the driver who had smashed into her car while she was stopped at a traffic light.
4. The instructor ————— at the students who were caught cheating on the exam.
5. The students thought the exam was too hard because a ————— number of them failed it.
6. When my horn got stuck, the ————— honking drove everyone crazy until I could get it stopped.
7. What is ————— behavior to one person may seem timid to another.
8. Only a person who is used to living in harsh conditions would appreciate a trip to Antarctica's ————— landscape.
9. The coastal town where we grew up is the ————— that draws me and my cousins together each summer.
10. I ————— a surprisingly good meal from the leftovers in my refrigerator.

THINKING DEEPER

Ideas for discussion and writing

1. Discuss the arguments for and against racial profiling. Why do police use the tactic? Why do some people rail against it? Do you think racial profiling is or is not justified?

2. At the time of this writing (1999) the author says that crime rates are tumbling and that racial profiling may have outlived its usefulness. Do you agree or disagree? Using your library's resources, research crime statistics for your area. What conclusions can you draw?

3. Discuss how this selection illustrates the Part 4 theme, *Hard Questions*. For example, in paragraph 14 the author says about racial profiling, "I asked myself a harder question: Hadn't I done the same thing myself?," recalling his experience as a taxi driver when he had refused to stop for black men who were casually dressed. A hard question for you to discuss and answer is, "Have you engaged in racial profiling?"

4. Write about a time when you felt singled out because of your race, or the way you were dressed, or for some other reason. What were your feelings, thoughts, or reactions?

FIRST THOUGHTS

To prepare yourself for the reading selection, answer the following questions, either on your own or in a group discussion.

1. Do you think most people are or are not willing to donate their organs after death?

2. Do you think there should be financial incentives for those who donate their organs?

3. Preview the title, headnote, and first one or two paragraphs. What do you think will follow?

WORD ALERT

taboo (4) something that is forbidden either because of social custom or because it is morally offensive

incentive (7) a reward or punishment that influences one's actions or behavior

ethical (8) of or relating to standards of right conduct

compensation (8) something given or received as payment

oxymoron (8) a contradiction in terms, such as *deafening silence*

altruistic (11) unselfish

paradox (17) A seemingly contradictory statement that may nonetheless be true.

procurement (17) the act of acquiring, obtaining, or getting by special effort

unseemly (18) not in good taste, improper, inappropriate

❧ A $300 Solution to Organ-Donation Dilemma?

ELLEN GOODMAN

Ellen Goodman is a member of the Washington Post *Writers Group. In her column, which is widely syndicated, she writes about a variety of social and political issues. In this selection, she comments on Pennsylvania's offer to pay the funeral costs to families of organ donors.*

© 1999, The Washington Post Writers Group. Reprinted with permission.

I T WOULD BE NICE to think of this as a simple problem of supply and demand. A test case for Economics 101. A problem for the market-place. 1

Over here, we have 66,000 potential customers on a waiting list. Over there, we have 5,500 products. How do you satisfy all these customers? Where's the supply to meet the demand? 2

But we aren't talking about a shortage of *Star Wars* tickets or Beanie Babies. We are talking about a shortage of human organs. We are talking about people who die, waiting for a liver or a heart or a lung. We are talking about thousands who might have left behind a legacy of life. 3

Until now, we've kept economics out of this group portrait. Although there are reports of kidneys for sale in poor countries, Americans don't put organs on the free market. We not only have a **taboo** against buying organs, we have a law against it. 4

Now the state of Pennsylvania is going to try a new experiment— or perhaps an end run—around this taboo. The details will be announced soon by an advisory board. But the outline is already clear. The state is beginning a three-year program to pay $300 to help donors' families pay for funeral costs. 5

State officials insist they are not in the organ-buying business. The money is low; the check goes to the funeral parlor. They prefer to think of this as a reward, a societal thank-you note for the gift. 6

But they also hope that the program will provide an **incentive.** This is a test—just a test—to see whether a financial incentive of a few hundred dollars will increase the number of organ donors. 7

In short, Pennsylvania is trying to find an **ethical** line between reward and **compensation,** between a thank-you note and a paycheck. The Keystone State is creating that ethical **oxymoron,** a paid gift. 8

I understand the motive behind this, even the desperation. Some weeks ago, after writing about the organ legacy of my cousin Keren, I heard from dozens of grateful and needy families. There has been a long and frustrating attempt to increase the number of folks who check off the donor box on their drivers license, and the number of families that give permission at moments of enormous grief. 9

In Pennsylvania, a center of transplant surgery, there are personal stories that reinforce the thinking behind this $300 difference. And stories that raise doubts. 10

Consider the death of John White, a 20-year-old whose organs helped a dozen others but whose family was left to raise funds for a funeral. Surely, the family deserved the $300. Consider, on the other 11

hand, the parents of 2-year-old donor Max Kaner: "When we decided
to donate, it was purely **altruistic.**"

Is one person's reward another person's insult? Is money an incen- 12
tive or a turnoff?

This is not the first discussion of economics and donors. Some 13
economists have talked of a futures market in organs. Others have
suggested that we offer a tax write-off such as the one for charity to
those who sign on as a donor.

But unease and suspicion already shadow the feelings of some 14
families faced with this choice. A $300 reward inevitably would mean
more to poorer families. Does that start us on the business plan that
has already made a flourishing market for "donor" eggs?

What happens if the Pennsylvania experiment begins a bidding 15
war? Pennsylvania offers $300 for a funeral. Do I hear another bid?
New York offers $600? California offers $1,200? SOLD!

This experiment will be conducted under the eyes of an ethics 16
panel. But when all is said and done, it is by no means clear how the
panel can measure success.

Joseph Moreno, an ethicist at the University of Virginia, said this 17
offers a **paradox:** "If they do increase the supply of organs, one would
infer that families were price-sensitive. I'm not sure that's a good thing.
If, on the other hand, it doesn't increase the organ-**procurement** rate,
well, then families aren't price-sensitive, but we also haven't gotten
any more organs."

Society should offer collective gratitude to donors and families. 18
But there is something **unseemly** and ultimately destructive in this $300
solution. In the end, it undermines the value that encourages donation,
a value that says there is something money can't buy: altruism.

COMPREHENSION CHECK

Purpose and Main Idea

1. What is the author's topic?
   a. organ diseases
   b. organ transplants
   c. organ donation
   d. the organ shortage
2. Which of the following is the best statement of the author's central idea?
   a. Organs needed for transplants are in short supply.

    b. Some people die waiting for an organ transplant.

    c. The sale of human organs for transplants is illegal in the United States.

    d. Pennsylvania's solution to the organ shortage problem is unseemly.

3.   The author's *primary* purpose is to

    a. inform readers that there is a shortage of organs for transplants.

    b. persuade readers that financial incentives for organ donors are unethical.

    c. express sympathy for those who need organ transplants but are unable to get them.

    d. entertain readers with a true-life account of an organ transplant.

Details

4.   Americans don't offer organs for sale because

    a. there is not enough supply to meet the demand.

    b. we cannot ensure quality control.

    c. there is both a taboo and a law against it.

    d. we have plenty of organs available for transplant.

5.   Pennsylvania has decided to help donors' families pay for funeral costs by offering them

    a. $300.

    b. $600.

    c. $1,200.

    d. credit.

6.   Discussions of economics and organ donors have included which one of the following suggestions?

    a. bidding on organs

    b. a tax write-off

    c. repealing the law against selling organs

    d. buying organs overseas

7.   The author cites all but which one of the following disadvantages of Pennsylvania's experiment?

    a. A financial reward would mean more to poorer families.

    b. It might cause a bidding war among states.

    c. According to Joseph Moreno, it might not guarantee an increased number of organs.

    d. It would encourage the value of altruism.

8. The author's organizational pattern in paragraph 11 is
    a. definition.
    b. process.
    c. sequence.
    d. contrast.

Inferences

9. In paragraph 8, the author calls Pennsylvania's financial incen-
    tive "that ethical oxymoron, a paid gift." What does she mean?
    a. The people of Pennsylvania are unethical.
    b. Pennsylvania has no right to make this offer.
    c. If you have to pay for it, it's not a gift.
    d. It is illegal to pay the funeral costs of organ donors.

10. Which one of the following words from paragraph 18 suggests
    that the author is against paying a portion of the funeral costs to
    organ donors' families?
    a. gratitude
    b. unseemly
    c. encourages
    d. altruism

WORKING WITH WORDS

Complete the sentences below with these words from Word Alert:

compensation	altruistic	ethical
procurement	oxymoron	paradox
incentive	unseemly	taboo

1. Just because an action is legal does not necessarily mean that it
    is _____ .
2. A few couples have chosen to get married in _____ places such
    as shopping malls and pool halls.
3. Most societies have a _____ against incest.
4. Many people who contribute to charities do so for _____ rea-
    sons rather than for the tax benefit.
5. Children who earn the money to buy their own cars may have a
    greater _____ to take care of them than children whose parents
    buy cars for them.
6. Linda's job is the _____ of props, such as cars, furniture, and
    other items used on movie sets.

7. An old joke says that the term *military intelligence* is
    a(n) _____ .

8. Salma's choice of a mate seemed a(n) _____ to her friends be-
    cause he was so unlike her.

9. If you choose a job based on financial _____ rather than on
    personal satisfaction, you may be unhappy in the long run.

THINKING DEEPER

Ideas for discussion and writing

1. Discuss Pennsylvania's $300 solution to the organ donation
    dilemma as explained in this selection. Do you agree or disagree
    with the author's conclusions in paragraph 18, and why?

2. Discuss what you think would be a fair way to allocate organs to
    those who need them.

3. Discuss how this selection illustrates the Part 4 theme, *Hard
    Questions.* For example, who should get organ transplants, who
    should pay for them, and what are the ethics involved in using
    animal organs and tissue for transplant purposes? These are all
    hard questions for which answers and opinions vary. What are
    your opinions on these issues?

4. Write about someone you know who has received an organ from
    a donor and its effect on his or her life. If you do not know such a
    person, then write about your own views on organ donation and
    why you would or would not choose to be an organ donor.

FIRST THOUGHTS

To prepare yourself for the reading selection, answer the following questions, either on your own or in a group discussion.

1. What do you know about physician-assisted suicide?

2. What is your position on physician-assisted suicide?

3. Preview the title, headnote, and first one or two paragraphs. What do you think will follow?

WORD ALERT

neurological (1) having to do with the nervous system
vulnerable (2) at risk of injury or attack
infirm (2) weak in body, feeble
stampede (2) headlong rush or flight
autonomy (3) self-determination, self-regulation
euthanasia (3) the act of ending the life of someone suffering from a terminal or incurable illness
compassionate (4) sympathetic, being deeply aware of others' suffering
fatal (5) causing or capable of causing death

ࣶ Some Dying Patients Need Help

CHARLES F. McKHANN

Charles F. McKhann, M.D., is professor of surgery at the Yale University School of Medicine and author of A Time to Die: The Place for Physician Assistance. *In this selection, he argues in favor of legalizing physician-assisted suicide. The selection ran in the* AARP Bulletin, *May 1999, as one of two opposing views written in answer to the question "Should physician-assisted suicide be legalized by the states?"*

IN SPITE OF MEDICINE'S best efforts there are people who suffer severely at the end of life, and there always will be. "Bad deaths" in-   1 clude cancer, AIDS and some **neurological** disorders. The aging of our population adds to these an accumulation of frightening disabilities, such as blindness and immobility. Recognition of these problems is transforming us from a society that did not want to think about death at all into one that is increasingly concerned about how life may end. We would like to avoid unnecessary pain and suffering, to retain a reasonable degree of human dignity and self-respect, and many would like to have some control over events at the end of life. Most people hope to live long, healthy lives and also to be assured that they will be spared the worst at the end. The fact is that we have now reached a point where the same medical profession that has added years to our lives can also provide more comfortable deaths for the few who need such help, if it is given the chance to do so legally.

Much is being said about the risks of physician-assisted suicide. 2 The primary focus is on abuse of the individual at the hands of a physician or a family that wants to rid themselves of a burdensome individual. Opponents also feel that assisted suicide would be directed at more **vulnerable** members of society, such as the aged, **infirm,** disabled, poor, minorities and even women. However, health care in the United States finds it easy to neglect these vulnerable people: They will be the last and least likely to benefit from any change in our laws. The new Oregon law addresses potential abuse very specifically, as an article in the October 1998 *Bulletin* pointed out, and there has been no **stampede** to assisted dying in that state.

A second concern is that voluntary shortening of life as an expres- 3 sion of **autonomy** would eventually lead to involuntary **euthanasia,** in which peoples' lives would be ended against their wills, at the insistence of others, even the state. But if the final step in ending life must be the taking of some medication by the patient himself (i.e., suicide), this possibility is remote indeed.

Physicians have always helped people die, and even now some do 4 so from time to time. Many more say that they would if only it were legal. Until the laws are changed, people who are concerned should ask their doctors while they are still well, or early in a serious illness, if the doctor would provide help in the face of severe suffering. As patients become more insistent, help will become more commonplace. However, it will remain unfair to place all the risk on the shoulders of **compassionate** physicians, because as a society we are unable to pass more humane laws.

Eventually new laws must be enacted by state legislatures composed 5 of people who are very sensitive to opposition, primarily from well-organized and well-financed religious groups. Since dying individuals will be unable to complain or vote, the responsibility is really with the healthy 65 percent of the population who say they want to have the laws changed. All of us must think about what we would want if we developed a **fatal** illness with serious suffering, and then push hard for more permissive laws now.

COMPREHENSION CHECK

Purpose and Main Idea

1. What is the author's topic?
    a. fatal illnesses
    b. medical care
    c. physician-assisted suicide
    d. insurance risks

2. The central idea of the selection is stated in
    a. paragraph 1, first sentence "In spite of. . . ."
    b. paragraph 1, second sentence "'Bad deaths'. . . ."
    c. paragraph 1, fourth sentence "Recognition of. . . ."
    d. paragraph 1, last sentence "The fact is. . . ."

3. The author's *primary* purpose is to
    a. entertain readers with sympathetic stories of the terminally ill.
    b. inform readers that people have always suffered at the end of life.
    c. express his view that physician-assisted suicide should be legal.
    d. persuade healthy readers that it is their responsibility to change the laws regarding euthanasia.

Details

4. According to the author, "bad deaths" include all but which one of the following?
    a. heart attack
    b. AIDS
    c. cancer
    d. some neurological disorders

5. Which one of the following is *not* one of the author's stated reasons in support of physician-assisted suicide?
    a. to avoid unnecessary pain and suffering
    b. to retain reasonable dignity and self-respect

    c. to exercise religious freedom

    d. to maintain some control over events at the end of life

6. According to the author, which one of the following would be the least likely to benefit from a change in the laws regarding physician-assisted suicide?

    a. young people

    b. the financially well off

    c. those in good health

    d. minorities and women

7. According to the author, which one of the following would prevent involuntary euthanasia?

    a. legalizing physician-assisted suicide

    b. requiring that the patient end his or her own life by taking medication

    c. leaving the decision to end a life in the hands of the state

    d. allowing relatives to decide whether a patient's life should be ended

8. The phrase "a second concern" in paragraph 3 signals the reader that

    a. ideas are being contrasted.

    b. an additional idea follows.

    c. events are related by time.

    d. an effect follows a stated cause.

Inferences

9. Of the author's following reasons in support of legalizing physician-assisted suicide, which one seems the most common-sense view?

    a. As a society, we are becoming increasingly concerned about how life may end.

    b. As patients become more insistent, help will become more commonplace.

    c. Physicians have always helped people die.

    d. Some people suffer severely at the end of life.

10. At the end of paragraph 5, the author is asking readers to

    a. make their own decisions.

    b. put themselves in the place of those who are suffering.

    c. let government make decisions about medical issues.

    d. look to religious groups for guidance.

WORKING WITH WORDS

Complete the sentences below with these words from Word Alert:

> neurological   euthanasia   stampede   fatal
> vulnerable   autonomy   infirm   compassionate

1. Many gunshot wounds are not _____, and patients are able to recover from them.
2. _____, sometimes called "mercy killing," is a topic of much controversy.
3. Children's inexperience makes them _____ to offers of gifts from people who are out to harm them.
4. When the department store opened its doors, a _____ of consumers rushed to the sales racks.
5. You can make a useful contribution to society by volunteering as a nursing home aide, doing small tasks for the _____.
6. Students who have a high degree of _____ are usually able to manage their time and control their concentration.
7. People who have _____ disorders such as cerebral palsy may need long-term care.
8. Because Jane enjoys working at her local homeless shelter, her friends call her a _____ person.

THINKING DEEPER

Ideas for discussion and writing

1. What are the author's reasons in favor of physician-assisted suicide and where does he state them?
2. Does the author state opposing views? What other reasons can you think of either for or against physician-assisted suicide?
3. Discuss how this selection illustrates the Part 4 theme, *Hard Questions*. For example, this author and the one in the next selection were asked the hard question "Should physician-assisted suicide be legalized by the states?" Individuals and state governments are also asking this question. Discuss what you know of the controversy surrounding physician-assisted suicide and whether your state is debating or considering legalizing it.
4. Do you agree or disagree that physician-assisted suicide should be legal? Explain your reasons in writing.

FIRST THOUGHTS

To prepare yourself for the reading selection, answer the following questions, either on your own or in a group discussion.

1. If you have read Selection 36, what additional questions do you have about physician-assisted suicide? If you did not read the selection, then what thoughts do you have about this issue?

2. What other issues are involved in caring for the dying?

3. Preview the title, headnote, and first one or two paragraphs. What do you think will follow?

WORD ALERT

abhorrent (1) regarded with horror or loathing
chronic (3) long-lasting, continuing, recurrent
impoverished (4) reduced to poverty
rational (6) reasoned, logical
diminishing (6) decreasing, lessening, making smaller
parlaying (11) betting

❧ Suicide Issue Diverts Us from the Real Problems

JOANNE LYNN

Joanne Lynn, M.D., is director of the Center to Improve Care of the Dying at George Washington University and president of Americans for Better Care of the Dying. In this selection, she argues against legalizing physician-assisted suicide. The selection ran in the AARP Bulletin, *May 1999, as one of two opposing views written in answer to the question "Should physician-assisted suicide be legalized by the states?"*

M ANY PEOPLE THINK that deciding whether to legalize physician- 1 assisted suicide is a clear-cut issue. They either oppose legalization because they find any killing **abhorrent,** or favor it because they believe people should be allowed to make choices without government interference.

Neither of these positions, though, takes into account the very difficult end-of-life issues that confront us. I oppose legalization of physician-assisted suicide because it risks killing people who could and should live their last days comfortably—if only we fixed our health-care system. 2

Until about 50 years ago, most people died suddenly—usually from infections and accidents. Now most of us grow old and then die slowly from a **chronic** illness like cancer or heart disease. Living longer is a good thing, but we need improved health services to live well until the end of life. 3

With better care for people with terminal illnesses, physician-assisted suicide would no longer need to be an option. No patient would have to be overwhelmed by pain, feel alone and afraid or be **impoverished** by medical expenses. 4

Now, however, many people do face those and other problems. One reason is because our medical system badly mismatches spending with actual patient needs. Medicare, for example, was set up to assure that individuals could get surgery when they needed it; the program was not set up to provide continuity of care, pain control or family support, the things dying patients most need. Medicare makes it easier to get a heart transplant than to get pain medicine or home-health aides. 5

Supporters and opponents of legalizing physician-assisted suicide agree we have not learned how to support very sick people and their families. Advocates contend, however, that physician-assisted suicide is still a choice, and that the risks can be contained. They imagine a **rational** person who has painful symptoms but a loving family, predictable illness and adequate finances. In truth, most of us will come to our last months of life with **diminishing** resources, some confusion and uncertainty about the course of our illness—and this occurs in a badly functioning health system that provides few real choices. 6

What is the physician to do when a patient asks for suicide assistance because his care is bankrupting his spouse, his pain is unrelieved, prescription drugs are too costly or the thought of going to a Medicaid nursing home is too threatening? 7

Our first response must be to change the care system—not to make it easier to "choose" to be dead. Assisted suicide is a sideshow that is taking our attention away from urgently needed health-care reform. 8

What can you do? First, educate yourself. People can ordinarily 9
live well despite serious illness. Various books, including our "Hand-
book for Mortals" (Oxford University Press, 1999), can show you how.

Second, you can be an advocate for change in the care system. 10
Americans for Better Care of the Dying posts its "Agitator's Guide" and
its legislative agenda on the Web at www.abcd-caring.com. Or you can
request copies by writing to: Americans for Better Care of the Dying,
2175 K St. N.W., Suite 810, Washington, D.C. 20037.

Seriously ill people should be able to live comfortably and with 11
dignity to the end. Legalizing physician-assisted suicide is not the answer, as it runs the risk of **parlaying** the vulnerability of the elderly and
the very sick into a "choice" to die. Instead we should work toward real,
enduring improvement in end-of-life care.

COMPREHENSION CHECK

Purpose and Main Idea

1. What is the author's topic?
   a. the suicide issue
   b. end-of-life issues
   c. managed health care
   d. Medicare

2. The central idea of the selection is stated in
   a. paragraph 1, first sentence "Many people. . . ."
   b. paragraph 1, second sentence "They either. . . ."
   c. paragraph 2, first sentence "Neither of. . . ."
   d. paragraph 2, last sentence "I oppose. . . ."

3. The author's *primary* purpose is to
   a. express distrust of government involvement in health care.
   b. entertain readers with a true-life account of health care in
      nursing homes.
   c. persuade readers to work toward improvement in end-of-life
      care.
   d. inform readers that health-care issues other than legalizing
      euthanasia confront us.

Details

4. The author opposes physician-assisted suicide because
   a. she believes people should be allowed to make choices with-
      out government interference.

    b. she finds all killing abhorrent.
    c. it risks killing people who could and should live out their last
       days comfortably.
    d. physicians should not be involved.

5. According to the author, to live well until the end of life, we need
    a. improved health services.
    b. better health insurance.
    c. the option of physician-assisted suicide.
    d. government involvement in health care.

6. Both supporters and opponents of legalizing physician-assisted
   suicide agree that
    a. patients should be free to choose suicide.
    b. physician-assisted suicide has too many risks.
    c. we do not know how to support the very sick.
    d. our health-care system functions adequately.

7. The author offers all but which one of the following as solutions
   to the problem of inadequate end-of-life care?
    a. Reform the care system.
    b. Educate yourself.
    c. Be an advocate for change.
    d. Legalize physician-assisted suicide.

8. Paragraphs 4 and 5 are related by
    a. comparison and contrast.
    b. generalization then example.
    c. cause and effect.
    d. steps in a process.

Inferences

9. The author would probably agree that which one of the following
   would be a real improvement in health care for an elderly patient
   who is terminally ill?
    a. increased Medicare benefits
    b. prescription drugs at affordable prices
    c. legalization of physician-assisted suicide
    d. confinement in a nursing home

10. The author calls assisted suicide a "sideshow" because it
    a. puts people at odds with each other.
    b. diverts attention from the real issues.
    c. offers patients the right to choose.
    d. is clouded in legal controversy.

WORKING WITH WORDS

Complete the sentences below with these words from Word Alert:

impoverished   parlaying   rational
diminishing   abhorrent   chronic

1. _____ headache sufferers hope for a remedy that not only will stop the pain but will keep the headache from recurring.
2. A crash in the stock market could leave some investors so _____ that it might take them years to regain their wealth.
3. Although the hurricane had been severe, we could tell from the _____ wind and rain that the storm would soon be over.
4. To many parents, the thought of their child getting a tattoo or a pierced navel is _____ .
5. Fred made the mistake of _____ his lottery winnings on another bet and lost everything.
6. It is not _____ to have test anxiety when you have studied sufficiently and know the material.

THINKING DEEPER

Ideas for discussion and writing

1. What opposing views on legalizing assisted suicide does the author state, and how does she counter these views?
2. Using what you have learned from both this selection and Selection 36, form a small group and prepare an argument either for or against physician-assisted suicide. List the points of your argument on a sheet of paper. Be prepared to make and defend your argument in class.
3. Discuss how this selection illustrates the Part 4 theme, *Hard Questions.* For example, the authors of Selections 36 and 37 answered the hard question "Should physician-assisted suicide be legalized by the states?" Discuss how their views differ. Which author's views come closest to your own?
4. Did reading these selections change or reaffirm your views on physician-assisted suicide or other health-care issues? Write about your reactions.

FIRST THOUGHTS

To prepare yourself for the reading selection, answer the following questions, either on your own or in a group discussion.

1. Is the death penalty legal in your state?
2. Are you in favor of or against the death penalty and why?
3. Preview the title, headnote, and first one or two paragraphs. What do you think will follow?

WORD ALERT

exasperation (1) great annoyance or impatience
gurney (3) a metal stretcher with legs on wheels
botched (6) ruined as a result of clumsiness
negotiate (8) to arrange or settle by agreement
inflicting (12) imposing, dealing out something that is a punishment or a burden

❧ In Opposition to the Death Penalty

A. E. P. WALL

A. E. P. Wall is a veteran journalist. He wrote this commentary on the death penalty for The Orlando Sentinel.

WHEN O.J. SIMPSON'S souvenirs were auctioned, one bidder said   1
he spent $16,000 for items that he planned to burn. This was to show his **exasperation** with the not-guilty verdict in Simpson's trial, which was the trial of the century just before former President Clinton's U.S. Senate trial of the century and just after Paula Jones nominated Clinton as defendant in the sexual-harassment trial of the century. You might think that the laid-back national attitude toward pranks of a capital nature, or those that miss being high crimes by several inches,

would bring a sense of hope to the 2,000 people or so now living on death row in U.S. prisons.

Everybody has read about innocent men saved from unjust exe- 2 cution by the state, which is we, you and I. Nobody knows how many innocent men we've killed in the past, legally correct but morally unpardonable.

Has the time come to grant celebrity status to those who await 3 death by artificial lightning in the electric chair or by an artificial drug overdose on a prison **gurney?**

Jesse Joseph Tafero became famous too late. After the state of 4 Florida replaced a natural sponge with a synthetic sponge in the headpiece, flames shot out from Tafero's head. He kept on breathing until three jolts of electricity were applied. Nobody in a position of authority to stop this kind of thing considers it to be cruel and unusual.

Pedro Medina was not the right kind of Florida celebrity either. 5 With the first jolt of electricity, flames sparked from the mask over his face. There was smoke, and there was the stench of burned flesh.

There have been a couple of dozen **botched** executions through- 6 out the country during the past decade and a half.

Most of the folk who await death at the hands of the American 7 public are poor. Some are mentally disabled. Four out of 10 are African-American.

If only they had the Senate Democrats to judge them, they might 8 **negotiate** life without parole—reasonable in capital cases—and reversible if the prisoner is later found to be innocent, leaving fewer scars on the nation's body politic.

In Florida, two influential groups oppose the death penalty out- 9 right. It is no longer politically correct to describe them, or anyone, as strange bedfellows, but the Catholic Church in the United States and the American Civil Liberties Union are on the same side. The Catholic Church goes further, also defending the life of the unborn.

Florida has a Catholic population of about 2 million, more than 10 300,000 of them in the Diocese of Orlando. ACLU members are not that numerous, but they tend to make themselves heard, even without a pulpit.

Among those Catholic millions is the governor, Jeb Bush, a widely 11 respected member of a family that is becoming what the Kennedys were once thought to be. There's no sign so far that he agrees with the Catholic bishops, who formally declared their opposition to capital punishment in 1974. Pope John Paul II wrote in his encyclical *The*

Gospel of Life that cases that might justify executions are rare if not practically nonexistent.

The ACLU believes that the death penalty is always unconstitu- 12 tional under the Eighth Amendment, which forbids **inflicting** "cruel and unusual" punishment, and the Fourteenth Amendment because the discriminatory choice of capital punishment victims violates the equal protection granted to all persons, citizens or not.

Whether the jury has six members or a dozen or a hundred, it may 13 define the law in its own language. That may be the language of the streets, the language of race, the language of privilege or the language of politics. A jury gives one person $50 million, sends another to death row, frees one to write a book celebrating the triumph of lawyerly talent.

A chap named Thucydides[1] said that in a democracy, the law as- 14 sures equal justice to all. The massing of more than 2,000 prisoners to await execution in American prisons came about 2,400 years later, most of them equal, at least in poverty.

Thomas Jefferson defined it more sharply. In his first Inaugural 15 Address, he saluted "equal and exact justice to all. . . ."

There's nothing equal or exact about the death penalty. The theory 16 of vengeance that supports hanging, electrocution, shooting or drug- ging to death by the state is not applied equally. If it were, convicted rapists would be raped by the official state rapist. A motorist, found guilty of driving while drunk and hitting a pedestrian, would be placed into the middle of the street and run down by the official state drunk.

If the ACLU and the Catholic Church and others as disparate can 17 agree on the injustice of rubbing out criminals, whether through frustra- tion or thirst for blood, maybe justice, even exact justice, has a chance.

COMPREHENSION CHECK

Purpose and Main Idea

1. What is the author's topic?
    a. famous trials
    b. the death penalty
    c. types of executions
    d. unjust execution

2. The central idea of the selection is stated in

---

[1] Thucydides was a Greek historian (c. 460–400 B.C.) noted for his account of the Pelo- ponnesian War.

    a. paragraph 2 "Nobody knows. . . ."
    b. paragraph 6 "There have been. . . ."
    c. paragraph 12 "The ACLU believes. . . ."
    d. paragraph 16 "There's nothing equal. . . ."

3. The author's *primary* purpose is to
    a. express opposition to the death penalty.
    b. persuade us that the death penalty is unjust.
    c. inform us that a controversy surrounds the death penalty.
    d. entertain us with accounts of trials of the century.

Details

4. According to the author, how many people in U.S. prisons are awaiting execution?
    a. 2,000
    b. 2,400
    c. 16,000
    d. 300,000

5. Most of the prisoners awaiting execution fall into all but which one of the following categories?
    a. poor people
    b. the mentally disabled
    c. young offenders
    d. African Americans

6. Two influential groups in Florida that oppose the death penalty are the ACLU (American Civil Liberties Union) and
    a. the Florida Senate.
    b. the Catholic Church.
    c. the American Bar Association.
    d. Democratic party members.

7. The author's evidence against the death penalty includes all but which one of the following?
    a. Innocent men have been executed.
    b. Executions have been botched.
    c. The death penalty is applied unequally.
    d. Poll results show widespread opposition.

8. In paragraphs 4 and 5, what purpose do the examples of Tafero and Medina serve?
    a. They prove that discrimination against minorities exists.
    b. Both show how Florida deals with capital punishment.
    c. Both are examples of botched executions.
    d. They appeal to a reader's sense of humor.

Inferences

9. Which one of the following best supports the legal argument against the death penalty?
    a. the Eighth and Fourteenth Amendments
    b. the trials of Simpson, Clinton, and Jones
    c. Tafero's and Medina's executions
    d. the ACLU's objections to capital punishment

10. The author's argument is invalid because
    a. he resorts to stereotyping.
    b. his language is emotionally charged.
    c. the evidence is insufficient.
    d. the argument is one-sided.

WORKING WITH WORDS

Complete the sentences below with these words from Word Alert:

exasperation   negotiate   gurney
inflicting   botched

1. Union leaders and management worked together to _____ the terms of their contract.

2. The accident victim was placed on a _____ and rushed to the emergency room.

3. May I borrow a piece of paper? I've _____ this one by writing answers to the wrong questions.

4. Many prisoners are guilty of fighting and _____ wounds on one another when no one is looking.

5. The students reacted with _____ when they saw how many of their test answers were incorrect.

THINKING DEEPER

Ideas for discussion and writing

1. Working with group members, list and discuss the author's evidence against the death penalty, and rank his reasons from most convincing to least convincing. Share your results with the rest of the class.

2. What evidence can you offer in favor of the death penalty? Working with group members, list, discuss, and rank the evidence from most to least convincing. Share your results with the rest of the class.

3. Discuss how this selection illustrates the Part 4 theme, *Hard Questions*. For example, whether to retain or abolish the death penalty has been a hard question for some states. How has your state addressed this issue, and do you agree with your lawmakers' decisions? Discuss and explain your answer.

4. Review the lists of evidence generated for discussion items 1 and 2, then write a paper in which you explain why you are either for or against the death penalty.

FIRST THOUGHTS

To prepare yourself for the reading selection, answer the following questions, either on your own or in a group discussion.

1. What have you heard or read about prisoners who were wrongly accused?
2. In your opinion, what is the single most important reason to be for or against the death penalty?
3. Preview the title, headnote, and first one or two paragraphs. What do you think will follow?

WORD ALERT

recede (3) withdraw, retreat, move back or away from
complied (7) acted in accordance with another's command, request, rule, or wishes
flagging (9) declining, weakening
exculpatory (11) acting or tending to clear of guilt or blame
moratorium (11) an authorized period of delay, suspension
scrutiny (13) close, careful observation or examination
tyranny (13) absolute power, especially when exercised unjustly or cruelly

❧ In Defense of the Death Penalty

MARIANNE MEANS

Marianne Means is a journalist for Hearst Newspapers. She wrote this commentary on the death penalty for The Orlando Sentinel.

WITHIN THE SPAN of a few days, Pope John Paul II pleaded for the 1 life of a convicted killer and college students uncovered evidence that a death-row inmate may have been wrongly sentenced—and the legitimacy of the death penalty was in for another political thumping.

Here we go again.   2

The ultimate punishment has become a quietly accepted fact of 3
American life only in the past few years. The Supreme Court ruled
back in 1976 that it was constitutionally OK if applied fairly and ap-
propriately. Controversy over the issue was slow to **recede** even though
a majority of the public and most national politicians long supported
the concept.

Opponents have continued to fight capital punishment. They 4
hold candlelight vigils before scheduled executions, help death-row
inmates file endless appeals, glamorize killers by selling sympathetic
books and raise their voices in moral outrage.

But throughout the country, the 38 states that permit the death 5
penalty have executed 500 convicted murderers in the past 23 years
with increasingly less public attention. Now, however, fresh ammuni-
tion is reviving the old arguments about whether capital punishment
can ever be morally justified or administered in a way that does not
sometimes mistakenly kill innocent men.

During his visit to St. Louis last month, the Pope tried to revive 6
the issue with strong statements condemning the death penalty.
He also asked Missouri Gov. Mel Carnahan to commute the death
sentence of Darrell Mease, who was due to die by lethal injection in
two weeks.

The governor **complied,** although there was no question at trial 7
that Mease was guilty of hiding for three days to ambush a 69-year-old
man, his wife and their paraplegic grandson. He shot the three and
then walked up to them to shoot each one again in the face in what
was described as the most cold-blooded killing ever to take place in
the region. His only defense was post-traumatic stress from Vietnam.

The incident dramatized the Pope's belief that the state has no 8
right to take any life, even that of someone who has brutally taken the
life of another. But his choice for salvation was not a sympathetic one;
the victims' families and friends, among others, felt that the killer deserved to die.

But to the degree that the Pope's example energizes Catholic offi- 9
cials, we may see the church try to revive its **flagging** efforts to get
Catholics to fight the death penalty. (Polls show that lay Catholics support capital punishment by a 2-to-1 margin, roughly equal to that of
Protestants.)

A more immediate reaction was prompted by the discovery of 10
Northwestern University journalism students that Anthony Porter,
who was due to be executed for the 1982 shooting deaths of two

teenagers, may be innocent. The students found a Milwaukee man who confessed to the murders for which Porter was convicted.

Death-penalty opponents point out that such mistakes are more 11 common than we realize. In Chicago, alone, 10 death-row inmates have been released since 1977 after the discovery of new **exculpatory** evidence. The cry has gone up for a **moratorium** on executions and drastic revisions in the way the sentence is imposed. Even Chicago Mayor Richard Daley, who calls himself "pro death," now supports a temporary halt to executions.

Yet the possibility of error—still relatively rare—is not, in itself, 12 sufficient to justify abandoning the death penalty.

Obviously an execution, being uniquely irreversible, calls for extra 13 **scrutiny.** But a great nation cannot tremble before laws to protect the safety of its citizens out of fear that they may be applied imperfectly. That would amount to **tyranny** of the few over the many.

If found guilty, those three white, Texas men who are charged with 14 dragging a black man to his death behind a pickup truck do not deserve a taxpayer subsidy to loaf in a prison cell. Karla Faye Tucker, executed for hacking two people to death with a pickax, didn't deserve it either—despite her belated conversion to Christianity.

Justice requires the ultimate repayment in kind for the ultimate 15 evil of robbing another living, breathing human being of life.

COMPREHENSION CHECK

Purpose and Main Idea

1. What is the author's topic?
    a. the wrongly accused
    b. criminals' rights
    c. the death penalty
    d. victims' rights

2. The central idea of the selection is stated in
    a. paragraph 3 "The ultimate. . . ."
    b. paragraph 5 "Now, however. . . ."
    c. paragraph 12 "Yet the possibility. . . ."
    d. paragraph 15 "Justice requires. . . ."

3. The author's *primary* purpose is to
    a. inform readers of new arguments against the death penalty.
    b. entertain us with profiles of death-row inmates.

    c. express concern about innocent people who have been executed.

    d. persuade readers that we need the death penalty.

Details

4. According to the author, who supports capital punishment?
   a. Pope John Paul II
   b. a majority of the public and most politicians
   c. the families of death-row inmates
   d. Northwestern University journalism students

5. According to the author, opponents of capital punishment have done all but which of the following?
   a. asserted the rights of criminals' victims
   b. held candlelight vigils
   c. helped death-row inmates file appeals
   d. glamorized killers and aroused sympathy for them

6. Although 10 death-row inmates were released from a Chicago prison after new evidence proved them innocent, the possibility of error in sentencing, according to the author, is
   a. frequent.
   b. unproven.
   c. rare.
   d. nonexistent.

7. Which one of the following may, in fact, be innocent of the 1982 murder for which he was convicted?
   a. Darrell Mease
   b. Mel Carnahan
   c. Anthony Porter
   d. a white Texas male

8. The organizational pattern in paragraph 11 is
   a. generalization then example.
   b. cause and effect.
   c. sequence.
   d. process.

Inferences

9. The author's choice of words in paragraph 14 can best be described as
   a. neutral.
   b. inappropriate.

c. emotionally charged.

d. descriptive.

10. The statement "Justice requires. . . ." (paragraph 15) is similar in meaning to which one of the following?

    a. Justice is blind.

    b. An eye for an eye.

    c. My kingdom for a horse.

    d. Render unto Caesar that which is Caesar's.

WORKING WITH WORDS

Complete the sentences below with these words from Word Alert:

exculpatory   flagging   scrutiny   recede
moratorium   complied   tyranny

1. Rolanda sat on the beach, watching the waves crash on shore then _____.

2. The schoolteacher quickly changed activities when he saw that the children's interest was _____.

3. After a shooting at the local high school, the mayor called for a _____ on selling guns until the case was resolved.

4. Our _____ of the map revealed to us that we were headed in the wrong direction.

5. The students _____ with their instructor's request to work in small groups on their assignments.

6. New _____ evidence proved that the person accused of vandalizing public property was out of town when the crime occurred.

7. Early settlers came to the New World to escape the _____ of their former rulers.

THINKING DEEPER

Ideas for discussion and writing

1. Where does the author state her position on the death penalty? What evidence does she give to support her position? Does she acknowledge and answer the claims of the opposition? Where?

2. Working with a partner or group, find another article on the death penalty. Use your library's resources or do your research on the Internet. Read the article and take notes on the author's evidence. How does the author's evidence compare to that of Means and Wall? What new evidence or information does your article contain? Present your findings to the rest of the class.

3. Discuss how this selection illustrates the Part 4 theme, *Hard Questions*. For example, Selections 38 and 39 address the death penalty from opposing points of view. How has each author answered the hard question "Should we keep the death penalty?" Discuss each author's evidence and choice of words. With which author do you most agree and why?

4. Write about what you have learned from reading Selections 38 and 39 and the article you researched for discussion item 2. Explain why your position on the death penalty either has or has not changed.

FIRST THOUGHTS

To prepare yourself for the reading selection, answer the following questions, either on your own or in a group discussion.

1. What percentage of American marriages would you estimate have ended in divorce?

2. What economic and social pressures face children of divorced parents?

3. Preview the title, headnote, and first one or two paragraphs. What do you think will follow?

WORD ALERT

In a textbook chapter, the words to watch may appear in boldface, italics, or a special color.

custody (2) legal responsibility for children, awarded to a parent following divorce

naturalistic (5) refers to research in which subjects are observed in normal or natural circumstances

externalizing (6) acting out impulses and feelings

authoritative (6) a parenting style that exercises high control with warmth and nurturing

authoritarian (6) a parenting style that exercises high control without warmth

permissive (6) a parenting style that involves either making few demands on children or avoiding child-rearing responsibilities altogether

internalizing (7) holding feelings and impulses inside

joint custody (11) a legal arrangement whereby parents share custody of children

❧ Divorce and Its Effects on Children

KELVIN L. SEIFERT AND ROBERT J. HOFFNUNG

This textbook reading is excerpted from Chapter 13 of Childhood and Adolescent Development, *fifth edition. The*

*entire chapter is about psychosocial development in middle
childhood. The excerpt focuses on parenting and family life.
When reading from textbooks, remember that headings
may signal topics, main ideas, or important details.*

M OST PARENTS WHO divorce must make major adjustments in 1
their lives, and these adjustments often affect their children
deeply. First, many divorcing parents face sudden economic pressures. Some find themselves financially responsible for two house-
holds, that of their former spouse and children and that of the new
spouse and children. Many divorced mothers must take on new or
additional employment to meet their household responsibilities,
but even so their standard of living frequently declines. For many of
these women, a reduction of economic resources often is accompanied by dependence on welfare; poorer-quality housing, neighborhoods, schools, and child care; and the need to move to a
neighborhood they can afford, which often leads to loss of social support for the child from familiar friends, neighbors, and teachers. In
contrast, both noncustodial and custodial fathers are more likely to
maintain or improve their standard of living following divorce (Hetherington et al., 1998).

Divorce involves many psychological pressures as well. The par- 2
ent who takes primary **custody** of the children must learn to manage
a household alone, which is a major physical and psychological burden. Some parents may feel deeply isolated from relatives or friends to
whom they used to feel close. If relatives do live nearby, divorcing parents often must rely on them for the first time, simply to procure help
with child care and household work. Even before actual separation
and divorce, many such families go through long periods of distress,
tension, and discord. For most, these pressures continue to create
stress for two or three years following separation (Corey, 1998; Hetherington et al., 1998).

Divorce is especially hard for school-age children. Having out- 3
grown the self-centeredness of the preschool years, school-age children increasingly identify with and rely on their parents as role
models to help them establish their own sense of who they are and
how they should behave. At a time when children are just learning to
be independent from home life, divorce threatens the safe base they
have come to rely on to help make increasing independence possible.
The loyalty conflicts frequently created by parents who are competing

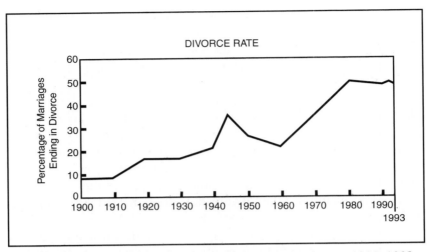

FIGURE 13.2   Percentage of U.S. Marriages Ending in Divorce, 1900–1993

Since the mid–1980s, approximately half of all marriages in the United States have ended in divorce.
Source: U.S. Bureau of the Census (1995)

for their children's allegiance can make children fearful that they will lose one of their parents in the process.

Judith Wallerstein and Sandra Blakeslee (1996) conducted a long-   4
term follow-up study of middle-SES[1] children who were between six and eight years old at the time of their parents' divorce. She found that even ten years later, these children were burdened by fear of disappointment in love relationships, lowered expectations, and a sense of powerlessness. When compared to children who were older or younger at the time of the breakup, school-age children fared far worse in their emotional adjustment and overall competence, including school and social relationships. The profound unhappiness with current relationships and concerns regarding future ones that these children experienced often were masked by their overall conformity to social expectations (see Table 13.2).

Some critics have questioned the degree to which Wallerstein &   5
Blakeslee's findings, which were based on **naturalistic,** case study techniques with a middle-class sample, represent the entire population of parents and children of divorce. Future research using more

_____

[1] socioeconomic status

TABLE 13.2 The Psychological Tasks of Children of Divorce

Task 1: Understanding the divorce	Children must first learn to accurately perceive the immediate changes that divorce brings. Later they learn to distinguish between fantasized fears of being abandoned or losing their parents and reality so that they can evaluate their parents' actions and draw useful lessons for their own lives.
Task 2: Strategic withdrawal	Children and adolescents need to get on with their own lives as quickly as possible and get back, physically and emotionally, to the normal tasks of growing up. This poses a dual challenge to children, who must actively remove themselves emotionally from parental distress and conflict to safeguard their individual identities and separate life course.
Task 3: Dealing with loss	Children must overcome two profound losses: the loss of the intact family, together with the symbolic and real protection it provided, and the loss of the presence of one parent, usually the father, from their lives. They must overcome the powerful sense of rejection, humiliation, unlovableness, and powerlessness they feel and feelings of self-blame for causing the divorce.
Task 4: Dealing with anger	The major task for children is to resolve their anger at being hurt by the very people they depend on for protection and love. They must recognize their parents as human beings capable of making mistakes and respect them for their efforts and courage.
Task 5: Working out guilt	Young children often feel responsible for divorce, thinking their misbehavior may have caused one parent to leave. They need to separate from guilty "ties that bind" them too closely to a troubled parent and go on with their own lives.
Task 6: Accepting the permanence of the divorce	At first, children's strong need to deny the divorce can help them cope with the powerful realities they face. Over time, they must accept the divorce as a permanent state of affairs.
Task 7: Taking a chance on love	Achieving realistic hope regarding relationships may be the most important task for both the child and society. Children must create and sustain a realistic vision of their own capacity to love and be loved, knowing that separation and divorce are always possible. Mastering this last task—which depends on successfully negotiating all of the others—leads to psychological freedom from the past and to a second chance.

Source: Adapted from Wallerstein and Blakeslee (1989, 1996).

quantitative approaches and families from a broader range of backgrounds will help determine the validity of their findings (Hetherington et al., 1998).

DIFFERENT EFFECTS ON BOYS AND GIRLS

On the whole, girls and boys tend to respond differently to divorce. [6] Boys often express their distress in **externalizing** ways, becoming more aggressive, willful, and disobedient during the period surrounding separation and divorce. They often lose access to the parent with whom they identify more strongly—their father—because the majority of divorced children live with their mothers and are more frequently victims of parental power struggles and inconsistencies in matters of discipline. In a study of children six years after divorce, Mavris Hetherington (1988, 1991) found that whereas mothers and daughters had reestablished close and positive relationships, problems between mothers and sons persisted. Whereas the most common parenting style for divorced mothers with daughters was **authoritative,** the most common style with sons was **authoritarian** and the next most common **permissive,** suggesting that mothers either tried to control their sons' behavior with power assertiveness or gave up trying.

Girls appear to become less aggressive as a result of divorce, tend [7] to worry more about schoolwork, and often take on more household responsibilities. This suggests they are **internalizing,** or holding inside, their distress by trying to act more helpful and responsible than usual (Block et al., 1981). Daughters of divorced parents may also become overly preoccupied with their relationships with males. They are more likely to become involved in dating and sexual activities at an early age, sometimes before the end of elementary school, and more likely to get pregnant and have conflict-ridden relationships with males during their teen years. Girls may also encounter increased risk of sexual abuse from stepparents and parents' dating partners in the period following divorce (Wallerstein & Blakeslee, 1996).

Perhaps the most important effort parents can make to minimize [8] the negative effects of divorce is to try to reduce their own conflicts and to cooperate in providing the best parenting possible for their children. Also important is the appropriate use of professional help to successfully work out postdivorce arrangements, resolve emotional conflicts more effectively, and develop the skills needed to sustain strong and supportive parent-child relationships. Finally, close relationships with mothers who are warm and supportive but still provide firm, consistent control and supervision, particularly in the period immediately following divorce, are associated with positive adjustment for both girls and boys (Armatz et al., 1995; Simons & Johnson, 1996; Stolberg & Walsh, 1988).

CUSTODY ARRANGEMENTS

Relationships between parents and children frequently deteriorate 9 during and immediately after a divorce. The parent with physical custody of the children (usually the mother) finds herself dealing not only with her children but also with major new responsibilities for earning a living and making peace—at least in her mind—with the reality of divorce. Parents without physical custody of the children (usually fathers) do not face these daily hassles, but they do report feeling rootless, dissatisfied, and unjustly cut off from their children. Seeing his children every other week or on school vacations may prevent a father from knowing them intimately and being part of their everyday lives, and lead him to become increasingly reliant on special events (such as going to Disney World), when contacts do occur. Noncustodial parents may also believe their financial and emotional support for their children goes unappreciated. Perhaps for these reasons, although fathers often increase the amount of time they spend with their children immediately after divorce, they soon decrease such time well below what it was before the divorce (Hetherington et al., 1998).

For noncustodial fathers and mothers alike, both the quantity and 10 quality of parent-child relationships differ from those of parents who have custody. Noncustodial mothers are, on the average, less competent than custodial mothers in controlling and monitoring their children's behavior, although they are more effective than noncustodial fathers. Noncustodial mothers are also more interested in and better informed about their children's activities; more supportive, sensitive, and responsive to their children's needs; and better able to communicate with their children than noncustodial fathers are (Hetherington et al., 1998). The postdivorce parenting of fathers is less predictable than that of noncustodial mothers. Some fathers who were previously attached to and involved with their children find their new role too limited and painful, and drift away from their children. Others, however, rise to the occasion and become more involved with their children. The quality of the noncustodial father's relationship with his children and the circumstances in which contacts with them occur are much more important than frequency of visits. When noncustodial

fathers remain actively involved in their children's activities and emotional lives, positive developmental outcomes are likely. Even limited
contact with noncustodial fathers can enhance children's adjustment
when it occurs under supportive, low-conflict conditions (Clarke-
Stewart & Hayward, 1996; Simons & Beaman, 1996).

Sometimes parents are able to establish **joint custody,** a legal   11
arrangement in which parental rights and responsibilities continue to
be shared in a relatively equal manner. The mechanics of the arrangement vary with the child's age and the family's circumstances. The
children may live with each parent during alternate weeks, parts of
weeks, or even parts of the year. Or, when the children are older, one or
more may live with one parent and the rest with the other parent. Joint
custody tends to promote greater contact with both parents after divorce, facilitate fathers' involvement, and make mothers' parenting
responsibilities less burdensome. Its success, however, depends on
parents' willingness and ability to rearrange their lives and maintain
the levels of mutual respect and cooperation required to make this
arrangement work (Arditti, 1992).

COMPREHENSION CHECK

Purpose and Main Idea

1. What is the authors' topic?
   a. custody arrangements
   b. effects of divorce
   c. parenting styles
   d. children's behavior

2. Which one of the following best states the authors' central idea?
   a. The law provides different custody arrangements for parents,
      depending on the circumstances of the divorce.
   b. Children's behavior, to a large extent, depends on the parent-
      ing style to which they are exposed.
   c. The adjustments that parents must make following divorce
      affect their children in several ways.
   d. Boys and girls may react differently when families are recom-
      bined following divorce and remarriage.

3. The authors' primary purpose in this excerpt is to do which one
   of the following?
   a. inform readers about the high rate of divorce in the United
      States

    b. express a preference for the traditional family
    c. persuade parents to work out problems for their children's sake
    d. explain how children react following their parents' divorce

Details

4. The authors cite all but which one of the following as economic pressures that divorced mothers may face?
    a. managing a household alone
    b. the need for additional or new employment
    c. poorer-quality housing
    d. a decline in their standard of living

5. According to the authors, divorce is especially hard on which one of the following groups?
    a. adolescents
    b. school-age children
    c. preschoolers
    d. young adults

6. Whose research showed that divorced mothers fared better at reestablishing positive relationships with daughters than with sons?
    a. Coley (1998)
    b. Block et al. (1981)
    c. Mavris Hetherington (1988, 1991)
    d. Wallerstein and Blakeslee (1996)

7. According to the authors, what is the most important way in which parents can minimize the negative effects of divorce?
    a. develop good parenting skills
    b. provide firm, consistent control and supervision
    c. seek professional help
    d. cooperate and reduce conflict

8. What is the authors' primary pattern of development in paragraphs 6 and 7?
    a. The authors *compare* boys' and girls' behavior following divorce.
    b. They explain *causes and effects* of divorce on children.
    c. They list stages in the *process* of recovering from divorce.
    d. The authors *classify* children's responses to divorce.

Inferences

9. Figure 13.2 shows that the greatest increase in the percentage of marriages ending in divorce occurred during which periods?
   a. 1900–1920
   b. 1920–1940
   c. 1940–1945
   d. 1960–1980

10. In Table 13.2, overcoming feelings of rejection and self-blame is a psychological task that falls into which category?
    a. understanding the divorce
    b. strategic withdrawal
    c. dealing with loss
    d. working out guilt

WORKING WITH WORDS

Complete the sentences below with these words from Word Alert:

> internalizing   authoritarian   naturalistic   permissive
> externalizing   joint custody   authoritative   custody

1. Following a divorce, parents must work out _____ arrangements.
2. Those who allow their children to run and play in restaurants have a _____ parenting style
3. Students in an education course were asked to conduct a _____ study in which they observed play behavior among kindergarteners.
4. Children who hit and bully others are _____ their anger.
5. Divorced parents who share child-rearing responsibilities equally have a _____ arrangement.
6. _____ parents are loving and caring, while insisting that their children follow rules.
7. A child who is more cooperative than usual may be _____ , or holding back, feelings of distress.
8. Parents whose style is _____ may be uncommunicative and lack warmth in dealing with their children.

THINKING DEEPER

Ideas for discussion and writing

1. In this selection, the authors explain the effects of custody arrangements on the children of divorce. Are their views similar to or different from those expressed by Nick Sheff in "My Long-Distance Life" (Selection 31)?

2. Seifert and Hoffnung in this selection and Barbara Dafoe White-head in Selection 32 discuss the effects of divorce on children. How do these authors differ in terms of the problems they identify and their solutions for minimizing the negative effects of divorce on children?

3. Discuss how the effects of divorce on children explained in this excerpt relate to the Part 4 theme, *Hard Questions*. For example, studies have shown, as in this excerpt, that divorce affects children differently but often negatively. Children of divorce are more likely to do poorly in school, get involved in drugs, become unwed parents, and have other adjustment problems than are children of intact families. Whether to divorce or to stay married is a hard question for some couples, and what we as a society can or should do about the high divorce rate is another hard question. What do you think about divorce and its effects in general, and what alternatives exist for troubled couples?

4. A key to understanding your textbooks is to learn the terms introduced in each chapter. One way to learn terms is to make 3" by 5" flashcards for frequent review. On one side of the card, write the term and a memory cue that identifies the source of the term, such as a course or textbook chapter. On the other side of the card, write a definition. Using the examples in Figures 4.1A and 4.1B as a guide, make a set of flashcards for the terms listed in Word Alert. If you prefer, choose terms that you need to review from one of your other courses.

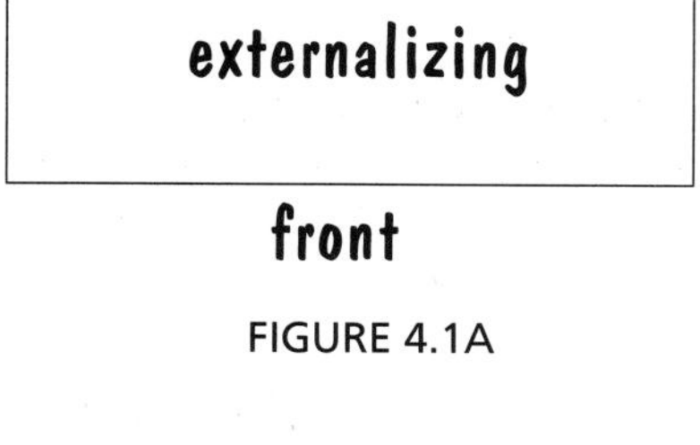

```
 _____
|                ( human )|
|                (  dev.  )|
|                          |
|     externalizing        |
|                          |
|_____|
```

front

FIGURE 4.1A

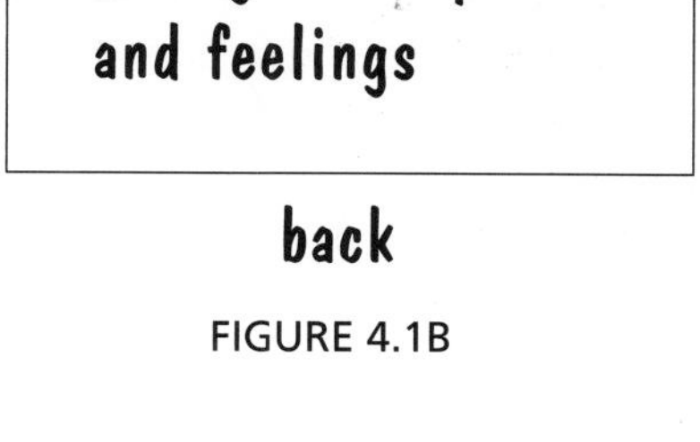

```
 _____
|                          |
|  acting out impulses     |
|  and feelings            |
|                          |
|_____|
```

back

FIGURE 4.1B

PART FIVE

America at Work

❧

If you are a young college student, you may view college as an essential step toward landing your first real job. If you are an older student, you may be seeking the opportunity college provides to rethink, retrain, and restart your life for a better future.

Work not only provides the means to a good life, but also makes up a large part of your identity. Asked to describe themselves, most Americans answer by explaining what they do for a living. Because work takes up such a big part of your life, you will be happiest if you choose a career that enables you to earn money while doing something that you love doing.

The Part 5 selections are about people who have found meaningful work and the skills that ensure career success. As you read and think about the selections, ask yourself these questions: What kind of world do I want to live in? What kind of person do I want to be? What kind of work will I enjoy?

FIRST THOUGHTS

To prepare yourself for the reading selection, answer the following questions, either on your own or in a group discussion.

1. Have you spent time in a country whose culture is quite different from your own? What did you learn from the experience?

2. If you had a choice between either remaining in a secure profession or striking out on your own, which would you choose and why?

3. Preview the title, headnote, and first one or two paragraphs. What do you think will follow?

WORD ALERT

esteem (3) favorable regard, respect
debate (4) to consider, discuss, or argue pros and cons
equatorial (6) relating to the equator, or the imaginary line around the earth's middle
complex (7) complicated, intricate
intangible (12) incapable of being perceived through the senses
elite (15) having intellectual, social, or economic status

❧ A Year of African Life Opened My Eyes

JOANN HORNAK

In this essay from Newsweek's *"My Turn" column, author JoAnn Hornak writes about her work as a volunteer in a developing country. Hornak's year in Africa was a time of self-discovery.*

Newsweek, May 13, 2002, pp. 14–15

A NYONE WHO HAS considered following a dream career is often told 1 by well-meaning family and friends, "Don't quit your day job." I didn't listen.

Three years ago, while I was working as a prosecuting attorney, I 2 took a year's leave of absence to pursue a goal I'd had since college: to volunteer in a developing country. During the year in Tanzania, I made several discoveries that ultimately led me to change careers when I returned home.

In Africa I worked on research proposals with several Tanzanian 3 attorneys, including Julius, a struggling public-interest lawyer at the East Africa Law Society. One of my first surprises was to find a country where lawyers are held in the highest **esteem**. That may be because with a population of about 30 million, Tanzania has fewer than 600 lawyers.

One day Julius and I had lunch at a café in Arusha, a tourist town 4 and starting point for safaris to the Serengeti and the Ngorongoro Crater. One of our favorite pastimes was discussing the many differences between life in the United States and in Tanzania. Dessert presented another opening for **debate**.

Julius ordered a dish of vanilla and banana ice cream, two of three 5 flavors offered on the menu. I told him that in the United States we have at least 50 flavors, some mixed with chocolate chips, chunks of cookie dough or caramel swirls, sweets that were difficult to describe because they don't exist in Tanzania. I thought he'd be interested and ask a lot of questions, so I wasn't prepared for his response.

"That's too many," he said, and then went back to enjoying his two 6 plain scoops melting in the **equatorial** heat. Considering that he longed to visit the United States someday, I was surprised by his lack of curiosity. But his observation struck me.

I thought about how **complex** U.S. life can be with our countless 7 lifestyle-and-consumer options. In Tanzania I'd learned to live without luxuries like constant running water and electricity, a refrigerator, car, television, telephone and shopping malls. I grew to prefer the lack of choices, the time not spent in making the perfect selection.

My housemates, Katie from Toronto and Ruth from England, felt 8 the same way. Near the end of our year, we talked about returning to our First World homes.

"I'm afraid to go back," said Katie.   9

"I'm going to stay in my village and not leave for a month," said 10 Ruth, who grew up in Calne, population 800.

"We don't have villages! What am I going to do?" I worried. I loved 11 the simple, slow pace of African life that had given me time to spend hours each day writing. I felt I loved it enough to leave the practice of law and make writing my new career. But when I returned home, reality struck. What if I failed? How would I pay my bills? I was afraid.

I went back to the district attorney's office. For months I resisted 12 the decision to take a leap of faith and quit my job that for nearly 10 years had provided a steady paycheck, health insurance, four weeks' paid vacation and the **intangible** benefits of a successful profession. I'm the first and only person in my family to have earned a college degree. To pay for undergrad and law school, I had always had part-time jobs and taken out student loans. I was reluctant to let go of a career I'd worked hard to achieve.

But often I'd think back to a conversation I had had at a confer- 13 ence in Nairobi a month before returning to the United States. It was at the Carnivore Restaurant, and I was sitting next to Edwin Mtei, former executive director of the International Monetary Fund. Over dinner of Cape buffalo, crocodile and zebra, Mtei asked if I was going back to my job as a prosecutor. I told him that I was thinking of other possibilities, that I hoped to try something new.

"You people have so many choices. You'd never hear a Tanzanian 14 say that. There are so few jobs, we need to take whatever comes along," he said. He wasn't bitter, just pointing out something I hadn't appreciated until I'd spent a year abroad: that I live in a country that gives me the opportunity to reinvent myself.

How could I not try to become a writer when, by accident of birth, 15 I had the option and my friends like Julius, the so-called **elite** in Tanzania, didn't? I finally realized that the only things holding me back were fear and the golden handcuffs.

I gave notice at the D.A.'s office last August. The past nine months 16 haven't been easy, but I can honestly say my only regret is that I wish I'd done this sooner.

COMPREHENSION CHECK

Purpose and Main Idea

1. What is the author's topic?
    a. working as a volunteer
    b. changing jobs or careers
    c. African life and culture
    d. a year among the Tanzanians
2. The author's central idea is stated in which one of the following sentences?

a. paragraph 2, first sentence: "Three years ago. . . ."
b. paragraph 2, last sentence: "During the year. . . ."
c. paragraph 3 first sentence: "In Africa I worked. . . ."
d. paragraph 16, last sentence: "The past nine. . . ."

3. The author's purpose is to
   a. persuade readers to volunteer for worthy causes.
   b. inform readers about life in an African village.
   c. explain why she changed jobs and started over.
   d. entertain readers with a story about African life.

Details

4. The author's work in Tanzania involved which one of the following?
   a. legal aid for the poor
   b. social work
   c. planting crops
   d. research proposals

5. When the author told her friend Julius about the many flavors of ice cream available in the United States, she was surprised by his lack of
   a. knowledge.
   b. understanding.
   c. curiosity.
   d. concern.

6. The author says that while in Tanzania, she learned to live without all but which one of the following?
   a. radio
   b. electricity
   c. shopping malls
   d. television

7. The author resisted changing careers for all but which one of the following reasons?
   a. fear of failure
   b. not knowing what she wanted to do
   c. wondering how she would pay her bills
   d. the intangible benefits of a successful profession

8. The details in paragraph 12 are organized by which one of the following patterns?
   a. classification
   b. comparison and contrast

c. cause and effect

d. generalization and example

Inferences

9. Which one of the following best explains what the author means when she says that life in the United States is "complex"?

    a. The future is uncertain for those who change careers.

    b. We do not appreciate the luxuries we have.

    c. Americans are overscheduled.

    d. We have many choices and opportunities.

10. In paragraph 15, second sentence, "golden handcuffs" most likely refers to which one of the following?

    a. personal luxuries

    b. career opportunities

    c. salary and benefits

    d. family and friends

WORKING WITH WORDS

Complete the sentences below with these words from Word Alert:

intangible   debate   complex
equatorial   esteem   elite

1. Many students hope to get into one of the _____ schools, such as Harvard or Yale.

2. Personal satisfaction is one of the _____ benefits of being self-employed.

3. During an election year, voters have an opportunity to hear the candidates _____ issues.

4. The tropical climate in some of the world's _____ regions draws tourists.

5. Some problems are too _____ to be solved with a simple answer.

6. Voters want to elect a president who not only is qualified to do the job but is also worthy of their _____ .

THINKING DEEPER

Ideas for discussion and writing

1. Have you ever done any volunteer work, either at home or in another country? What are some volunteer services and organizations in your area? What are some of the benefits and rewards of volunteering?

2. What purpose does the ice cream example in paragraphs 5 and 6 serve? What does this example tell you about life in the United States as compared to that in Tanzania?

3. Discuss how the author's year of African life relates to the Part 5 theme, *America at Work*. For example, deciding to change jobs or careers can be one of life's most stressful choices, yet most people change jobs several times during their lives. The process can be a learning experience. What did the author learn about herself, her career, and her outlook for the future?

4. Write about either a time when you volunteered for an organization or a time when you were able to help someone solve a problem or achieve a goal. What happened? What did you learn?

FIRST THOUGHTS

To prepare yourself for the reading selection, answer the following questions, either on your own or in a group discussion.

1. What do the terms *white-collar* and *blue-collar* mean to you?
2. Although employers value both education and experience, in what kind of job might the possession of one make up for a lack in the other?
3. Preview the title, headnote, and first one or two paragraphs. What do you think will follow?

WORD ALERT

deflating (1) reducing the importance of
apoplectic (4) filled with extreme anger or rage
reveling (6) taking great pleasure
dawdling (11) wasting time
flummoxed (13) confused, perplexed
vestige (14) visible trace, remnant

❧ White-Collar Man in a Blue-Collar World

BOB MULDOON

When companies downsize, many employees find that they must take jobs for which they are unprepared. In this essay from Newsweek, *the author tells of his experiences while learning new skills.*

CAN YOU DRIVE a forklift? Those five **deflating** words instantly 1 alerted me that my prep-school background and advanced degrees would mean nothing on the new job.

Newsweek, February 4, 2002, p. 13

Alas, I have two Ivy League master's degrees—and two left 2
thumbs. And neither the degrees nor the digits are serving me well in
these times, when many a displaced white-collar worker has gone
blue collar. Or, in my case, "green collar"—laying down lush, hydroseeded lawns.

Like thousands last year, I was downsized from one of those siz- 3
zling dot-coms, now dot-gone. Faced with a shrinking job market, I
turned to manual labor. It's a common trend, now that unemployment
is at 5.8 percent. But the transition is seldom seamless.

While the new boss was mildly disgusted when I couldn't drive the 4
forklift ("The guy I just fired could"), he was **apoplectic** when he
tossed me a wrench to open a hydrant and saw me tightening it with
all my strength. "Wrong direction!" he exploded. "Lefty loosey; righty
tighty."

I didn't know that. Indeed, there is a whole tool kit of basic skills 5
that Andover, Bates, Columbia and Harvard never equipped me with.
These include (but are not limited to) any task involving the use of a
tool, or any with a small or large gas-powered machine.

But there are moments when I shine. I can read the Latin on every 6
public building we pass. And when the boss once had to leave a note
to a customer, he needed help spelling a certain word. "R- e-c-e-i-v-e,"
I said crisply, **reveling** in the rare, value-added moment. "I before e,
except after c."

When the truckdriver from Quebec arrived with an 18-wheeler of 7
mulch and I began conversing in near-flawless Parisian French about
his long journey and breakfast of croissants, my boss's eyes lit up. But
when it came time to tell him to "attach the metal chain to the forklift
and remove the pallets," all I could muster was a vacuous stare. Evidently I'd been absent from French class the day trucking was covered.
I was reduced to grunting and clutching at his sleeve to convey the
message.

In hydroseeding, we spread a green slurry of water, seed, fertilizer 8
and mulch. This mixture applies the seed evenly, protects it from wind
and rain, and retains water for germination. It's all the rage in suburbia. My main responsibility is to guide 200 feet of heavy, serpentine
hose while the boss sprays the slime. But there's more to my job than
wrestling the anaconda.

Sometimes the hose gets clogged. Sometimes the chain comes off 9
the mixer. And sometimes I have to use the side mirrors to move the
60,000-pound truck in reverse. All these situations require an all-
around mechanical common sense that is as important to the blue-

collar worker as the ability to navigate Microsoft Office is to the white-collar one. These are the "value subtracted" moments my background has not prepared me for.

So I'm happy when those occasions arise when I can offer the ben- 10 efits of my education. Like when a butterfly flutters by in the field and I can identify it—authoritatively—as a great spangled fritillary. Or when I can edit the punctuation in our "How to Care for Your Newly Hydroseeded Lawn" flier.

Of course, it annoys the hell out of my boss how rarely my skill set 11 actually helps us out. And it amazes him how I'm forever **dawdling** with my coffee and misplacing it at job sites. Or how I'm morbidly preoccupied with safety—like the time, fearing electrocution, when I refused to hold up a low-hanging cable wire to allow our tall truck to pass beneath. ("It carries a signal, not a current!" he hollered, grabbing it for dramatic effect.)

In some ways, ours is a clash of cultures. On days off, the boss 12 changes the oil in his pickup, retiles his kitchen floor or does brickwork; I take my car through the automatic wash, go bird watching or read "Nicholas Nickleby." This last tickles him—so mighty are my struggles reading maps. ("Turn it in the direction we're traveling," he snaps, spinning it 180 degrees.)

All my life I've been trained in the manipulation of abstractions 13 (words, symbols, figures), so when it now comes to the manipulation of tangibles (nuts, bolts, maps), I'm **flummoxed.** So much that it's become a running joke with my boss that, whenever there is a choice to push or pull, turn left or right, I invariably err. At these moments, he signals my misjudgment in a chortling, sing-song voice: "Fifty-fifty."

But I'm just as strong as he is, and can match him bale for bale, 14 hoisting the 50-pound sacks of seed we fill the truck with. So there is the basis for a bit of grudging respect. And for all of my drawbacks, I am at least reliable—a **vestige,** perhaps, of the grim "show up at your desk at all costs (if only to sit there)" ethic.

But still it caught me off guard when, with the air now cold and the 15 hydroseeding season over, the boss inquired recently: "Can you drive a snowplow?"

COMPREHENSION CHECK

Purpose and Main Idea

1. What is the author's topic?
   a. feeling ill-prepared for his job

    b. skills required of blue-collar workers

    c. the advantages of an Ivy League education

    d. downsizing in today's job market

2. Which one of the following states the author's thesis?
   a. paragraph 2, first sentence: "Alas, I have two. . . ."
   b. paragraph 2, second sentence: "And neither the degrees. . . ."
   c. paragraph 3, first sentence: "Like thousands. . . ."
   d. paragraph 5, second sentence: "Indeed, there is a. . . ."

3. The author's *primary* purpose is to do which one of the following?
   a. entertain us with anecdotes of on-the-job mistakes
   b. inform us of the differences between white- and blue-collar
      jobs
   c. persuade us to prepare for a changing job market
   d. express his dilemma at being caught between two worlds

Details

4. The author was educated at all but which one of the following?
   a. Andover
   b. Baylor
   c. Columbia
   d. Harvard

5. The author's "skill set" includes all but which one of the following?
   a. using tools
   b. spelling
   c. identifying butterflies
   d. speaking a foreign language

6. The author is "flummoxed" by all but which one of the following?
   a. nuts
   b. bolts
   c. maps
   d. figures

7. The author and his boss are matched in what respect?
   a. size
   b. culture
   c. strength
   d. experience

8. Paragraph 12 is organized by which one of the following?
   a. process
   b. contrast
   c. definition
   d. cause and effect

Inferences

9. The author would probably agree that which one of the following job skills is of equal importance to both blue-collar and white-collar workers?
   a. computer skills
   b. facility with language
   c. critical thinking ability
   d. using and troubleshooting equipment

10. The author's attitude toward his education in general seems to be one of
    a. disappointment.
    b. pride.
    c. indifference.
    d. anger.

WORKING WITH WORDS

Complete the sentences below with these words from Word Alert:

flummoxed   deflating   vestige
apoplectic   reveling   dawdling

1. Holding the trophy high in the air, the athlete was _____ in victory.

2. The murder victim's family became _____ when the jury reached a verdict of not guilty.

3. The more time you spend _____ and the less time you spend engaged in productive activity, the less you will accomplish.

4. Some students were able to solve the equation, while others were _____ by it.

5. Why can't you be more encouraging of my work instead of always making those _____ remarks?

6. The table's surface had been painted over, leaving only a _____ of its original color.

THINKING DEEPER

Ideas for discussion and writing

1. What practical value do you see in the courses you are taking now? How will the information presented in these courses help you in your career or your personal life? How can you avoid some of the problems the author is facing?

2. Define the terms *white-collar* and *blue-collar* as applied to workers. What does the author's attitude toward each seem to be? Find evidence in the reading selection to support your answer.

3. Discuss how this selection relates to the Part 5 theme, *America at Work*. For example, both this selection and Selection 41 are about people who changed jobs. How do these authors' reasons for changing jobs, their experiences, and the new jobs they chose differ? What do they have in common?

4. Write about a piece of information you have learned from one of your courses that has changed the way you think.

FIRST THOUGHTS

To prepare yourself for the reading selection, answer the following questions, either on your own or in a group discussion.

1. Have you ever considered cooking for a living? What skills do you think the job of chef requires?

2. Do you know what a research chef is? If not, make an educated guess.

3. Preview the title, headnote, and first one or two paragraphs. What do you think will follow?

WORD ALERT

culinary (1) of or relating to cooking
precision (7) exactness, as in performance or amount
collaborative (10) of or relating to working cooperatively with others
accredited (13) having met an applied standard
zest (19) spirited enjoyment, gusto
knack (19) ability or talent

❧ You're a What? Research Chef

OLIVIA CROSBY

Olivia Crosby is a contributing editor of the Occupational
Outlook Quarterly, *from which this selection came. If you
like to cook, or if you just enjoy eating, Crosby's review of a
fascinating career will provide a fresh insight into the food
industry.*

WHEN ANNE ALBERTINE gets creative in the kitchen, millions taste 1
the results. As a research chef, she mixes good taste with good
science, creating recipes for Taco Bell restaurants at its corporate
headquarters in Irvine, California. Her tacos, chalupas, and burritos

---

Occupational Outlook Quarterly, Fall 2002, pp. 46–47.

fill the menus of more than 6,500 restaurants. "My team and I make restaurant quality food that can be mass produced," says Anne, "so the **culinary** quality—the freshness, taste, and texture— has to hold up."

Research chefs, also called product development or food innova- 2 tion chefs, create new foods for restaurant chains, coffee shops, and food manufacturing companies. They blend culinary training with a knowledge of food science. "As chefs, we can make food that tastes good and has visual appeal," says Anne. "We can weave flavors together." But research chefs also understand food preservation, mass production, and the technical terms used by scientists. And they use this knowledge in their recipes.

Research chefs get ideas for new menu items from many different 3 sources. They often use the results of customer surveys to determine what customers crave. Suggestions are general. They might include requests for a large portion size, a low price, or a certain flavor, such as smoky or sweet. Research chefs give the ideas substance by creating several different recipes to match these characteristics. "My job is to create options," says Anne. For every product that makes it to the public, researchers cook up 30 to 100 alternative recipes that never make it out of the laboratory.

Research chefs also find inspiration by following trends in con- 4 sumer tastes. They sample the menus of fine restaurants, often traveling abroad to stir up their creativity. And chefs read culinary magazines and study cookbooks, searching for recipes to modify.

With a set of food qualities in mind, research chefs start experi- 5 menting with ingredients. Anne often begins her day with a trip to the grocery store. "I pick up fresh ingredients," she says, "then go play in my test kitchen." She might try different styles of chopping, compare grilling an ingredient with frying it, or contrast vacuum-packed ingredients with frozen ones. In one recipe, Anne was striving for the just right level of spiciness and the best type of cheese to give a toasty flavor. She uses her technical expertise to pick ingredients that will taste good when cooked in bulk, under the real world conditions of a restaurant.

Anne's recipes also need to be convenient. To make a burrito that 6 was portable, for example, she decided to grill it. The grilling process seared the burrito so it would stay closed, even when it held more food than the other burritos did.

A research chef's test kitchen is similar to the kitchen of any pro- 7 fessional chef, with heavy-duty mixers, salamanders—tools for browning the tops of food—and other gadgets. But a research chef's kitchen is designed for **precision.** Graduated cylinders stand in for measuring cups, and scientific balances that are accurate to the milligram replace the standard countertop scales. Large-batch recipes have to be detailed and accurate so that they can be reproduced in every restaurant. "We strive for quality and consistency," says Anne.

At each stage of development, recipes are tested with customers. 8 In the first testing session, a focus group of customers might choose among 50 or more pictures and written descriptions of possible menu items. "I let the customers tell me what they like," says Anne. "I'm cooking for them, not myself."

Eventually, focus groups taste samples of the most appealing of 9 the proposed foods. Responses are taken during experiments conducted in sensory labs by food scientists and marketers. Anne observes and learns from these experiments. "People might say a product is too messy, too spicy, or too expensive, so I tweak it," she says. "With food, small changes in ingredients can make a dramatic impact."

When Anne isn't fine-tuning recipes, she meets with other mem- 10 bers of the staff. "Development is a **collaborative** process," she says. Financial experts check a recipe's profitability. Market researchers confirm its popularity. Food scientists concentrate on food safety and other considerations. And training and operations managers ensure that the restaurant crews will be able to make the food quickly and well.

Meetings like these highlight non-food-related skills that research 11 chefs need in their jobs: good communication skills and the ability to persuade. "You have to prove your hunches," says Anne. She gives evidence that her ideas will be successful, especially when they require a large monetary investment, such as new restaurant equipment.

Research chefs who work for food manufacturers instead of 12 restaurant chains perform slightly different tasks. They help food scientists develop flavor additives and prepared and frozen foods. They consult with restaurant chefs to learn what they need and explain flavor possibilities. If the restaurant wants a lemon flavor, for example, should it be acidic, sweet, or peely? Should it be liquid or dry? Research chefs translate the specifications of the restaurant into the technical language of scientists. Research chefs also test food scientists' products, using them in recipes to make sure they taste good.

To gain their unique mixture of skills, most research chefs earn a 13 degree in culinary arts from a school **accredited** by the American Culinary Federation. And they take additional classes in food science and chemistry. Anne received a bachelor's degree in general science and worked in consumer product development before following her love of cooking and getting her culinary arts degree. After graduating, she completed several internships with chefs experienced in fine dining, an experience she recommends highly. "Intern with as many different people as you can," she says. "It's important to learn different techniques and to build contacts in the industry."

The Research Chefs Association offers certification to research 14 chefs who have culinary education, 3 to 5 years of experience in both research and culinary arts, and a passing score on the certification exam. The Association also offers a culinary scientist certification to those who have a bachelor's degree in food science, at least 8 weeks of accredited culinary education, research experience, and a passing score on a written cooking exam.

The Research Chefs Association had almost 1,400 members this 15 year, but the number of research chefs may be higher or lower than that number because not every member is a research chef and not every research chef is a member. According to a survey taken at the association conference in 1999, earnings varied widely for research chefs, but many experienced chefs earned between $70,000 and $90,000 per year. This suggests that research chefs often earn more than other chefs do. The Bureau of Labor Statistics does not collect data on research chefs.

The benefits of working as a research chef extend beyond earn- 16 ings. Unlike restaurant and cafeteria chefs, who usually work weekends and evenings to prepare meals and supervise kitchen staff, most research chefs work standard business hours. And although they have deadlines to meet, research chefs usually work at a more relaxed pace than their restaurant counterparts.

The chance to be innovative adds spice to the job. "I'm always 17 looking for a new way to achieve something in a recipe," says Anne.

And when a recipe succeeds, research chefs share it with a wide 18 audience. "I love seeing a product go national," Anne says. She also enjoys seeing people eating and liking her creations—and if people discover what her job is, they often tell her which of her menu items are their favorites.

Knowing that her creations are popular adds **zest** to Anne's work, 19 but the work itself is what she likes best. By mixing a passion for food, a **knack** for science, and a flair for creativity, she wrote a recipe for a career she loves.

COMPREHENSION CHECK

Purpose and Main Idea

1. What is the author's topic?
   a. cooking
   b. the food industry
   c. a research chef
   d. how to be a chef

2. Which one of the following best states the author's central idea?
   a. A research chef is different from an ordinary chef.
   b. What it means to be a research chef may surprise you.
   c. Research chefs create recipes for restaurant chains.
   d. Research chefs have skills other than cooking.

3. What is the author's primary purpose?
   a. to express interesting facts about the food industry
   b. to inform readers about the qualifications required of a chef
   c. to persuade the reader to consider becoming a research chef
   d. to explain what a research chef is

Details

4. Culinary quality includes all but which one of the following?
   a. freshness
   b. taste
   c. variety
   d. texture

5. Which one of the following items would you *not* find in a research chef's kitchen?
   a. measuring cups
   b. heavy-duty mixers
   c. scientific balances
   d. tools for browning

6. The Research Chefs Association is responsible for which one of the following?
   a. awarding degrees
   b. job placement
   c. training
   d. certification

7. According to the author, what ingredient will give food a toasty flavor?
   a. onions

    b. cheese

    c. pepper

    d. bread crumbs

8. Which one of the following is the author's overall organizational pattern?

    a. Process: She explains how to become a research chef.

    b. Comparison: She compares research chefs with restaurant chefs.

    c. Definition: She answers the question, "What is a research chef?"

    d. Cause and effect: She explains why Anne became a research chef.

Inferences

9. In paragraph 9, *tweak* means which one of the following?

    a. mix

    b. cook

    c. season

    d. change

10. The author would probably agree that in addition to cooking skills, which one of the following types of workplace skills is most important for a research chef?

    a. personal skills

    b. computer skills

    c. resource allocation

    d. information gathering and filing

WORKING WITH WORDS

Complete the sentences below with these words from Word Alert:

accredited	precision	knack
collaborative	culinary	zest

1. One of the team members who had a _____ for drawing agreed to make posters to publicize the team's fundraising event.

2. Colleges work hard to maintain their status as _____ institutions.

3. Good interpersonal skills are essential in today's workplace, as so much of the work done is a _____ effort.

4. A student seeking a career as a research chef should major in _____ arts.

5. In an interview, an applicant who shows a certain _____ for the job will be more impressive than one who is indifferent.

6. Race car engines are so highly tuned that they require the use of _____ tools.

THINKING DEEPER

Ideas for discussion and writing

1. Using the author's examples, explain how a research chef differs from an ordinary chef.

2. An author can define a term by using examples, by comparing and contrasting, by stating what something is not in order to show what it is, by examining its parts or functions, or by showing how it works or what it does. Which of these methods does the author use to explain *research chef*? Find as many examples as you can in the selection.

3. Discuss how this selection relates to the Part 5 theme, *America at Work*. For instance, this author explains the skills and personal qualities that one needs in order to be a research chef. What are these skills and qualities? Would this job appeal to you as a career goal? Why or why not?

4. Write about a personal quality you have that you think most employers would value and explain your reasons.

FIRST THOUGHTS

To prepare yourself for the reading selection, answer the following questions, either on your own or in a group discussion.

1. What is e-learning? If you do not know, what do you think it might be?

2. What tutorial or other Web-based training programs have you used, and how effective were they?

3. Preview the title, headnote, and first one or two paragraphs. What do you think will follow?

WORD ALERT

proprietary (4) exclusively owned by an individual or corporation, trademarked

initiatives (6) enterprises, ventures, business opportunities

supplant (11) replace

chitchat (11) casual conversation

kiosks (16) small freestanding structures used as newsstands or booths

tutorial (17) private instruction

❧ E-Learning as Easy as ABC

HARRY WESSEL

> Orlando Sentinel *staff writer Harry Wessel writes of the business community's increased interest in Web-based training as more and more employers and employees take advantage of this learning opportunity.*

CHRIS POTTER, A 10-year employee at Home Depot, can tell you a lot 1
about caulk. She doesn't usually work in the paint department where caulk is sold, but Home Depot employees are encouraged to learn as much as they can about every aspect of the store.

Orlando Sentinel, February 26, 2003, pp. G1 and G8

Potter, whose main responsibility is setting work schedules for the 2
200-plus employees at the East Colonial Drive store in Orlando, chalks
up her caulk knowledge to the outlet's new E-Learning Center.

"Eventually, I want to learn everything," says Potter, 40, of Or- 3
lando. "E-learning has expanded my knowledge."

E-learning—computer-based training delivered via the Internet 4
or **proprietary** intranet sites—is expanding knowledge in workplaces
nationwide. It has been used to train Home Depot associates on products and forklift safety. Darden Restaurant managers and hourly workers have used it to learn a new software system. Duke University
Health System employees have used it to learn new federal requirements on patient confidentiality.

Although still in its infancy—1999 is most often cited as the year 5
things really started rolling—e-learning is well-established at America's
largest companies.

"About 85 percent of Fortune 1,000 companies have significant 6
e-learning **initiatives** under way," says Elliott Masie of the Masie Center, a learning research think tank in Saratoga Springs, N.Y.

These companies have not abandoned traditional training meth- 7
ods, Masie says. He estimates that e-learning accounts for 5 percent to
15 percent of the training their employees receive. Although he expects that percentage to rise in the future, he says e-learning works
best when it's blended with other training techniques.

In the next few years, "we may see a mild to moderate decline in 8
the number of traditional classes," Masie predicts, "but that doesn't
mean trainers will go out of business."

Pat Galagan agrees. She's the founding editor of *Learning Circuit*, 9
an electronic e-learning magazine published by the American Society
of Training & Development. Companies that offer e-learning to employees always combine it with other forms of training, from classroom instruction to videotapes to paper manuals. "You don't do one
or the other. It's a bit of this and that," she says.

Most training will continue to be delivered the old-fashioned way, 10
Galagan says, with no more than about a third of training delivered via
e-learning in even the most progressive companies. "The average,
everyday companies will be doing about 10 percent of their training
via e-learning," he predicts.

Though no one expects e-learning to **supplant** classroom train- 11
ing, it does have its advantages. "It cuts out the **chitchat** before class,
the teacher explaining something a second time when you're ready to
proceed quickly," says Margaret Driscoll, director of strategy and ventures for IBM E-Learning. With Web-based training, "those who don't

get it the first time can get remedial learning that brings them up to speed."

Another advantage, Driscoll says, is that companies can easily 12 track who has been through training and who hasn't.

That's a big plus at Ryder System, the Miami-based truck leasing 13 company. "Being in a regulated industry, if there's a problem and we need to prove someone was trained, we have it documented in one place," says Jeff Wright, Ryder's e-learning manager.

E-learning is spreading into the workplace, and it's not just for the 14 computer savvy. Orlando-based Darden, with more than 135,000 employees and 1,200 restaurants nationwide, recently introduced a PeopleSoft software system that employees can use to access benefits and other information through its intranet site.

"How do you train 135,000 people how to use PeopleSoft?" asks 15 Randy Babitt, Darden's director of operations development. "In the old days, we'd have to print up 135,000 manuals, with different ones for different jobs. We'd have to send them out to all the restaurants. Managers would have to attend meetings out of their offices, spending a day or two learning the system with a manual and trainer, go back to their restaurants and have weekend meetings with all the employees for a couple of hours."

With e-learning computer **kiosks** now placed in Darden restau- 16 rants, employees individually can learn how to use the software system, with instruction tailored for their job and at a time convenient to them. If they only have a few minutes here and there, that's fine. The e-learning program will bookmark where they left off.

Even employees who have never used a computer before can be 17 served by the system, Babitt says. Working with Get Thinking, an Orlando company that specializes in Web- and computer-based training, Darden offers an e-learning program that leads the uninitiated through a **tutorial** on computer use. "All an employee has to do is click once, and it walks you through it," Babitt says.

Large employers often are faced with training a lot of employees 18 with differing schedules spread over a wide geographic area. The challenge takes on more urgency when the training is required by law.

That's the case with health-care providers, who are required to fol- 19 low the new federal Health Insurance Portability and Accountability Act, better known as HIPAA.

In the past four months, the Duke University Health System in 20 North Carolina already has had more than 12,000 of its doctors, nurses and other health-care providers complete their HIPAA training via e-learning.

"Without online learning, it would definitely have taken more 21
time and effort," says Terry Seelinger, e-learning manager for the Duke
health system. Despite a few technical problems, those who have
taken the training like being able to do it at their convenience. The
slide-show format allows someone to go through the training in about
20 to 25 minutes. "The content is not real high-tech, but it's constructed well," Seelinger says. And the system keeps track of who has
completed the training.

The content is considerably more high-tech for Home Depot 22
workers. Its e-learning lessons use text, sound and animation to deliver information. In its tutorial on cabinets, for example, an animated
department manager walks down a Home Depot aisle to both show
and explain products.

The East Colonial store had its two E-Learning Center touch- 23
screen computer stations installed last July, and since then more than
half the store's employees have taken at least one e-learning lesson, reports Shannon Elven, the store's human-resources manager.

By the end of this year, every employee will have taken some 24
e-learning courses, she says.

That pattern will be repeated in more than 1,500 Home Depot 25
stores nationwide, says Charlie Gardner, director of e-learning in
Home Depot's Atlanta headquarters. He reports that 100,000 Home
Depot employees already have been through the four-hour e-learning
training course for forklifts, and tens of thousands more will be going
through a 16-hour e-learning program for cashiers.

Home Depot's "Cashier College" used to take three days of tradi- 26
tional training, usually at a district facility to which employees had to
travel. Now it will take two days and be done at the employee's store.

E-learning "has saved us an incredible number of training hours," 27
Gardner says. He expects that five to 10 years from now, as much as
half of all training that Home Depot employees receive will be via
e-learning.

Elliott Masie, the Saratoga Springs learning researcher, says get- 28
ting this kind of individualized, Web-based training is welcomed by
employees because having up-to-date information on products
"makes them look good to customers." But there's another advantage:

Unlike in a traditional classroom setting, employees can learn 29
"without the embarrassment of getting something wrong," Masie
says. "People don't want to look stupid in front of other people."

COMPREHENSION CHECK

Purpose and Main Idea

1. What is the author's topic?
   a. computers
   b. the Internet
   c. Web-based learning
   d. tutorial programs

2. Which one of the following states the author's central idea?
   a. E-learning is expanding knowledge in workplaces nationwide.
   b. E-learning is spreading because of its advantages, such as convenience and accessibility.
   c. E-learning is not just for the computer-savvy, but also works well for those who have little Web experience.
   d. Though still new, e-learning is well established at America's largest businesses.

3. Which one of the following is the author's *primary* purpose?
   a. to entertain readers with examples of interesting Web activities
   b. to express concern that e-learning may replace traditional instruction
   c. to persuade readers to use Web-based training programs
   d. to inform readers about e-learning and its expansion and advantages

Details

4. Which one of the following companies used e-learning to help employees learn PeopleSoft, a software system?
   a. Home Depot
   b. Duke University
   c. Darden Restaurants
   d. the Ryder System

5. Which one of the following estimates that e-learning accounts for 5 to 15 percent of the training that employees of *Fortune* 1,000 companies receive?
   a. Elliott Masie
   b. Jeff Wright
   c. Chris Potter
   d. Randy Babbitt

6. Margaret Driscoll cites all but which one of the following advantages of e-learning?
   a. Companies can track who has been trained.

     b. It provides opportunities for users to interact.

     c. It cuts out chitchat before class.

     d. Remedial learning is available for those who need it.

7. According to the author, companies that provide e-learning always combine it with other forms of training, including all but which one of the following?

     a. classroom instruction

     b. videotapes

     c. paper manuals

     d. lectures by recognized experts

8. What is the *dominant* organizational pattern of paragraph 4?

     a. process

     b. definition

     c. generalization then example

     d. cause and effect

Inferences

9. What is the best meaning of *uninitiated* in this sentence from paragraph 17: "Darden offers an e-learning program that leads the uninitiated through a tutorial on computer use"?

     a. uneducated

     b. unqualified

     c. inadequate

     d. inexperienced

10. Most of the professionals cited in this selection would be most likely to agree with which one of the following?

     a. Because of e-learning, a college degree will become less important.

     b. Companies that don't use e-learning will be at a disadvantage in the marketplace.

     c. E-learning is the easiest and most convenient way to learn on-the-job skills.

     d. E-learning will not replace traditional types of training.

WORKING WITH WORDS

Complete the sentences below with these words from Word Alert:

     initiatives   tutorial   supplant

     proprietary   chitchat   kiosks

1. Some people would rather bypass the _____ and skip to serious discussion.

2. My word processing program comes with a _____ that explains its use.

3. Although other instructional modes may be more effective, they will probably never _____ the lecture entirely.

4. Be sure to check the _____ on campus for flyers that may announce upcoming events.

5. Even if some _____ fail, the company has enough other ventures going to make up the difference.

6. Because McDonald's has a _____ interest in its golden arches, it would very likely sue another company that tried to copy its logo.

THINKING DEEPER

Ideas for discussion and writing

1. What purpose do the author's many examples of companies, e-learning initiatives, and spokespeople serve?

2. In the last paragraph, the author quotes Elliott Masie as saying, "People don't want to look stupid in front of other people." Masie believes that e-learning helps people learn without the embarrassment of being wrong. How important is it to not appear wrong or uninformed? Does the fear of being wrong affect students' willingness to participate in class, for example? Does the fear of looking stupid prevent people from trying new things? What examples can you give? What are some ways to overcome the fear of being wrong?

3. Discuss how this selection relates to the Part 5 theme, *America at Work*. For example, what can you conclude from this selection about the importance of having some computer skills, no matter what career you choose? What computer skills will you use in the career you have chosen?

4. Think about your education, either now or in the past. Then write about a learning method that works well for you and why.

FIRST THOUGHTS

To prepare yourself for the reading selection, answer the following questions, either on your own or in a group discussion.

1. Are four-letter words ever appropriate in the workplace? Why or why not?
2. Do you think men or women swear more? Why?
3. Preview the title, headnote, and first one or two paragraphs. What do you think will follow?

WORD ALERT

conveying (1) communicating, imparting
specious (3) seemingly true, but actually false
intimidates (9) discourages or forces
expletives (11) exclamations or oaths, curse words
pretentious (12) demanding undeserved distinction or merit
defuse (13) make less dangerous or hostile

❧ Foul Language Could Be a Curse on Your Career

JACQUELINE FITZGERALD

What message do your speech habits send? Jacqueline Fitzgerald says that cursing is not the best way to fit in at work. The author is a reporter for the Chicago Tribune.

AUTHOR JAMES O'CONNOR says there's one area where working 1 women should not catch up with men: When it comes to **conveying** strength, swearing will hurt, not help, your image.

"In an effort to advance in the work force and to fit in, women 2 picked up one of men's worst habits," says O'Connor, author of *Cuss Control: The Complete Book on How to Curb Your Cursing* (Three Rivers Press, $12.95).

Orlando Sentinel, January 1, 2003, pp. G1 and G4

People who swear as a way of sounding strong are using **specious** 3 reasoning, says O'Connor. "It would be like saying, 'If I shout loud enough, I'll win the argument.'"

Nicola Summers, a salesperson at the Lynch Auto Group in 4 Chicago, says she frequently encounters women who curse. "It's like they want to outdo the men," she says.

And in her male-dominated field, men may have an edge in the 5 swearing stakes. "It's a culture, that's what they do," she says. "They're used to it being all guys, and it's the biggest playground there is."

Summers, who doesn't swear, says her co-workers are "very re- 6 spectful . . . they calm it down or stop it if I walk in."

Another mistake is thinking that in an informal workplace no one 7 would take offense to four-letter words. "A lot of women swear today simply because that's the way the language and the culture have evolved—from a time when ladies didn't swear and gentlemen didn't swear in front of ladies, which was a double standard," O'Connor says. Now "they figure, everybody swears. And people assume nobody minds."

Etiquette consultant Ann Marie Sabath says that assumption is 8 risky. "Swearing means different things to different people," she says, "and you never know whom you might offend."

If you cuss to communicate displeasure to subordinates, realize 9 that you're creating negative energy. "It **intimidates** rather than motivates," O'Connor says.

Sabath and O'Connor agree that relying on curse words to express 10 yourself could hurt your chances for promotion. "It's such an unwritten rule," says Sabath. "We've all done it, but [chronic swearers] are proving that they are allowing their emotions to control them rather than their logic. It just shows you have no class or that you have a very limited vocabulary."

Career experts Marjorie Brody and Pamela Holland say hanging 11 out on a lower rung of the career ladder isn't the worst of it. In their book *Help! Was That a Career Limiting Move?* (Career Skills Press $10.95), they write: "We can only assume that individuals who spew **expletives** and insults would be shocked to realize that they are committing career suicide. . . . These words are inappropriate everywhere, but particularly in a work environment."

They also caution against sarcasm, gossip and **pretentious** lan- 12 guage as well as jargon, buzzwords and acronyms.

If you want to cut down on cussing, experts advise the following: 13

- Commit to changing, perhaps as a New Year's resolution. If you don't swear in your personal life, it will be second nature for you to avoid it at work.
- When tempted, try counting or pausing for a deep breath before you speak.
- Substitute other words, like stinking, bungled or botched.
- Use humor to **defuse** tempers.

If a colleague swears regularly, tell the person that you've heard 14 enough. Or if you have unfinished business with the person, say: "I'd like to talk to you about this when you're ready to use more professional language."

In the case of a boss who uses foul language, consider banding 15 your department together to discuss the issue with him or her. If a superior or client swears when you've made a mistake, deal with the problem first, O'Connor says, then explain that you'd prefer to talk without swear words.

COMPREHENSION CHECK

Purpose and Main Idea

1. What is the author's topic?
   a. habits of conversation
   b. usage of four-letter words
   c. ethical behavior
   d. foul language at work

2. What is the author's central idea?
   a. When it comes to swearing, women are catching up with men.
   b. Foul language can hurt, not help, your career image.
   c. What is acceptable to one may not be acceptable to another.
   d. Most people today do not take offense at four-letter words.

3. The author's *primary* purpose is to do which one of the following?
   a. express concern that women are swearing as much as men
   b. inform readers that the use of four-letter words is increasing
   c. persuade readers to avoid using foul language at work
   d. explain when swearing may or may not be appropriate

Details

4. O'Connor says about swearing:
   a. Everybody does it.
   b. No one takes offense.

    c. Women picked it up from men.

    d. It's not a bad habit.

5. Ann Marie Sabath says that people who swear are allowing which one of the following to control them?

    a. emotions

    b. logic

    c. social pressure

    d. vocabulary limitations

6. Sabath and O'Connor agree that relying on curse words to express yourself could hurt your chances for which one of the following?

    a. an interview

    b. a better job

    c. a promotion

    d. a lasting relationship

7. What does O'Connor advise employees to do if they have a boss who swears?

    a. Ignore it unless it interferes with your work.

    b. To fit in, adopt your boss's language style.

    c. Band together to discuss the issue with him or her.

    d. Learn to accept others' differences.

8. Paragraph 13 is organized by which one of the following patterns?

    a. definition

    b. classification

    c. generalization then example

    d. process

Inferences

9. Brody and Holland would probably agree that the use of foreign phrases by an American is an example of which one of the following types of language?

    a. sarcastic

    b. pretentious

    c. jargon-filled

    d. professional

10. The title is a pun (play on words) whose understanding depends on the double meaning of which word?

    a. foul

    b. language

c. career

d. curse

WORKING WITH WORDS

Complete the sentences below with these words from Word Alert:

pretentious   expletives   specious

intimidates   conveying   defuse

1. When the two athletes got into a fight, the coach used humor to _____ the situation.

2. Instead of resorting to _____ when you are angry, try presenting your case calmly and rationally.

3. One way of _____ your thanks is by sending personal notes or giving gifts.

4. Those who try to adopt the habits of another culture may seem more _____ than well traveled.

5. A boss who _____ employees is not likely to get their whole-hearted cooperation.

6. It would be a _____ argument to say that if one glass of wine a day is good for you, then several glasses may be even better.

THINKING DEEPER

Ideas for discussion and writing

1. The authors' sources seem to take it for granted that foul language is common in the workplace. Do you think this is true? What about on campus or in other public places: How common is foul language, and how does it affect you? Are you offended or indifferent, and why?

2. To what extent do you think foul language is a habit? Review Brody and Holland's suggestions for cutting down on cussing in paragraphs 13 and 14. Can these suggestions work? Why or why not? What other suggestions do you have for those who want to clean up their language?

3. Discuss how this selection relates to the Part 5 theme, *America at Work*. For example, the way you speak can send a positive or

negative message to employers. On the one hand, job applicants are told, "Be yourself." On the other hand, they are advised to "dress for success" or to create a good impression. In terms of dress, attitude, and behavior, what are some general rules or guidelines on how to present yourself to employers?

4. Employers expect you to have confidence in your strengths. Write about a skill you possess that you think everyone would benefit from having.

FIRST THOUGHTS

To prepare yourself for the reading selection, answer the following questions, either on your own or in a group discussion.

1. If you live with someone, which one of you does most of the housework?
2. Do people seem to do more or less housework today than they did in years past? Why do you think so?
3. Preview the title, headnote, and first one or two paragraphs. What do you think will follow?

WORD ALERT

bustled (1) moved energetically and busily
grimy (3) dirty or sooty
slackers (6) those who avoid or neglect work or duty
succession (7) following in order, sequence
fanatic (8) one who is extremely enthusiastic, fervent, or zealous
shirking (11) avoiding responsibility

৯ Until Dust Do Us Part

DIRK JOHNSON

Dirk Johnson, writing for the Home section of Newsweek, *reports on a new study that reveals how the housework burden is shared among today's working couples.*

ONCE UPON A time, men were treated like indulged children in the 1 house, as women **bustled** about cleaning, sweeping, cooking. That was 50 years ago, some men say. That was this morning, some women say.

Want to start a fight? Ask about housework and the division of la- 2 bor. For that matter, ask what housework means. Does gardening count? How about running a snow blower?

Newsweek, March 25, 2002, p. 41

To settle the score, a new study from the University of Michigan ₃ examines how the housework burden is shared by women and men. The results: women still do much more than men, though men are getting better (actually, men were getting better until about 1985, and then stalled out). But the real news stood out like a streak of clean glass on a **grimy** window: nobody really cares that much about housework at all anymore. In 1965 women did 40 hours of housework a week, men a mere 12. Nowadays women are averaging 27 hours; men, closing the gap, average 16. That means housework has decreased even as average house size has ballooned.

None of this comes as a shock to Gale Zemel's 73-year-old mother, ₄ Lita. She simply won't visit her daughter—they go to mom's place or meet at a restaurant. "The clutter drives her nuts," said Gale, a 48-year-old office manager in Oak Park, Ill. "And it's true, the place is a mess."

For millions of Americans, it comes down to math. He works. She ₅ works. The kids need to be transported all over creation for soccer and piano lessons. People are too pooped to mop. "Who's got time to clean?" says Hiromi Ono, an author of the report by the Institute for Social Research at Ann Arbor, Mich.

Each of the 6,000 people in the study—from the United States and ₆ around the world—kept a daily record of the work they did around the house, from sweeping the kitchen floor to changing the oil. As it turned out, American men were much more helpful than Japanese men (four hours a week), but **slackers** compared to the Swedes (24 hours a week).

When it comes to thankless chores, of course, everyone thinks ₇ they're doing too much already and that their other half could be doing just a little bit more. "Every time my husband gets a raise," one suburban Chicago woman bristles, "he starts throwing his clothes all over the floor." Zemel's husband, David Mausner, will tell you he's a pretty helpful mate, a virtue he attributes to "having my consciousness raised in the '70s by a **succession** of girlfriends." Mausner says he's setting tables, clearing them, washing dishes and fixing whatever needs fixing. "When there's something that requires a tool, I'm the guy for the job." His wife sees it somewhat differently. "He does the dishes. Period."

Neither claims to be a **fanatic** about cleaning. Zemel acknowl- ₈ edges: "I don't even know where the iron is." Mausner says simply, "I guess I could do more."

People are working hard—just not at hunting dust bunnies. The ₉ Michigan researchers credit a strong job market in the 1990s for the phenomenon they term "vanishing housework." Women in their study averaged 24 hours of paid work outside the home, while men averaged 37. (For those keeping score, men total 53 combined hours of job and housework; women 51.)

Everybody is simply trying to do too much, says Cheryl Mendelson, the author of the surprise best-seller *Home Comforts: The Art and Science of Keeping House.* With families on the run, she says, the home has been reduced to a changing station, a pit-stop between wind sprints. 10

It's a question of priorities, and some things matter more than others. For all the demands on their time, most parents are not **shirking** when it comes the kids. Another recent study from the University of Michigan found that most parents—working and stay-at-home—spend more time with the children than parents did 20 years ago. Linda Rufer, a doctor in suburban Milwaukee, said housecleaning ranked a distant second to taking her three children to the Wisconsin Dells last weekend. "Either the house is clean or I see my kids," she said. "And as a pediatrician, it's bad form not to see the kids." For Rufer and plenty of others, the mess will be still there when they get home. The kids, on the other hand, grow up fast. And then they'll be gone. 11

COMPREHENSION CHECK

Purpose and Main Idea

1. What is the author's topic?
   a. marriage and family
   b. stay-at-home moms
   c. the truth about housework
   d. house husbands

2. Where is the central idea stated?
   a. paragraph 2, first sentence "Want to start. . . ."
   b. paragraph 3, first sentence: "To settle the score. . . ."
   c. paragraph 3, second sentence: "The results. . . ."
   d. paragraph 3, third sentence: "But the real news. . . ."

3. Which one of the following is the author's *primary* purpose?
   a. to express his own views about the study's results
   b. to inform readers about a University of Michigan study
   c. to persuade readers that the study was not very important
   d. to entertain readers with facts from the study

Details

4. According to the author, what is the real news about housework?
   a. Women do more of it than men.
   b. Men and women share the burden.

    c. Nobody really cares about it.

    d. Housework has decreased since 1965.

5. According to the study, which of the following were the most helpful around the house?

    a. American men

    b. Japanese men

    c. German men

    d. Swedish men

6. To what do the Michigan researchers credit "vanishing housework"?

    a. the 1990s job market

    b. too little time

    c. spending more time with kids

    d. increase in average house size

7. The study found that women averaged how many combined hours of job and housework?

    a. 24

    b. 37

    c. 51

    d. 53

8. The author's details consist mainly of

    a. opinions.

    b. facts.

    c. reasons.

    d. examples.

Inferences

9. Based on the details in paragraph 10, Cheryl Mendelson would probably agree that most people could benefit from which one of the following?

    a. sharing chores

    b. staying at home more

    c. hired help

    d. time management

10. According to the author, the Michigan study answered all but which one of the following questions?

    a. Who does the most housework?

    b. Who is the most helpful around the house?

    c. Why are men and women doing less housework than in the past?

    d. How can men and women improve their home management?

WORKING WITH WORDS

Complete the sentences below with these words from Word Alert:

succession   slackers   fanatic
shirking   bustled   grimy

1. Please do not wipe your _____ fingers on the clean white towel.
2. After a _____ of bad grades, my studying finally paid off with a high score on the next test.
3. A housecleaning _____ is someone who will almost take the dishes from in front of you while you are still eating.
4. Unlike the _____ who wait until the last minute to study for an exam, you should avoid procrastination by studying several days in advance.
5. The children _____ around their rooms, cleaning up before their mother came home.
6. Parents who do not make children behave in public places are _____ their disciplinary responsibilities.

THINKING DEEPER

Ideas for discussion and writing

1. How do today's families differ from families in the past in terms of who does housework, who takes care of the children, and who makes financial decisions? What are some of the reasons behind these differences?
2. What is the author's tone in this selection? For example, is it humorous, serious, scholarly? How would you describe it? Find words or examples in the selection to support your answer.
3. Discuss how this selection relates to the Part 5 theme, *America at Work*. For example, the Michigan researchers commented on the fact that two-income families have little time for housework. What are some of the advantages and disadvantages of both parents working? Use information from the selection and from your own experience to support your answer.
4. Reflect on your childhood. Write about an advantage or disadvantage you had that you hope your children will or will not have.

FIRST THOUGHTS

To prepare yourself for the reading selection, answer the following questions, either on your own or in a group discussion.

1. Is time management a problem for you? Why or why not?

2. Do you believe that children today have too much to do? Why or why not?

3. Preview the title, headnote, and first one or two paragraphs. What do you think will follow?

WORD ALERT

glee (1) delight, joy
hiatus (3) gap or interruption in space, time, or continuity
ample (6) large in size or extent, plentiful
parlance (6) a certain way of speaking, idiom
laudable (9) praiseworthy
respite (10) a short period of rest or relief, pause
contemptuous (11) feeling or showing disrespect or scorn

❧ Doing Nothing Is Something

ANNA QUINDLEN

Anna Quindlen is a journalist and novelist. Currently, she alternates with George F. Will as an author of Newsweek's *regular feature "The Last Word." In this selection, Quindlen reminisces about the days when children had summers off and career readiness could be postponed at least through childhood.*

SUMMER IS COMING soon. I can feel it in the softening of the air, but 1
I can see it, too, in the textbooks on my children's desks. The number of uncut pages at the back grows smaller and smaller. The loose-leaf is ragged at the edges, the binder plastic ripped at the corners. An

Anna Quindlen, *"Doing Nothing is Something."* Reprinted by permission of International Creative Management, Inc. Copyright © 2002 by Anna Quindlen. First appeared in Newsweek.

old remembered **glee** rises inside me. Summer is coming. Uniform skirts in mothballs. Pencils with their points left broken. Open windows. Day trips to the beach. Pickup games. Hanging out.

How boring it was.   2

Of course, it was the making of me, as a human being and a writer. 3 Downtime is where we become ourselves, looking into the middle distance, kicking at the curb, lying on the grass or sitting on the stoop and staring at the tedious blue of the summer sky. I don't believe you can write poetry, or compose music, or become an actor without downtime, and plenty of it, a **hiatus** that passes for boredom but is really the quiet moving of the wheels inside that fuel creativity.

And that, to me, is one of the saddest things about the lives of 4 American children today. Soccer leagues, acting classes, tutors—the calendar of the average middle-class kid is so over the top that soon Palm handhelds will be sold in Toys "R" Us. Our children are as overscheduled as we are, and that is saying something.

This has become so bad that parents have arranged to schedule 5 times for unscheduled time. Earlier this year the privileged suburb of Ridgewood, N.J., announced a Family Night, when there would be no homework, no athletic practices and no after-school events. This was terribly exciting until I realized that this was not one night a week, but one single night. There is even a free-time movement, and Web site: familylife1st.org. Among the frequently asked questions provided online: "What would families do with family time if they took it back?"

Let me make a suggestion for the kids involved: how about noth- 6 ing? It is not simply that it is pathetic to consider the lives of children who don't have a moment between piano and dance and homework to talk about their day or just search for split ends, an enormously satisfying leisure-time activity of my youth. There is also **ample** psychological research suggesting that what we might call "doing nothing" is when human beings actually do their best thinking, and when creativity comes to call. Perhaps we are creating an entire generation of people whose ability to think outside the box, as the current **parlance** of business has it, is being systematically stunted by scheduling.

A study by the University of Michigan quantified the downtime 7 deficit; in the last 20 years American kids have lost about four unstructured hours a week. There has even arisen a global Right to Play movement: in the Third World it is often about child labor, but in the United States it is about the sheer labor of being a perpetually busy child. In Omaha, Neb., a group of parents recently lobbied for additional recess. Hooray, and yikes.

How did this happen? Adults did it. There is a culture of adult dis- 8
trust that suggests that a kid who is not playing softball or attending
science-enrichment programs—or both—is huffing or boosting cars:
if kids are left alone, they will not stare into the middle distance and
consider the meaning of life and how come your nose in pictures
never looks the way you think it should, but instead will get into trouble. There is also the culture of cutthroat and unquestioning competition that leads even the parents of preschoolers to gab about prestigious
colleges without a trace of irony: this suggests that any class in which
you do not enroll your first grader will put him at a disadvantage in,
say, law school.

Finally, there is a culture of workplace presence (as opposed to 9
productivity). Try as we might to suggest that all these enrichment activities are for the good of the kid, there is ample evidence that they are
really for the convenience of parents with way too little leisure time of
their own. Stories about the resignation of presidential aide Karen
Hughes unfailingly reported her dedication to family time by noting
that she arranged to get home at 5:30 one night a week to have dinner
with her son. If one weekday dinner out of five is considered **laudable,**
what does that say about what's become commonplace?

Summer is coming. It used to be a time apart for kids, a **respite** 10
from the clock and the copybook, the organized day. Every once in a
while, either guilty or overwhelmed or tired of listening to me keen
about my monumental boredom, my mother would send me to some
rinky-dink park program that consisted almost entirely of three-
legged races and making things out of Popsicle sticks. Now, instead,
there are music camps, sports camps, fat camps, probably thin camps.
I mourn hanging out in the backyard. I mourn playing Wiffle ball in
the street without a sponsor and matching shirts. I mourn drawing in
the dirt with a stick.

Maybe that kind of summer is gone for good. Maybe this is the 11
leading edge of a new way of living that not only has no room for con-
templation but is **contemptuous** of it. But if downtime cannot be
squeezed during the school year into the life of frantic and often joyless activity with which our children are saddled while their parents
pursue frantic and often joyless activity of their own, what about summer? Do most adults really want to stand in line for Space Mountain or
sit in traffic to get to a shore house that doesn't have enough saucepans?
Might it be even more enriching for their children to stay at home and
do nothing? For those who say they will only watch TV or play on the
computer, a piece of technical advice: the cable box can be unhooked,

the modem removed. Perhaps it is not too late for American kids to be given the gift of enforced boredom for at least a week or two, staring into space, bored out of their gourds, exploring the inside of their own heads. "To contemplate is to toil, to think is to do," said Victor Hugo. "Go outside and play," said Prudence Quindlen. Both of them were right.

COMPREHENSION CHECK

Purpose and Main Idea

1. What is the author's topic?
   a. doing nothing
   b. the importance of free time
   c. overscheduled children
   d. childhood activities

2. What is the author's central idea?
   a. Summer used to be a time for doing nothing.
   b. Family life is often joyless and overscheduled.
   c. Kids today have more to do than their parents did.
   d. Downtime has benefits that our children are missing.

3. What is the author's *primary* purpose?
   a. to entertain us with memories of her childhood summers
   b. to convince readers that their lives are overscheduled
   c. to persuade parents that children need more free time
   d. to inform us about the ways children spend their summers

Details

4. According to the author, "doing nothing" is which one of the following?
   a. a period of inactivity
   b. the right of every child
   c. when people do their best thinking
   d. the natural result of boredom

5. As evidence of a "downtime deficit," the author cites which one of the following?
   a. Nebraska parents who lobbied for more recess
   b. a University of Michigan study
   c. the website familylife1st.org
   d. a global Right to Play movement

6. The author says that summer used to be all but which one of the following?
   a. a time apart for kids
   b. a respite from clock and copybook
   c. a time for camps
   d. a time for hanging out

7 The author suggests that enrichment activities are really for
   a. filling leisure time.
   b. the good of the children.
   c. teaching kids skills.
   d. parents' convenience.

8. Paragraph 3 is organized by which one of the following patterns?
   a. process
   b. definition
   c. contrast
   d. generalization then example

Inferences

9. What does the author mean in paragraph 9 by a "culture of work-place presence"?
   a. not being present and not being productive
   b. being both present and productive
   c. being present but not productive
   d. not being present but still being productive

10. Which one of the following best states the meaning of the Victor Hugo quotation in paragraph 11, "To contemplate is to toil, to think is to do"?
   a. Thought leads to action.
   b. Thinking is hard work.
   c. Everyone should take time to think.
   d. Thought and work are two different things.

WORKING WITH WORDS

Complete the sentences below with these words from Word Alert:

contemptuous   laudable   hiatus   glee
parlance   respite   ample

1. The children shouted with _____ when they saw the new puppy.

2. While summer may seem only a brief _____ to some, for others it stretches out endlessly.

3. Volunteering for organizations such as a hospice or your local hospital is a _____ activity.

4. Some voters were _____ of the candidates' obviously insincere attempts to appeal to their interests.

5. After working in the yard for several hours, we were glad to have a _____ from our labor.

6. Though we eat small amounts most of the time, our feast is _____ at Thanksgiving.

7. In business _____ a "state-of-the-art" computer is one that is current or up to date.

THINKING DEEPER

Ideas for discussion and writing

1. Anna Quindlen says that children have too much to do, that their endless activities are more for their parents' benefit than for their benefit, and that downtime, or free time, is a good thing. Do you agree or disagree with these assertions and why?

2. In paragraph 11 the author suggests that parents and children are leading lives of "frantic and often joyless activity." Using examples from the selection, explain what she means.

3. Discuss how this selection relates to the Part 5 theme, *America at Work*. For example, the author sees humor in parents of preschoolers who are already thinking about their children's careers. She suggests that working parents' lack of time for their families has led to the problem of the overscheduled child. In her own case, she credits her summers of "doing nothing" for making her the writer that she is. As you think about your own career plans, how will you balance work and leisure time? What success have you had so far in learning to manage your time?

4. Think about your childhood summers. Were they like the ones Anna Quindlen remembers, or were you one of the overscheduled children she describes? Write about one childhood summer that stands out in your memory.

FIRST THOUGHTS

To prepare yourself for the reading selection, answer the following questions, either on your own or in a group discussion.

1. How often do you use the Internet, and for what?

2. What are the advantages and disadvantages of using the Internet for job hunting?

3. Preview the title, headnote, and first one or two paragraphs. What do you think will follow?

WORD ALERT

In a textbook chapter, the words to watch may appear in boldface, italics, or a special color.

network (4) to interact with others for mutual assistance or support
prominent (4) widely known, eminent
vital (7) of great importance, essential
cybersearch (9) an Internet search of websites to find information
search engines (14) software used to find information on the Internet
promotional (15) contributing to the progress or growth of, advancing
global (34) worldwide, comprehensive, total

❧ Pounding the Virtual Pavement

SUSAN D. GREENE AND MELANIE C. L. MARTEL

This textbook reading is excerpted from Chapter 10 of The Ultimate Job Hunter's Guidebook, *fourth edition. The entire chapter is about job hunting online. The excerpt focuses on the application of the Internet to career researching. When reading from textbooks, remember that headings may signal topics, main ideas, or important details.*

THE NEW MEDIUM FOR JOB SEEKERS

Athough reading classified ads, cold calling, letter writing, and net- 1
working have traditionally been the most widely used means of finding a job, the Internet has emerged as one of the most important tools
in the job-search process. With its extensive, easily accessible information, its powerful searching capabilities, and its instant channels of
communication, it has revolutionized the way people look for jobs
and the way companies recruit.

WHAT IS THE INTERNET?

The Internet is a vast system of millions of interconnected computer 2
networks. This network links individuals, businesses, universities, libraries, and governments throughout the world. Unlike virtually any
other medium, no one owns or operates it—it's just there. Although
the Internet was a government initiative started in the 1960s, its boom
in commercial and educational markets in the past decade or so has
sparked new ways of doing business and communicating globally.

The World Wide Web is the fastest-growing part of the Internet. 3
Using a Web browser, people can view information from web sites that
other companies or individuals have created. A formatting language,
HTML (hypertext markup language), is used to create web pages and
establish hypertext links to other web sites. Most Web browsers allow
users to view text, graphics, video, and animation on the Web as well
as to hear audio. It is also possible to download software programs,
conduct online discussions, and purchase items.

USING THE INTERNET TO JOB-HUNT

The Internet can provide great tools to assist in your job search. You 4
can **network;** exchange correspondence; gather research on careers,
trends, industries, and individual companies; search for job openings;
post your résumé; get career advice from professional counselors; and
exchange ideas with other job hunters. The Internet is used by many
prominent companies to list job openings, accept employee applica-
tions, and even conduct interviews online. In fact, the Internet has
been called the future of recruiting.

IT'S FAST; IT'S CONVENIENT

One of the best characteristics of the Internet is its convenience. You 5
can go online at any time; it's "open" twenty-four hours a day. Doing
your research or networking in the evening or on weekends is no
problem. Unlike a library or business, the Internet is there whenever
you need it.

You should keep in mind, however, that not all information on the 6
Internet is accurate, current, or necessarily true. Be sure to evaluate
carefully the quality of Internet data before using it to make an important decision.

Also, the Internet is not a replacement for other types of research 7
and job-hunting tools. Printed materials such as magazines, newspapers, books, and directories are still **vital** to a comprehensive job
search.

SHOW EMPLOYERS YOU KNOW YOUR WAY AROUND THE INTERNET

Although your level of success on the Internet depends in part on the 8
kind of job you're seeking and how skilled you are in online comput-
ing, use of the Internet should still be a major component of your job
search. Beyond providing listings of specific job openings, it is an in-
valuable research tool.

At the very least, job seekers who conduct a **cybersearch** demon- 9
strate to employers a basic knowledge of personal computers and the
Internet. In today's intensely competitive job market, every little advantage counts.

ACCESSING THE INTERNET

If you don't have a computer, don't despair. Many public libraries and 10
schools offer Internet access through their computers. Take advantage
of free resources if you are currently unable to invest in your own
computer equipment.

If you do have your own computer and are a student, you can 11
most likely get online free of charge through your school. Visit your
school's computer center to obtain any necessary software and to
learn what requirements you must meet.

If you are not a student, to get online you'll need a personal com- 12
puter, an Internet service provider, and a browser to view the World
Wide Web. You can use a service provider that offers the Internet and

e-mail only, or an online service that provides Internet access as well as many other online features such as America Online. Service charges vary according to many factors, but they typically range from $15 to $25 a month for unlimited use.

BOOSTING YOUR JOB SEARCH

You can use the Internet to enhance your job search in many ways, as   13
explained in this section.

Industry research

Begin by checking trade periodicals. Most publications have their own   14
web sites that highlight key stories relevant to the industry. Next, find the industry's main web sites by checking major **search engines** like Yahoo! at *www.yahoo.com,* and Excite at *www.excite.com.* Finally, look for discussion groups in the chosen industry. These groups often produce discussion lists about industry-related information and keep articles from back issues of trade periodicals at their web sites.

Company research

If you have identified a specific company as your desired potential   15
employer, you'll want to know everything you can about it, to better target your cover letter and appear knowledgeable in an interview. Begin by finding the company's web site. Try doing a search using the company's name followed by *.com.* If that doesn't bring up the site you seek, try a keyword search using a major search engine. Most likely, you can also find the company's web site address listed in any of its ads and **promotional** literature. If you still strike out, give the company a call—most will gladly give out their web address over the phone with no questions asked.

What will you find at a company web site? Usually, it contains in-   16
formation about the company's products or services. It may also give background on key personnel. Many corporate web sites list the company's job openings and allow you to apply online. You may also find press releases about recent noteworthy events at the company.

Another way to research a company is to search career web sites,   17
some of which feature a section, called Employer Profiles, that gives detailed information on employers around the world. If the company in which you're interested is publicly held, check out its stock—

information such as its general price range and recent history can help you assess how the company is doing.

A final way of learning about an individual company is to become 18 familiar with its competitors. If you don't know offhand who they are, use search engines to find other companies in the same industry. Also, Hoover's Online (*www.hoovers.com*) is a first-rate resource. If a company is listed on Hoover's, often its competitors, and hyperlinks to their web sites, will be referenced.

Job openings databases

Career sites download and index job postings every day. The organiza- 19 tion of these databases allows you to search postings by location, job title, and required skills.

When using these databases, however, keep in mind that posted 20 vacancies are sometimes out-of-date. Employers may forget to remove them once the position has been filled, or they may leave them online while the new hire is being "tried out." Other postings are sometimes designed merely to get information about job seekers into the databases of recruiters. Despite these drawbacks, employment databases are valuable job-searching tools. . . .

Résumé banks

You can enter your résumé into a data bank available to human re- 21 sources professionals and recruiters. Don't get frustrated if you receive some responses that don't match your career objectives. Sometimes machines, not humans, match job openings to candidates.

Before posting your résumé to a particular data bank, be sure to 22 investigate what type of employer would likely search that bank. Also, find out how long your résumé stays online. Most résumé banks provide this information on their web sites or answer specific questions by e-mail.

Online career discussion groups

Discussion groups are online networks in which you exchange infor- 23 mation with other job seekers and professionals through text messages. You enter a *chat room*, where you can ask questions, give and get advice, share war stories, exchange leads, and obtain information from specialists in different fields. To find a discussion group, use search engines or visit the major career sites. . . .

Electronic bulletin boards.

Like a corkboard in your local grocery store or laundromat, these 24 boards are for posting and reading notices. They contain thousands of help-wanted classifieds and enable job seekers to post their résumés. Most electronic bulletin boards charge nothing for their services; the few that charge nominal fees usually provide more services, such as categorizing your résumé for easy access to employers or ensuring confidentiality. Job listings are run by individuals, associations, civic groups, and corporations. There are a lot of listings, so be prepared to sift through them to find the ones relevant to your situation. To find these bulletin boards, visit some of the major career sites. . . .

Newspaper classifieds

With the Internet, you are no longer restricted to looking at classified 25 ads only in your local newspaper. Many major newspapers, including the *New York Times, Washington Post, Chicago Tribune, Los Angeles Times,* and the *Boston Globe,* as well as many smaller newspapers, now post their classified employment ads online. Just go to the website for the individual publication, and find the link to the classifieds section.

Additionally, some newspapers use the Internet to offer more de- 26 tails about jobs that appear in the print classified ads. That is, a classified ad in the newspaper might contain a Web ID code that you would use at the newspaper's web site to see an expanded listing. That listing should help you better identify opportunities that match your qualifications, write a more targeted cover letter, and prepare for an interview. The listing might also offer you a way to apply online.

Career guidance and job-search help

Nearly all commercial online services and the Internet have areas de- 27 voted exclusively to helping job seekers manage their searches. These sites often include résumé templates, articles about job searching and career management, and discussion forums about careers. . . .

Your own web site

On your résumé and in your cover letters, you can refer to your per- 28
sonal home page—a great place to strut your stuff. The average size is
usually four to twenty pages. Use your web site to give more detailed
information about your background. Include work samples, photos,
letters of recommendation, awards, and anything else that demonstrates to a prospective employer that you're the right person for the
job. Many books and software packages are available to help you create your own web site, or you can enlist the services of a professional
web designer.

E-mail

Electronic-mail messages are a key component of modern communi- 29
cations, ranking with the telephone, traditional paper mail, and fac-
simile (fax) machines. One of the nice things about e-mail is that you
can address your communication directly to an individual and have a
good chance of it reaching him without interference from a secretary
or other type of gatekeeper, because your e-mail goes straight to that
individual's computer. Furthermore, you're more likely to receive a response to an e-mail than to other types of communication, because
the professional is already seated at the computer and can dash off a
quick, informal e-mail reply to your request.

E-mail is an excellent tool for finding out if a position has been 30
filled, showing initial interest in a job, requesting more information,
and inquiring about the status of a position you've applied for. It's fast,
easy, and amazingly effective. To increase the chances that your e-mail
will generate action, be sure it contains the following items: a statement that clearly identifies the purpose of the e-mail, relevant facts to
support the purpose, a request specifying the next step to be taken,
and a time frame in which you would appreciate a reply. Finally, don't
forget to check your e-mail daily. A prospective employer who chooses
to contact you by e-mail and does not get a fast response might go on
to the next candidate.

Career products and services

You can search through ads to locate products or services that might 31
prove useful in your job search. Books about all aspects of job hunting,
résumé software, career counselors, and networking services are just a

few examples. Once again, use search engines and also the major career web sites to find the products and services you want.

Salary research

Salary guides on the Internet can help you develop a realistic picture 32 of what you might expect to earn in a particular profession. That information can be valuable to you when negotiating for a position. Many major career sites contain salary data.

Learning about a geographic area

You can use the Internet to obtain data about a specific place you may 33 be considering for relocation. For example, you can learn about the cost of living, housing options, and schools in that area.

Here's some advice for the hesitant: Don't be intimidated by com- 34 puters and the Internet. Both are more user friendly than ever before. There are plenty of books that can help you get started if you need a little push. Also, the Internet has gained **global** acceptance, so one of your friends or teachers can no doubt offer advice or help. Don't put off using this valuable tool.

COMPREHENSION CHECK

Purpose and Main Idea
1. What is the authors' topic?
   a. what the Internet is
   b. how the Internet works
   c. using the Internet as a career tool
   d. why you should use the Internet
2. What is the authors' central idea?
   a. paragraph 1, first sentence: "Although reading. . . ."
   b. paragraph 1, last sentence: "With its extensive. . . ."
   c. paragraph 2, last sentence: "Although the Internet. . . ."
   d. paragraph 4, first sentence: "The Internet can. . . ."
3. Which one of the following is the authors' *primary* purpose?
   a. to teach students how to use the Internet for job seeking
   b. to inform students about job sites available on the Internet
   c. to persuade students to make greater use of the Internet
   d. to express concern that many students are computer illiterate

Details

4. Many prominent companies do all but which one of the following on the Internet?
    a. list job openings
    b. conduct interviews
    c. accept applications
    d. hire employees

5. To research a company, the authors suggest that you begin by doing which one of the following?
    a. Call the company.
    b. Find the company's website.
    c. Check the company's promotional literature.
    d. Become familiar with its competitors.

6. According to the authors, which one of the following is a "first-rate resource" for finding a company's competitors?
    a. *www.careershop.com*
    b. *www.hotjobs.com*
    c. *www.hoovers.com*
    d. *www.excite.com*

7. When using email to inquire about a job, be sure to include all but which one of the following items?
    a. a statement of purpose
    b. a list of your qualifications
    c. relevant facts
    d. a time frame for reply

8. Which one of the following is the authors' *primary* organizational pattern?
    a. Definition: They state what the Internet is.
    b. Comparison: They list the advantages and disadvantages of using the Internet to research careers.
    c. Process: They explain how to use the Internet as a career tool.
    d. Cause and effect: They give several reasons to use the Internet for a job hunt.

Inferences

9. Which one of the following best explains why the Internet has been called the future of recruiting?
    a. It saves employers time and money.
    b. It replaces other job-hunting tools.

c. It is "open" twenty-four hours a day.

d. It enables prominent companies to list job openings.

10. Which one of the following is the best restatement of the authors' title, "Pounding the Virtual Pavement"?

a. Getting a Job Is Like Taking a Walk

b. No One Ever Said Job Hunting Was Easy

c. Walking the Walk, Talking the Talk

d. Same Search, Different Medium

WORKING WITH WORDS

Complete the sentences below with these words from Word Alert:

search engines   promotional   network   vital
cybersearch   prominent   global

1. Students who are new to college will do well to _____ with helpful others.

2. Time management and goal setting are _____ to a successful academic career.

3. Use major _____ to help you find the websites of companies that interest you.

4. The Student Government Association met to determine what kind of _____ materials would convince more students to get involved.

5. Conducting a _____ is one way to demonstrate your online skills.

6. Dell is one of many _____ companies that have opened offices overseas.

7. American business has a _____ outreach that extends to remote areas of the world.

THINKING DEEPER

Ideas for discussion and writing

1. The opening paragraphs of a major section of a textbook chapter introduce the topic and build background for the information

that follows. With that in mind, what purpose do you think paragraphs 1 through 3 of this selection serve? What assumption do the authors make about their readers' computer skills?

2. Have you ever done a career search, filled out a job application, or submitted a résumé online? If so, what were your results? If not, which of the authors' suggestions do you think will be most helpful to you in your next job search?

3. Discuss how this selection relates to the Part 5 theme, *America at Work*. For example, the authors suggest that not only does an online career search help you simplify the job-hunting process, but it also gives you some practical experience in using the Internet. What helpful advice do you have for those who are job hunting? What Internet sites or other career resources have you used?

4. Go to one or more of these websites and research a career that interests you. Information on the Internet changes daily, so if these sites are not in service, ask your instructor or a librarian for help. Then write a paragraph explaining the results of your search.

America's CareerInfoNet	*www.acinet.org*
America's Job Bank	*www.ajb.dni.us*
Careerbuilder	*www.careerbuilder.com*
CareersOnLine	*www.careersonline.com*
Hotjobs	*www.hotjobs.com*

FIRST THOUGHTS

To prepare yourself for the reading selection, answer the following questions, either on your own or in a group discussion.

1. What does the word *communication* mean to you?
2. What barriers to good communication have you noticed?
3. Preview the title, headnote, and first one or two paragraphs. What do you think will follow?

WORD ALERT

In a textbook chapter, the words to watch may appear in boldface, italics, or a special color.

denotation (6) a word's literal, dictionary meaning
connotation (6) a word's subjective, emotional meaning
slang (11) an expression identified with a specific group of people
jargon (11) technical terminology used within specialized groups
euphemisms (11) inoffensive expressions that replace words that may offend
abstract word (13) a word that identifies an idea or feeling instead of a concrete object
concrete word (13) a word that identifies something that can be seen or touched
noise (25) environmental or competing distractions that hinder effective communication

❧ Barriers to Communication

SCOT OBER

This textbook reading is excerpted from Chapter 1 of Contemporary Business Communication, *fifth edition. The entire chapter is about understanding business communication. The excerpt focuses on communication barriers, a core concern. When reading from textbooks, remember that headings may signal topics, main ideas, or important details.*

CONSIDERING THE COMPLEX nature of the communication process, 1
your messages may not always be received exactly as you intended. As a matter of fact, sometimes your messages will not be received at all; at other times, they will be received incompletely or
inaccurately. Some of the obstacles to effective and efficient communication are verbal; others are nonverbal. As illustrated in Figure 1.5,
these barriers can create an impenetrable "brick wall" that makes effective communication impossible.

VERBAL BARRIERS

Verbal barriers are related to what you write or say. They include inad- 2
equate knowledge or vocabulary, differences in interpretation, language differences, inappropriate use of expressions, overabstraction
and ambiguity, and polarization.

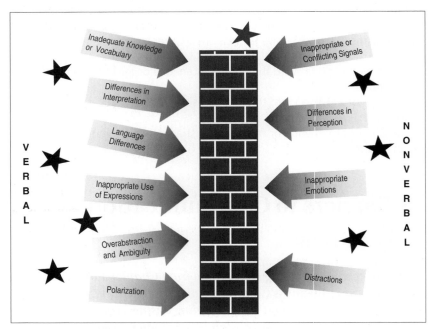

FIGURE 1.5   Verbal and Nonverbal Barriers to Communication

Inadequate Knowledge or Vocabulary

Before you can even begin to think about how you will communicate 3
an idea, you must, first of all, *have* the idea; that is, you must *have* sufficient knowledge about the topic to know what you want to say. Regardless of your level of technical expertise, this may not be as simple
as it sounds. Assume, for example, that you are Larry Haas, manager of
the finance department at Urban Systems. Dave Kaplan, president of
the company, has asked you to evaluate an investment opportunity.
You've completed all the necessary research and are now ready to
write your report. Or are you?

Have you analyzed your audience? Do you know how much the 4
president knows about the investment so that you'll know how much
background information to include? Do you know how familiar Dave
is with investment terminology? Can you safely use abbreviations like
NPV and *RRR,* or will you have to spell out and perhaps define *net
present value* and *required rate of return?* Do you know whether the
president would prefer to have your conclusions at the beginning of
the report, followed by your analysis, or at the end? What tone should
the report take? The answers to such questions will be important if
you are to achieve your objective in writing the report.

Differences in Interpretation

Sometimes senders and receivers attribute different meanings to the 5
same word or attribute the same meaning to different words. When
this happens, miscommunication can occur.

Every word has both a denotative and a connotative meaning. **De-** 6
notation refers to the literal, dictionary meaning of a word. **Connota-**
tion refers to the subjective, emotional meaning that you attach to a
word. For example, the denotative meaning of the word *plastic* is "a
synthetic material that can be easily molded into different forms." For
some people, the word also has a negative connotative meaning—
"cheap or artificial substitute."

Most of the interpretation problems occur because of the per- 7
sonal reactions engendered by the connotative meaning of a word. Do
you have a positive, neutral, or negative reaction to the terms *broad,
bad, aggressive, hard-hitting, workaholic, corporate raider, head-
hunter, gay, golden parachute,* or *wasted?* Are your reactions likely to
be the same as everyone else's? The problem with some terms is not

only that people assign different meanings to the term but also that the term itself might cause such an emotional reaction that the receiver is "turned off" to any further communication with the sender.

Language Differences

In an ideal world, all managers would know the language of each culture with which they deal. International businesspeople often say that you can buy in your native language anywhere in the world, but you can sell only in the language of the local community. 8

Most of the correspondence between American or Canadian firms and foreign firms is in English; in other cases, the services of a qualified interpreter (for oral communication) or translator (for written communication) may be available. But even with such services, problems can occur. Consider, for example, the following blunders[11]: 9

- In Brazil, where Portuguese is spoken, a U.S. airline advertised that its Boeing 747s had "rendezvous lounges," without realizing that *rendezvous* in Portuguese implies prostitution.
- In China, Kentucky Fried Chicken's slogan "Finger-lickin' good" was translated "So good you suck your fingers."
- In Puerto Rico, General Motors had difficulties advertising Chevrolet's Nova model because the name sounds like the Spanish phrase *No va,* which means "It doesn't go."

To ensure that the intended meaning is not lost during translation, legal, technical, and all other important documents should first be translated into the second language and then retranslated into English. Be aware, however, that communication difficulties can arise even among native English speakers. For example, a British advertisement for Electrolux vacuum cleaners displayed the headline "Nothing Sucks Like An Electrolux." Copywriters in the United States and Canada would never use this wording! 10

Inappropriate Use of Expressions

Expressions are groups of words whose intended meanings are different from their literal interpretations. Examples include slang, jargon, and euphemisms. 11

- **Slang** is an expression, often short-lived, that is identified with a specific group of people. Here, for example, are some slang terms (and their meanings) currently popular on college campuses[12]:

  As if—"In your dreams"
  Barbie—A painstakingly dressed and groomed female
  Brain burp—A random thought
  Circle of death—A lousy pizza
  My bad—My fault
  Zoo a course—To fail
  McPaper—A quickly or poorly written paper
  Mad—Very (as in "mad cool")
  Posse—Group of friends
  Velveeta—Something or someone cheesy

  Teenagers, construction workers, immigrants, knowledge professionals, and just about every other subgroup you can imagine all have their own sets of slang. Using appropriate slang in everyday speech presents no problem; it conveys precise information and may indicate group membership. Problems arise, however, when the sender uses slang that the receiver doesn't understand. Slang that sends a negative nonverbal message about the sender can also be a source of problems.

- **Jargon** is the technical terminology used within specialized groups; it has sometimes been called "the pros' prose." As with slang, the problem is not in using jargon—jargon provides a very precise and efficient way of communicating with those familiar with it. The problem comes either in using jargon with someone who doesn't understand it or in using jargon in an effort to impress others.

- **Euphemisms** are inoffensive expressions used in place of words that may offend or suggest something unpleasant. Sensitive writers and speakers use euphemisms occasionally, especially to describe bodily functions. How many ways, for example, can you think of to say that someone has died?

Slang, jargon, and euphemisms all have important roles to play in business communication—so long as they're used with appropriate people and in appropriate contexts. They can, however, prove to be barriers to effective communication when used to impress, when used too often, or when used in inappropriate settings. 12

Overabstraction and Ambiguity

An **abstract word** identifies an idea or a feeling instead of a concrete 13
object. For example, *communication* is an abstract word, whereas
memorandum is a **concrete word,** a word that identifies something
that can be seen or touched. Abstract words are necessary in order to
communicate about things you cannot see or touch. However, communication problems result when you use too many abstract words or
when you use too high a level of abstraction. The higher the level of
abstraction, the more difficult it is for the receiver to visualize exactly
what the sender has in mind. For example, which sentence communi-
cates more information: "I acquired an asset at the store" or "I bought
a laser printer at ComputerLand"?

Similar communication problems result from the overuse of am- 14
biguous terms such as *a few, some, several,* and *far away,* which have
too broad a meaning for use in much business communication.

Polarization

At times, some people act as though every situation is divided into two 15
opposite and distinct poles, with no allowance for a middle ground. Of
course, there are some true dichotomies. You are either male or female, and your company either will or will not make a profit this year.
But most aspects of life involve more than two alternatives.

For example, you might assume that a speaker either is telling the 16
truth or is lying. In fact, what the speaker actually says may be true,
but by selectively omitting some important information, he or she
may be giving an inaccurate impression. Is the speaker telling the
truth or not? Most likely, the answer lies somewhere in between. Likewise, you are not necessarily either tall or short, rich or poor, smart or
dumb. Competent communicators avoid inappropriate *either/or* logic
and instead make the effort to search for middle-ground words when
such language best describes a situation.

Incidentally, remember that what you do *not* say can also produce 17
barriers to communication. Suppose, for example, that you congratu-
late only one of the three people who took part in making a company
presentation. How would the other two presenters feel—even though
you said nothing negative about their performance? Or suppose you
tell one of them, "You really did an outstanding job this time." The pre-
senter's natural reaction is, "What was wrong with my performance
last time?" (And how about this announcement from the author's

seven-year-old son one day after school: "Hey, Dad, guess what? I didn't get my name on the board today." What's the implication?)

NONVERBAL BARRIERS

Not all communication problems are related to what you write or say. 18 Some are related to how you act. Nonverbal barriers to communication include inappropriate or conflicting signals, differences in perception, inappropriate emotions, and distractions.

Inappropriate or Conflicting Signals

Suppose a well-qualified applicant for an administrative assistant po- 19 sition submits a résumé with a typographical error, or an accountant's personal office is in such disorder that she can't find the papers she needs for a meeting with a client. When verbal and nonverbal signals conflict, the receiver tends to put more faith in the nonverbal signals because nonverbal messages are more difficult to manipulate than verbal messages.

Many nonverbal signals vary from culture to culture. Remember 20 also that the United States itself is a multicultural country: a banker from Boston, an art shop owner from San Francisco, and a farmer

word wise

SIGNS OF THE TIMES

In a New Hampshire jewelry store:	"Ears pierced while you wait."
On a bicycle-helmet mirror:	"Remember—objects in the mirror are actually behind you."
On a camera:	"This camera works only when there is film inside."
On a package of peanuts:	"Open packet and eat contents."
On a steering-wheel lock:	"Warning—Remove lock before driving."

from North Dakota are likely to both use and interpret nonverbal signals in quite different ways. What is appropriate in one context might not be appropriate in another.

Communication competence requires that you communicate 21 nonverbal messages that are consistent with your verbal messages and that are appropriate for the context.

Differences in Perception

Even when they hear the same speech or read the same document, 22 people of different ages, socioeconomic backgrounds, cultures, and so forth often form very different perceptions. We discussed earlier the mental filter by which each communication source is interpreted. Because each person is unique, with unique experiences, knowledge, and viewpoints, each person forms a different opinion about what he or she reads and hears.

Some people tend automatically to believe certain people and to 23 distrust other people. For example, when reading a memo from the company president, one employee may be so intimidated by the president that he or she accepts everything the president says, whereas another employee may have such negative feelings about the president that he or she believes nothing the president says.

Inappropriate Emotions

In most cases, a moderate level of emotional involvement intensifies 24 the communication and makes it more personal. However, too much emotional involvement can be an obstacle to communication. For example, excessive anger can create such an emotionally charged environment that reasonable discussion is not possible. Likewise, prejudice (automatically rejecting certain people or ideas), stereotyping (placing individuals into categories), and boredom all hinder effective communication. Such emotions tend to create a blocked mind that is closed to new ideas, rejecting or ignoring information that is contrary to one's prevailing belief.

Distractions

Any environmental or competing element that restricts one's ability to 25 concentrate on the communication task hinders effective communication. Such distractions are called **noise.** Examples of *environmental*

noise are poor acoustics, extreme temperature, uncomfortable seating, body odor, poor telephone connections, and illegible photo-
copies. Examples of *competing* noise are other important business to
attend to, too many meetings, and too many reports to read.

    Competent communicators make the effort to write and speak 26
clearly and consistently and try to avoid or minimize any verbal or
nonverbal barriers that might cause misunderstandings.

COMPREHENSION CHECK

Purpose and Main Idea

1. What is the author's topic?
   a. improving communication skills
   b. communication in the business world
   c. the communication process
   d. obstacles that hinder communication
2. What is the central idea of this selection?
   a. Communication is a complex process.
   b. Effective communication is essential for success in all fields.
   c. Verbal and nonverbal obstacles prevent good communication.
   d. Improving communication is easy if you follow several steps.
3. Which one of the following is the author's *primary* purpose?
   a. to teach readers what the barriers to communication are
   b. to inform readers about cultural differences in communication
   c. to persuade readers to improve their communication skills
   d. to express concern that communication can be
      misunderstood

Details

4. Verbal barriers to communication include all but which one of
   the following?
   a. inadequate knowledge
   b. differences in perception
   c. differences in interpretation
   d. inappropriate use of expressions
5. The author says all of the following about slang except which one?
   a. It is inappropriate in the workplace.
   b. It is no problem in everyday speech.
   c. It can be a barrier to effective communication.
   d. Most subgroups have their own slang.

6. According to the author, inappropriate emotions are a communi-
    cation barrier because they
    a. intensify communication.
    b. make communication more personal.
    c. create a blocked mind.
    d. restrict the ability to concentrate.
7. According to the author, which one of the following is a compet-
    ing distraction?
    a. poor acoustics
    b. uncomfortable seating
    c. temperature extremes
    d. too many meetings
8. Which one of the following is the *dominant* organizational pat-
    tern in paragraph 13?
    a. process
    b. cause and effect
    c. comparison
    d. definition

Inferences

9. Choose the *concrete* term in the following list:
    a. success
    b. trophy
    c. award
    d. honor
10. Based on the author's definitions, a student who says, "I can't
    take good notes in a lecture if I don't like the instructor" is
    allowing which one of the following to interfere with effective
    communication?
    a. a competing distraction
    b. a difference in perception
    c. polarization
    d. an inappropriate emotion

WORKING WITH WORDS

Complete the sentences below with these words from Word Alert:

abstract word   connotation   euphemism   noise
concrete word   denotation   jargon   slang

1. Good writers take time to find the right _____ that will appeal to readers' senses.
2. Although *slender* has a positive meaning, *skinny* has a negative _____ .
3. In some circles, "shooting hoops" is _____ for playing basketball.
4. The environmental _____ in the library that interferes with my studying consists of students talking and a lack of comfortable seating.
5. *Sanitation engineer* is a _____ for *janitor*.
6. Most politicians will resort to the _____ or idea rather than clearly explaining their views.
7. Look in a dictionary to find the _____ of a word.
8. Using today's business _____ , those who tell you to think outside the box just want you to be creative.

THINKING DEEPER

Ideas for discussion and writing

1. When asked to list the skills they value most, employers invariably will include communication skills. What are communication skills, and why are they essential in almost any career?
2. The author gives several examples of slang but no examples of jargon or euphemism. What examples can you give, and what do they mean? Using details from the selection, explain how jargon and euphemism can create barriers to communication.
3. Discuss how this selection relates to the Part 5 theme, *America at Work*. For example, most jobs or careers require you to interact with others. Discuss the role that communication skills will play in the career you have chosen.
4. Review Figure 1.5 on page 370 of the excerpt. What do the arrows and bricks stand for? Why do the arrows point the way they do? This type of figure is a *diagram*. Diagrams use pictures or illustrations to condense and simplify concepts or ideas, making them easier to remember. Read again paragraphs 25 and 26, then make a diagram to illustrate types of distractions.

SELECTION
50

FIRST THOUGHTS

To prepare yourself for the reading selection, answer the following questions, either on your own or in a group discussion.

1. When you are choosing a career, what are some important financial considerations?
2. What do you know about the benefits that are available to most employees of large companies?
3. Preview the title, headnote, and first one or two paragraphs. What do you think will follow?

WORD ALERT

In a textbook chapter, the words to watch may appear in boldface, italics, or a special color.

employee benefit (1) employment compensation other than cash payments
tax-sheltered (1) tax payments that are postponed, or deferred
flexible spending arrangement (7) a system that allows reimbursement of employee-paid expenses with pretax dollars
pretax dollars (8) money income that has not yet been taxed
qualified retirement plan (10) a retirement plan approved by the IRS; also called a tax-sheltered retirement plan

❧ Career-Related Decisions in Personal Finance

E. THOMAS GARMAN AND RAYMOND E. FORGUE

This textbook reading is excerpted from Chapter 1 of Personal Finance, *seventh edition. The entire chapter is about*

Adapted from "Career-Related Decisions in Personal Finance," in Garman and Forgue, PERSONAL FINANCE, 7/e, HMCo, 2003, pp. 22–27. Copyright © 2003 by Houghton Mifflin Company. Reprinted with permission.

the importance of personal finance. The excerpt focuses on personal finance as it relates to career planning. When reading from textbooks, remember that headings may signal topics, main ideas, or important details.

IMPORTANT FINANCIAL ASPECTS of one's working life will affect one's 1
success in personal finance. It is vital to make effective use of the employee benefits offered through an employer. An **employee benefit** is compensation for employment that does not take the form of wage, salaries, commissions, or other cash payments. Examples include paid holidays, health insurance, and a retirement plan. Some employee benefits are tax-sheltered, such as flexible spending accounts and retirement plans. **Tax-sheltered** means that the employee avoids paying current income taxes on the value of the benefits received from the employer. The taxes may be postponed, or deferred, until a later date (usually a good idea)—perhaps until retirement, when the individual's income tax rate might be lower. Smart decisions can increase your real income by thousands of dollars each year.

This section examines (1) comparisons of salary offers from employ- 2
ers located in cities that have different costs of living, (2) flexible spending accounts, and (3) employer-sponsored qualified retirement plans.

COMPARING SALARY OFFERS IN CITIES WITH DIFFERENT LIVING COSTS

Comparing salary offers from employers located in different cities can 3
be difficult without sufficient information on the approximate cost of living in each community. Sometimes those costs vary drastically. Data from the American Chamber of Commerce Researchers Association reveal, for example, that life in a high-cost city such as Boston is, on average, 30 percent more expensive than life in a lower-cost city such as Portland, Oregon. The Chamber data are reported in index form, with the "average cost" community given a rating of 100.

The following example demonstrates how to compare salary of- 4
fers in two different cities. In a recent year, the index was 130.6 for Boston (city 1) and 114.9 for Los Angeles (city 2). Let's assume you want to compare the buying power of a salary offer of $34,000 in Boston with a $31,000 offer in Los Angeles. The costs can be compared using Equations (1.5) and (1.6) on the following page.

$$\text{Salary in city 1} \times \frac{\text{index city 2}}{\text{index city 1}} = \text{equivalent salary in city 2} \qquad (1.5)$$

$$\text{Boston's \$34,000} \times \frac{114.9}{130.6} \text{ is equal to \$29,913 in Los Angeles}$$

Thus, the $34,000 Boston salary offer would buy $29,913 of goods and services in Los Angeles—an amount less than the $31,000 Los Angeles salary offer. All things being equal (and they are both nice cities), the Los Angeles offer is better.

To compare the buying power of salaries in the other direction, re- ⁵ verse the formula:

$$\text{Salary in city 2} \times \frac{\text{index city 1}}{\text{index city 2}} = \text{equivalent salary in city 2} \qquad (1.6)$$

$$\text{Los Angeles's \$31,000} \times \frac{130.6}{114.9} \text{ is equal to \$35,236 in Boston}$$

Thus, the $31,000 Los Angeles salary offer can buy $35,236 of goods and services in Boston—an amount higher than the $34,000 Boston salary offer. All things being equal, the Los Angeles offer is still better.

You may compare salary figures and the cost of living in different ⁶ communities in three ways:

1. By finding the index data in the American Chamber of Commerce Researchers Association's publication, *ACCRA Cost of Living Index* (found in your library or at *www.accra.org*).
2. By telephoning the local Chamber of Commerce in each city to obtain its researched-based index number.
3. By making a personal estimate of an index for each city based on your impressions.

For the fairest comparisons, be sure to add or subtract from the salary offers the value of employee benefits included or excluded, then do the calculations with the indexes.

TAX-SHELTERED FLEXIBLE SPENDING ACCOUNTS

One example of tax-sheltered employee benefits is the **flexible spend-** ⁷ **ing arrangement (FSA).** These employee benefits are now offered by more than half of all large employers. The government-approved plans allow payment of selected employee-paid expenses for medical

or dependent care to be reimbursed with pretax dollars. Under a typical FSA, the employee agrees to have a certain amount deducted from
each paycheck that is then deposited in a separate account. As qualified expenses are incurred, the employee requests and receives reim-
bursements from the account. FSA accounts can be used to pay for
three types of expenses: (1) care of a dependent younger than age 13;
(2) care of another dependent who is physically or mentally incapable
of caring for himself or herself and who resides in the taxpayer's home;
and (3) qualified, unreimbursed medical expenses. Examples of the
last kind of expenses include eye examinations, eyeglasses, routine
physical exams, and orthodontia work.

The tax advantage of an FSA occurs because the deducted 8
amounts of salary avoid federal income tax, Social Security taxes, and,
in most states, state income taxes, thereby allowing selected personal
expenses to be paid with pretax (rather than after-tax) income. Paying
the expenses with **pretax dollars** (money income that has not been
taxed by the government) lowers taxable income, decreases take-
home pay, and increases effective take-home pay because of the reim-
bursements. The resulting tax savings can be as high as 40 percent
of the amount placed in the account for someone in the 27 percent
federal and 6 percent state marginal tax brackets when the saved 7.65
percent Social Security and Medicare taxes are included (27% + 6% +
7.65%).

Before enrolling in an FSA, it is important to estimate your ex- 9
penses carefully so that the amount in the FSA does not exceed anticipated expenses. Internal Revenue Service (IRS) regulations do not
allow the plan to return unused amounts at the end of the plan year,
nor can money be transferred from one account to another, nor from
one plan year to another. Thus, unused amounts are forfeited and are
not returned to the employee—a condition called the "use it or lose it"
rule. A nominal monthly fee is assessed to participate in these programs,
and the maximum annual contribution is $8000. A negative aspect of
FSAs for most workers is that eventual Social Security retirement benefits may be slightly lower than anticipated (perhaps $10–$15 per
month) because Social Security taxable income is also reduced by the
amount of the FSA withholding.

EMPLOYER-SPONSORED QUALIFIED RETIREMENT PLANS

More than half of all workers are covered by an employer-sponsored 10
qualified retirement plan, also called a **tax-sheltered retirement
plan.** The most popular of these is the 401(k) plan offered by private

companies, although 403(b) and 457 plans are available for other workers. These retirement plans have been approved (qualified) by the IRS as vehicles in which to deposit tax-sheltered contributions. They offer tax advantages that can reduce a person's current income taxes and increase his or her retirement benefits. In particular, contributions to the retirement plans are exempt from current income taxes. Employer-sponsored qualified retirement plans provide two distinct advantages.

First Advantage: Tax-Deductible Contributions Create Larger Returns

Tax-sheltered retirement plans provide tremendous tax-deductibility 11 benefits compared with ordinary savings and investment plans. Because pretax contributions to qualified plans reduce income, the current year's tax liability is lowered. Thus, the money saved in taxes can be used to partially fund a larger contribution, which creates even greater returns.

As Table 1.2 illustrates, you can save substantial sums for retire- 12 ment with minimal effects on your monthly take-home pay. A single person with a monthly taxable income of $3000 in the 27 percent marginal tax bracket who places $500 into a tax-sheltered retirement plan [for an annual contribution of $6000 ($500 x 12)] reduces monthly take-home pay from $2400 to $2035, not an enormous amount. The net effect is that it costs that person only $365 to put away $500 per month into a retirement plan. The immediate "return on investment" equals a fantastic 36.99 percent ($135 ÷ $365). In essence, the taxpayer puts $365 into his or her retirement plan and the government contributes $135. (Alternatively, the taxpayer would pay the $135 to the government.) A taxpayer paying a higher marginal tax rate realizes even greater gains. Because a substantial part of your contributions to a tax-sheltered retirement plan comes from money that you would have paid in income taxes, it costs you less to save more.

Second Advantage: Tax-Deferred Growth Enhances Earnings

Because interest, dividends, and capital gains from qualified plans are 13 taxed only after funds are withdrawn from the plan, investments in tax-sheltered retirement plans grow tax-free. The benefits of tax deferral can be substantial.

TABLE 1.2 The Value of Tax-Sheltered Contributions

Monthly salary	$3000	Monthly salary	$3000
Pretax retirement plan		Pretax retirement plan	
contribution	0	contribution	500
Taxable income	3000	Taxable income	2500
Federal taxes	600	Federal taxes	465
Monthly take-home pay	2400	Monthly take-home pay	2035
You put away for retirement	0	Cost to put away $500 per month	365
		($2,400 – $2,035)	

For example, if a person in the 27 percent tax bracket invests 14 $2000 at the beginning of every year for 30 years and the investment earns an 8 percent taxable return compounded annually, the fund will grow to $162,700. If the same $2000 invested annually was instead compounded at 8 percent within a tax-sheltered program, it would grow to $244,700! The higher amount solely results from compounding without paying income taxes. Indeed, when the funds are finally taxed upon withdrawal some years later, the taxpayer may be in a lower marginal tax bracket.

HOW TO MAXIMIZE THE BENEFITS FROM A TAX-SHELTERED RETIREMENT PLAN

1. Start Early to Boost Your Retirement

Recall the rule of 72, which can be used to calculate the years it would 15 take a lump-sum investment to double. An 8 percent rate of return doubles an investment every nine years. So, waiting nine years to begin results in the loss of one doubling. However, it's the last doubling that is lost, as illustrated in Table 1.3. In that example, $48,000 is lost due to a hesitancy to invest $3000. That is quite an opportunity cost.

The opportunity costs are even greater when the start of regular, 16 continuing deposits is delayed. For example, a worker who starts saving $25 per week in a qualified retirement plan at age 23 will have about $450,000 by age 65, assuming an annual growth rate of 8 percent. Waiting until age 33 to start saving, instead of beginning at age 23, results in a retirement fund of *only* about $250,000. The cost of delay is nearly $200,000, even though ten years' worth of delayed deposits would have totaled only $13,000. Again, this effect occurs because most of the power of compounding appears in the last years of growth.

TABLE 1.3 How Starting Just Eight Years Later Will Affect Investment Growth (assuming $3,000 invested at 9 percent)

Starting Earlier		Starting Later	
Age	$ Value	Age	$ Value
23	$ 3,000	23	$0
31	6,000	31	3,000
39	12,000	39	6,000
47	24,000	47	12,000
55	48,000	55	24,000
63	96,000	63	48,000

2. Plan to Be a Millionaire

Being a millionaire is not as difficult as it might seem. Investing $214 17 per month in a tax-sheltered retirement plan earning 9 percent for 40 years will yield slightly more than $1 million (see Chapter 13 to learn how such rates of return are possible). Setting aside $214 may seem like a difficult task at first, but this amount can include employer contributions into the plan. Plus, as your income grows, you will be able to deposit larger amounts, resulting in a nest egg of perhaps $2 or $3 million. The best time to start is when your income jumps significantly. College graduates could start with their very first paycheck from a full-time job. Once you start living on the higher level of income, cutting back is difficult.

3. Saving Just 1 Percent More of Your Pay Makes a Big Difference

Employer restrictions limit the maximum amount that workers may 18 save in a qualified retirement plan to perhaps a total of 15 percent of income (including employee and employer contributions). Most workers, however, do not save the maximum amount. A 23-year-old worker earning $30,000 who saves just 1 percent more of his or her pay (only an extra $300 per year) will see a boost in the retirement fund at age 65 of $91,273 (assuming an annual growth rate of 8 percent).

4. Avoid Making Withdrawals from a Tax-Sheltered Retirement Plan

The tax sheltering of funds in a qualified plan actually represents a deferment of taxes rather than a permanent avoidance of them. Income 19 taxes must be paid when the funds are withdrawn. If money is withdrawn prior to a certain age—usually 59½—a 10 percent penalty may be assessed as well as the usual income tax. In addition to paying a penalty and the income tax due on funds withdrawn from a retirement plan, the worker loses the opportunity cost of keeping the funds invested. For example, assume that Ramsey Marshalla, a legal assistant from San Jose, California, withdraws $5000 from his employer-sponsored retirement plan for some reason (for example, to deal with an emergency, to pay bills, to buy a new vehicle when changing jobs, or to make a down payment on a home). As a result, Ramsey will not accumulate the $45,313 ($50,313–$5000) that amount would have earned over the next 30 years. When faced with a financial problem, you should borrow from a credit union or bank (see Chapter 7) before withdrawing money from a retirement plan.

COMPREHENSION CHECK

Purpose and Main Idea

1. What is the authors' topic?
   a. types of income
   b. career-related financial decisions
   c. employee benefits
   d. the decision-making process

2. Which sentence in paragraph 1 states the authors' central idea?
   a. first sentence: "Important financial. . . ."
   b. second sentence: "It is vital. . . ."
   c. fifth sentence: "Some employee benefits. . . ."
   d. last sentence: "Smart decisions. . . ."

3. What is the authors' purpose?
   a. to teach readers a step-by-step decision-making process
   b. to persuade readers to make salary and benefit comparisons
   c. to examine financial benefits, accounts, and plans that can save you money
   d. to express concern that many people do not make good financial decisions

Details

4. Which one of the following is *not* an employee benefit?
   a. salaries or wages
   b. paid holidays

    c. health insurance

    d. retirement plan

5. According to the authors, comparing salary offers from employers in different cities can be difficult without information on which one of the following?

    a. population densities

    b. employment opportunities

    c. the cost of living

    d. demographic data

6. Flexible spending accounts can be used for paying expenses for all but which one of the following?

    a. care of a dependent younger than age 13

    b. eyeglasses and eye examinations

    c. routine physical examinations

    d. mentally incapable dependents living away from home

7. The 401(k) plan is an example of which one of the following?

    a. a flexible spending arrangement

    b. a tax-sheltered retirement plan

    c. tax-exempt contributions

    d. taxable income

8. The authors' organizational pattern in paragraphs 10–14 is which one of the following?

    a. explaining the reasons for choosing a retirement plan

    b. sorting retirement plans into categories

    c. comparing the advantages of retirement plans to those of other savings

    d. explaining how retirement plans work

Inferences

9. Which one of the following best explains what the "use it or lose it" rule means as applied to flexible spending accounts?

    a. If you overestimate your expenses, you do not get to keep the money.

    b. Money left over can be deposited into another account.

    c. The plan can return to itself any unused amounts.

    d. You can transfer unused amounts from one year to another year.

10. Based on Table 1.3, a person who waits until age 39 to invest $3,000 at an 8 percent rate of return will have earned how much by age 63?

a. $12,000
b. $24,000
c. $48,000
d. $96,000

WORKING WITH WORDS

Complete the sentences below with these words from Word Alert:

pretax dollars   employee benefit
flexible spending arrangement   tax-sheltered
qualified retirement plan

1. A good investment plan may include one or more _____ annu-
   ities along with investments in stocks and bonds.
2. Through _____ employees can reduce their taxes and increase
   benefits.
3. The most popular _____ offered by private companies is the
   401(k).
4. Because of rising medical costs, health insurance is one _____
   you would not want to do without.
5. Some personal expenses can be paid with _____ rather than
   with after-tax income.

THINKING DEEPER

Ideas for discussion and writing

1. Personal finance is a broad topic that covers building income
   and managing money through budgeting, saving, investing, and
   using credit wisely. What successes or challenges have you had in
   these areas?
2. Setting goals is essential to financial success. What do you want
   in terms of a home, a neighborhood, material possessions, and
   advantages for yourself and your family? Answering these questions will help you determine how much income you will need in
   order to have the life you want.
3. Discuss how the advantages of flexible spending arrangements
   and retirement plans explained in this excerpt relate to the Part 5

theme, *America at Work*. For example, the authors suggest that employee benefits as well as salary should influence your career choice. What is your current career goal or major? What salary and benefits can you expect as an employee in your chosen field?

4. Table 1.2 shows that you can save a large amount of money for retirement with only a small reduction in take-home pay. Even if you have never earned a large salary or contributed part of your income to a retirement plan, the point you can take from Table 1.2 is that consistent savings may not affect your current quality of life and can net you a significant amount of money over time. What are your sources of income right now? Do you have a savings plan? Carefully consider the money that is available to you each month and your living expenses. What are some ways in which you can cut spending? Write a paragraph or short essay explaining what you, or any student, can do to save money.

ACKNOWLEDGMENTS

Selection 4: "What's in a Name?" by Deborah P. Work is reprinted by permission of the author. Selection 5: "My Spanish Standoff" by Gabriella Kuntz, ("My Turn"). From Newsweek, 5/4/98 © 1998 Newsweek, Inc. All rights reserved. Reprinted by permission. Selection 6: "The Good Daughter" by Caroline Hwang ("My Turn"). From Newsweek, 9/21/98 © 1998 Newsweek, Inc. All rights reserved. Reprinted by permission. Selection 7: "No Place Like Home" by Jennifer J. Crispin, NEWSWEEK, May 26, 1997, p. 16 ("My Turn" essay). From Newsweek, 5/26/97 © 1997 Newsweek, Inc. All rights reserved. Reprinted by permission. Selection 8: "Beyond the Gender Myths" by Margot Hornblower, TIME, October 19, 1998. © 1998 Time Inc. Reprinted by permission. Selection 9: "I Have a Dream" by Martin Luther King, Jr. Reprinted by arrangement with the Estate of Martin Luther King, Jr., c/o Writers House, Inc. as agent for the proprietor New York, NY. Copyright 1963 Dr. Martin Luther King, Jr., copyright renewed 1991 Coretta Scott King. Selection 10: Bernstein, Douglas A., and Peggy W. Nash, ESSENTIALS OF PSYCHOLOGY, 2nd edition, pp. 496–499. Copyright © 2002 by Houghton Mifflin Company. Reprinted with permission. Selection 11: "The Ritual of Fast Food" from THE RITUALS OF DINNER by Margaret Visser. Copyright © 1991 by Margaret Visser. Used by permission of Grove/Atlantic, Inc. Selection 12: Jeff Kunerth, "It's not guns, games or Net—it's a lack of listening" from THE ORLANDO SENTINEL, May 23, 1999. Reprinted by permission of THE ORLANDO SENTINEL. Selection 13: Barbara Lerner, "Killings

Show Moral Void that Psychology Cannot Fill," THE ORLANDO SEN-
TINEL, Sunday, May 2, 1999. Dr. Barbara Lerner, a psychologist and
writer in Chicago, wrote this article for the NATIONAL REVIEW. It was
reprinted in the ORLANDO SENTINEL, the DETROIT NEWS and
Canada's NATIONAL POST in April and May, 1999. Selection 14: "Why
Do Students at U.S. Military-base Schools Excel?" by William Raspberry. © **1999, The Washington Post Writers Group. Reprinted with
permission.** Selection 15: "Seeking Spirituality in a Time of Tragedy"
by Donna Britt, appeared in THE ORLANDO SENTINEL, May 4, 1999,
Op-Ed page. © **1999, The Washington Post Writers Group. Reprinted
with permission.** Selection 16: "I'm Afraid to Look, Afraid to Turn
Away" by Denise Gonsales, from NEWSWEEK, March 31, 2003, ("My
Turn" essay). © 2003 Newsweek, Inc. All rights reserved. Reprinted by
permission. Selection 17: "Cell Phones Destroy Solitude of Wilder-
ness," The Associated Press, July 5, 1999. Reprinted by permission.
Selection 18: Brief excerpt (as it appeared in an article for THE
ORLANDO SENTINEL) from Claudia Goldin and Lawrence F. Katz,
"The Power of the Pill" from JOURNAL OF POLITICAL ECONOMY
110:4 (2002), pp. 730–32. Copyright © 2002 by The University of
Chicago Press. Reprinted by permission. Selection 19: "The War on Tobacco: Where There's Smoke There's Money" by Dave Barry, MIAMI
HERALD, Sunday, October 24, 1999. Reprinted by permission of the
author. Selection 20: Berko, Roy M., Andrew D. Wolvin, and Darlyn R.
Wolvin, COMMUNICATING, 8th edition, pp. 220–223. Copyright ©
2001 by Houghton Mifflin Company. Reprinted with permission. Se-
lection 21: "I Saw Anne Frank Die" by Irma Sonnenberg Menkel. From
NEWSWEEK, July 21, 1997. All rights reserved. Reprinted by permis-
sion. Selection 22: From pp. 137–140 of SMALL COMFORTS by Tom
Bodett. Copyright © 1987 by Tom Bodett. Reprinted by permission of
Perseus Books Publishers, a member of Perseus Books, L.L.C. Permis-
sion conveyed through Copyright Clearance Center, Inc. Selection 23:
"How I Quit Smoking" by Helen Parramore, THE ORLANDO SEN-
TINEL, April 19, 1998. Reprinted by permission of the author. Selec-
tion 24: " Navigating My Eerie Landscape Alone" by Jim Bobryk. From
NEWSWEEK, March 8, 1999. All rights reserved. Reprinted by permis-
sion. Selection 25: "Drive" by Shannon Shelton from the ORLANDO
SENTINEL, May 18, 2003, p. C11. Reprinted by permission. Selection
26: "Longevity and Livability" by Argus J. Tresidder. From NEWS-
WEEK, March 2, 1998. All rights reserved. Reprinted by permission.
Selection 27: Republished with permission of WALL STREET JOUR-
NAL from "A Drag Racer Turns his Yugo's Handicap to His Advan-

tage" by Dan Morse, WALL STREET JOURNAL, May 25, 1999. Permission conveyed through Copyright Clearance Center, Inc. Selection 28: "Scholars and Descendants" Kathleen Teltsch, NEW YORK TIMES, November 11, 1990. Copyright © 2000 by the New York Times Co. Reprinted with permission. Selection 29: "Chapter 3", from THE GRAPES OF WRATH by John Steinbeck, copyright 1939, renewed © 1967 by John Steinbeck. Used by permission of Viking Penguin, a division of Penguin Putnam Group (USA) Inc. Selection 30: Norton, Mary Beth, David M. Katzman, David W. Blight, Howard P. Chudacoff, Thomas G. Peterson, William M. Tuttle, Jr., Paul D. Escott, and William J. Brophy, A PEOPLE AND A NATION, Brief Sixth Edition, pp. 501–503. Copyright © 2003 by Houghton Mifflin Company. Reprinted with permission. Selection 31: "My Long-Distance Life" by Nick Sheff, from NEWSWEEK, February 15, 1999. All rights reserved. Reprinted by permission. Selection 32: From THE DIVORCE CULTURE by Barbara Dafoe Whitehead. Copyright © 1997 by Barbara Dafoe Whitehead. Reprinted by permission of Alfred A. Knopf, a Division of Random House Inc. Selection 33: "Have Today's Schools Failed Male Students?" Patricia Dalton, as appeared in the ORLANDO SENTINEL May 23, 1999. Reprinted by permission of the author. Selection 34: "Correspondence/Black & Middle Class. Both a Victim of Racial Profiling— and a Practitioner" by Steven A. Holmes, NEW YORK TIMES, April 25, 1999. Copyright © 1999 by the New York Times Co. Reprinted with permission. Selection 35: "A $300 Solution to Organ-Donation Dilemma?" by Ellen Goodman, June 11, 1999, as appeared in THE ORLANDO SENTINEL. **© 1999, The Washington Post Writers Group. Reprinted with permission.** Selection 36: "Yes: Some Dying Patients Need Such Help" by Charles F. McKhann, AARP Bulletin, May 1999, Vol. 40, No. 5, p. 29. Reprinted by permission of the author. Selection 37: "No: 'Suicide' Issue Diverts Us from the Real Problems" by Joanne Lynn, AARP Bulletin, May 1999, Vol. 40, No. 5, p. 31. Reprinted by permission of the author. Selection 38: "In Opposition to Death Penalty" by A. E. P. Wall, THE ORLANDO SENTINEL, February 22, 1999. Reprinted by permission of the author. Selection 39: "In Defense of Death Penalty" by Marianne Means, in THE ORLANDO SENTINEL, February 22, 1999. Reprinted with special permission of King Features Syndicate. Selection 40: Seifert, Kelvin L. and Robert J. Hoffnung, "Divorce and its effects on Children," excerpted from Ch. 13 of CHILDHOOD AND ADOLESCENT DEVELOPMENT, 5/e, pp. 402–406. Copyright © 2000 by Houghton Mifflin Company. Reprinted with permission. Selection 41: Joann Hornak, "A Year of African Life Opened My Eyes." From

NEWSWEEK, May 13, 2002, © 2002 Newsweek, Inc. All rights reserved. Reprinted by permission. Selection 42: Bob Muldoon, "White-Collar Man in a Blue-Collar World." From NEWSWEEK, February 4, 2002, © 2002 Newsweek, Inc. All rights reserved. Reprinted by permission. Selection 43: Olivia Crosby, "You're a What? Research Chef," OCCUPATIONAL OUTLOOK QUARTERLY, Fall 2002, pp. 46–7. Public domain. Selection 44: Harry Wessel, "E-Learning As Easy As ABC," ORLANDO SENTINEL, February 26, 2003. Reprinted by permission. Selection 45: Jacqueline Fitzgerald, "Foul Language Could be a Curse on Your Career," from CHICAGO TRIBUNE as found in the ORLANDO SENTINEL, January 1, 2003. Reprinted by permission of THE CHICAGO TRIBUNE. Selection 46: Dirk Johnson, "Until Dust Do Us Part." From NEWSWEEK, March 25, 2002, © 2002 Newsweek, Inc. All rights reserved. Reprinted by permission. Selection 47: Anna Quindlen, "Doing Nothing is Something." Reprinted by permission of International Creative Management, Inc. Copyright © 2002 by Anna Quindlen. First appeared in Newsweek. Selection 48: "Pounding the Virtual Pavement" adapted from Ch. 10 of Greene and Martel, THE ULTIMATE JOB HUNTER'S GUIDEBOOK, Fourth Edition, 2004, pp. 147–152. Copyright © 2004 by Houghton Mifflin Company. Reprinted with permission. Selection 49: "Barriers to Communication," adapted from Ober, CONTEMPORARY BUSINESS COMMUNICATION, 5/e, HMCo, 2003, pp. 17–22. Copyright © 2003 by Houghton Mifflin Company. Reprinted with permission. Selection 50: Adapted from "Career-Related Decisions in Personal Finance," in Garman and Forgue, PERSONAL FINANCE, 7/e, HMCo, 2003, pp. 22–27. Copyright © 2003 by Houghton Mifflin Company. Reprinted with permission.

INDEX